T0326219

Macroeconomics and Markets in India

India was one of the better performers after the global financial crisis, and has done well despite opening out in a period of great international volatility. This book asks if this was due to luck or to good management. How much did macroeconomic policy contribute and did it do as much as it could have, on a reform path that was not standard? Are there any lessons from the Indian experience for the rest of the world? Senior Indian policy economists, market participants, and researchers address these interesting and important questions.

There are those who think financial reform has gone too fast - relaxations in foreign borrowing norms exposed firms to external shocks. Volatile capital flows impacted markets, although more liberalization of risk-sharing equity compared to debt flows, was effective in reducing domestic risk. But there are also those who think reform was too slow - choking financial development: many markets and instruments that could improve domestic financial intermediation and reduce risk were held back. Analysis suggests policy was able to find the correct timing, pace and combination of reforms and of caution, but improvement is always possible. Luck and inherent strengths of the economy helped absorb both policy mistakes and external shocks.

This book was previously published as a special issue of *Macroeconomics and Finance in Emerging Market Economies*.

Ashima Goyal is Professor at the Indira Gandhi Institute of Development Research, Mumbai, India. She has numerous research and policy publications, is editor of a Routledge journal in her research areas of Macroeconomics and International Finance and has received many fellowships, national and international awards. She is active in the Indian public debate, and has served on several boards and policy committees.

Macroeconomics and Markets in India

Good Luck or Good Policy?

Edited by
Ashima Goyal

Routledge
Taylor & Francis Group

LONDON AND NEW YORK

First published 2012
by Routledge
2 Park Square, Milton Park, Abingdon, Oxon, OX14 4RN

Simultaneously published in the USA and Canada
by Routledge
711 Third Avenue, New York, NY 10017

Routledge is an imprint of the Taylor & Francis Group, an informa business

This book is a reproduction of *Macroeconomics and Finance in Emerging Market Economies,* volume 2, issue 2. The Publisher requests to those authors who may be citing this book to state, also, the bibliographical details of the special issue on which the book was based.

British Library Cataloguing in Publication Data
A catalogue record for this book is available from the British Library

ISBN13: 978-0-415-69017-1

Typeset in Times
by Saxon Graphics Ltd, Derby

Publisher's Note
The publisher would like to make readers aware that the chapters in this book may be referred to as articles as they are identical to the articles published in the special issue. The publisher accepts responsibility for any inconsistencies that may have arisen in the course of preparing this volume for print.

Contents

CONTENTS

Notes on contributors

Indranil Bhattacharyya holds a Masters degree in Economics and has completed PhD coursework at Jawaharlal Nehru University, New Delhi. His research interests are primarily in monetary theory and policy and open economy macroeconomics. He has research publications in national and international journals in the area of monetary policy and financial markets in India.

Ranjan R. Chakravarty is Head, Research & Product Development Department, MCX Stock Exchange.

Saurabh Ghosh holds a Masters degree in Economics from Jawaharlal Nehru University, New Delhi and received his PhD from Indira Gandhi Institute of Development Research (IGIDR), Mumbai. His research interests are primarily in corporate finance, financial markets and monetary policy. He has research publications in national and international journals in the area of IPO performance, banking and financial markets in India.

Dr Shyamala Gopinath was Deputy Governor at the Reserve Bank of India at the time of writing this paper, in charge of departments relating to foreign exchange, reserve management, public debt management, government and bank accounts, payment and settlement systems, information technology and non-banking supervision. She is also a Certified Associate of the Indian Institute of Bankers.

Ashima Goyal is Professor at the Indira Gandhi Institute of Development Research, Mumbai, India. She has numerous research and policy publications, is editor of a Routledge journal in her research areas of Macroeconomics and International Finance and has received many fellowships, national and international awards. She is active in the Indian public debate, and has served on several boards and policy committees.

Dr Danish A. Hashim has an MA and a PhD in Economics. His research areas include commodity market, industrial economics, aviation economics, international economics, and macroeconomics. Prior to joining FTIL, Dr Hashim worked with the Confederation of Indian Industry (CII), the Indian Council for Research on International Economic Relations (ICRIER), the Institute of Economic Growth (IEG), etc.

Vivekanand Jayakumar received his PhD in economics in 2004 from Purdue University (Indiana, USA). He was a Visiting Assistant Professor of Economics at Colgate University (New York, USA) from 2004 to 2007. He is currently an Assistant Professor of Economics at the Sykes College of Business at the University of Tampa (Florida, USA). His fields of research are open-economy macroeconomics, international finance, monetary policy and economic growth.

R. Madhumathi is an Associate Professor in the Department of Management Studies at IIT Madras. She holds a PhD degree in Banking from the University of Madras.

D. Malathy is a Professor of Economics in the Department of Humanities and Social Sciences at IIT Madras. She holds a PhD degree in Economics (Econometrics) from the University of Madras.

Jamal Mecklai is the CEO of Mecklai Financial Services Ltd., a leading risk management consulting company based in India. He is a chemical engineer (IIT, Bombay) by education, a market analyst by inclination, and a lets-change-the-worlder by temperament.

Dr Rakesh Mohan is Distinguished Consulting Professor at the Stanford Centre for International Development at Stanford University. At the time of writing this paper, Dr. Mohan was Deputy Governor of the Reserve Bank of India. In the Reserve Bank of India Dr. Mohan looked after the Monetary Policy Department, Department of Statistical Analysis and Computer Services, Department of Economic Analysis and Policy, Secretary's Department, Financial Markets Department and also co-ordination work. He also co-chaired the G20 Working Group 'Enhancing Sound Regulation and Strengthening Transparency' (2009). He chaired the Working Group on 'Capital Flows and Emerging Market Economies' (2009) set up by the Committee on Global Financial System (CGFS), Bank of International Settlements (BIS).

K.P. Prabheesh was pursuing a PhD programme in Economics in the Department of Humanities and Social Sciences at IIT Madras, India at the time of writing this paper. He is now a faculty member with the Indian Institute of Technology Hyderabad.

D.G. Praveen is Assistant Vice President, Research & Product Development Department, MCX Stock Exchange.

Anis Shaikh is Head of Research at Mecklai Financial Services Ltd. He was studying medicine when India's liberalization process started and prompted a career switch to financial services. He is a Certified Financial Analyst.

Dr V. Shunmugam has a doctorate in Agricultural Economics. He heads the economic analysis and policy division at MCX and is responsible for analysis of market data and informing the participants and policymakers of the benefits of commodity futures in India. Earlier, he worked with United States Department of Agriculture for eight years reporting on Indian agricultural sector, trade, trade policy, etc.

Mrs Usha Thorat was Deputy Governor of the Reserve Bank of India (RBI) at the time of writing this paper. Her major responsibilities included banking regulation and supervision and currency management. She represented the RBI at the Basel Committee on Banking Supervision. She is, and has been on the boards of many financial institutions, including as chairperson. Earlier, she represented the RBI on the BIS Committee on Global Financial Systems, and was a member on the CPSSIOSCO Task Force on Securities Settlement Systems (1999–2001).

Arvind Virmani was Chief Economic Advisor, Ministry of Finance, India at the time of writing this paper. He was previously Principle Advisor, Planning Commission, and before that Director and Chief Executive, Indian Council for Research on International Economic Relations (ICRIER) and Member, Telecom Regulatory Authority of India (TRAI). Some of his past policy research is summarised in two books, *Accelerating*

Growth and Poverty Reduction – A Policy Framework for India's Development (Academic Foundation, 2004) and *Propelling India from Socialist Stagnation to Global Power, Vols. I and II* (Academic Foundation, 2006) and many articles.

Introduction: Good luck or good policy

Ashima Goyal

India was one of the better performers after the global financial crisis, and has done well despite opening out in a period of great international volatility. The book asks if this was due to luck or to good management. How much did macroeconomic policy contribute and did it do as much as it could have, on a reform path that was not standard? Are there any lessons from the Indian experience for the rest of the world? Senior Indian policy economists, market participants, and researchers address these interesting and important questions in this special issue.

Arvind Virmani presents the broad macroeconomic policy choices made. These set the stage on which the current crisis has played out. He suggests the selective opening out was based on a well-considered position that the country would be able to handle the resulting volatility. Rakesh Mohan argues the cost of opening out in a turbulent era proved to be low for India compared to other emerging markets, as it was accomplished without a crisis. He records the steady deepening of markets and policy institutions, together with restrictions on full capital account convertibility, and the intermediate approach to policy that have helped handle volatility. In his opinion, as India's global integration rises, more market development will be required. Jamal Mecklai and Anis Shaikh corroborate the market deepening by devising indices of FX market development and using them to benchmark Indian FX markets against other countries.

Shyamala Gopinath presents a report card for a healthy financial sector. It did not create negative shocks for the real sector and was well positioned to survive any adverse impact of a real sector slowdown. In some ways regulation was conservative, for example, in forbidding securitization, in others it was trend setting as in the use of countercyclical macro-prudential regulations that moderated a real estate boom. But both aspects saved the Indian financial sector from the global meltdown. Usha Thorat points to learning from past crisis as helping make Indian financial regulations more robust, while Vivekanand Jayakumar assesses India's prospects and positioning in view of continuing global risks such as unwinding of global imbalances.

There are, however, two views on removal of internal and external restrictions on the Indian financial sector. There are those who think reform has gone too fast—relaxations in foreign borrowing norms exposed firms to shocks from international credit markets, and from currency depreciation. Volatile equity flows impacted markets, although more liberalization of risk-sharing equity compared to debt flows, was effective in reducing domestic risk. But there are those who think reform was too slow—choking financial development: many markets and instruments that could improve domestic financial intermediation and volatility hedging have been held back. Shunmugam and Hashim explain the design problems that aborted India's attempt to start interest rate futures. Chakravarty and Praveen assess the long road ahead for Indian exchange traded currency derivative markets.

Policy has to act and react in real time, often with less than perfect information in challenging circumstances. But ultimately rigorous research will assess policy choices. In the two research papers in this volume Saurabh Ghosh and Indranil Bhattacharyya

1

record real improvement in Indian money market microstructure after 2002. Large inflows after 2002 were accumulated in reserves that crossed dollars 300 billion by 2009, and these reserves helped manage outflows during the crisis. Yet emerging market reserve accumulation is often attacked as an attempt to manipulate the exchange rate to encourage exports. K.P. Prabheesh, D. Malathy and R. Madhumathi estimate the determinants of reserve accumulation and find self-insurance against volatile inflows to be significant. Deviation of the real exchange rate from its trend is also significant. But since India had a current account deficit through the period, this cannot be regarded as undervaluation of the managed exchange rate.

For readers unfamiliar with the context in which these issues are addressed: after two decades of steady liberalizing reforms, India is now open in many aspects. Even so export share is less than 15 percent of GDP, and capital account convertibility is partial. The sub-prime crisis did not affect India but in the global freeze after the September 2008 demise of Lehman Brothers, export growth fell steeply, stock indices dropped as funds flowed out, the currency depreciated 20 percent, firms that had borrowed abroad were hit by widening spreads and the depreciating rupee. They were already suffering from aggressive monetary tightening—an overreaction to the oil shock. Industrial growth collapsed although the fall in annual aggregate growth was 2.4 percentage points and remained respectable at 6.7 percent. Policy response was rapid. Rates were cut steeply and the fiscal deficit ratio shot up to 10 percent.

In the absence of a financial crisis and when fundamentals are sound, recovery can be fast. This was the collective judgment as inflows resumed and stock indices began to recover in April 2009. India's diversified demand base, rise in government expenditure, robust agricultural income and services growth was able to support output growth until the lagged effects of rates cuts revived consumer demand and the infrastructure investment cycle, even though export growth remained sluggish until the end of 2010. Some industries began showing signs of recovery in March 2009. The vote for political stability in the 2009 elections helped dissolve the fear of contagion from the global crash. A booming economy helped reduce public debt. The country had crossed a critical threshold in its transitional catch-up phase of growth.

Did these inherent strengths of the economy absorb policy mistakes and external shocks? Openness has contributed greatly to the higher trend growth, and there has been real progress in building markets and policy infrastructure, but it is an open research question whether the cost of openness was kept to a minimum or was larger than it need have been. Was the impact of the global shock relatively low because the country could indeed handle volatility, or because openness had been restricted?

The last chapter assesses the contribution of Indian macroeconomic policies towards reducing the impact of shocks. A crisis is a shock impinging on a system, so the response can be used to deduce aspects of the system's structure. Such an analysis of the crisis and recovery suggests aggregate supply in India is elastic but subject to upward shocks. Policies attuned to this structure would be more effective. Both monetary and fiscal policy should identify measures that would reduce costs, while avoiding too large a demand contraction. The failure to do this was a policy mistake, but luck and inherent strengths of the economy helped absorb both policy failures and external shocks.

On the whole policy was able to find the correct timing, pace and combination of reforms and of caution, but the evaluation of Indian macroeconomic policies suggests possible improvements, such as better incentives for government expenditure management. One source of costs was self-insurance through the accumulation of reserves. Therefore reforms in the global financial architecture are also required to reduce the necessity of such insurance and the cost of engaging with the world.

Macro-economic management of the Indian economy: capital flows, interest rates, and inflation[1]

Arvind Virmani

Ministry of Finance, Government of India, New Delhi, India

This paper addresses the issue of surge in capital inflows into a relatively open emerging economy. One of the constraints in dealing with surges is that much of the theoretical analysis is motivated by developed economies with well developed capital and money markets, while emerging economies are characterised by missing market segments and incomplete integration of such markets. It tries to use the existing literature and empirical information on the concerned economy to derive practical policy suggestions for meeting and balancing the objectives of inflation control and sustained growth. One of the noteworthy recommendations is the introduction of an auctioning mechanism for the right to incur foreign debt. This is designed to correct or compensate for the negative externalities arising from such cross-border debt, given the possibility of sharp reversals arising from global external developments and global shocks. The auction of rights to borrow can act as a variable tax that taxes short term flows at a higher rate and adjusts to changing environment. A limited version of such auctions has been tried sucessfully under the supervision of the Securities and Exchange Board of India.

The global environment that gave rise to this issue in India has changed dramatically the US financial crisis and global recession. The analysis however, stands and may be useful when the global situation returns to normal and another emerging economy is faced with a similar situation.

1.   Introduction

Historical fears of inadequate reserves have been replaced by concerns about how to manage the increased inflows of foreign money. A sustained increase in net foreign earnings of the nation raises the possibility of Dutch disease. A global economy in a globalized world can be subject to the problems of success. High growth attracts foreign capital looking for profitable investment opportunities. In a positive cycle this inflow will indeed find profitable investment opportunities that others have missed and lead to even higher growth. However, if the growth opportunities do not materialize fast enough there is enormous pressure on the currency to appreciate, resulting in either an accumulation of reserves (followed by monetary expansion and inflation) or actual (nominal) appreciation or both. Appreciation can in turn reduce exports and overall growth of tradable goods and services. This negative cycle of greater foreign earnings leading to slowdown in the growth of tradable goods is known as Dutch disease.

The translation of capital inflows (equity and debt) into productive investment depends to an important extent on the development of financial markets that intermediate such flows. Thus the translation of such inflows into accelerated growth depends on how quickly we can develop missing markets for debt and risk. Larger capital inflows also provide a golden opportunity to accelerate the lifting of restrictions on imports of goods and services and the purchase of foreign exchange for external spending and investment abroad. The accumulation of reserves above the level that fulfils a national precautionary motive is a clear signal that such liberalization should be accelerated. Beyond this the issue is one of monetary and exchange rate management.

Empirical estimates suggest that the sweeping reforms of the 1990s have put the economy on a rising growth path since 1994–95.[2] This rising growth trend has been supported by subsequent reforms despite their relative modesty. If this trend persists unchanged then we would average a growth rate of 8.75% during 2007–2008 to 2011–2012.[3] To put this into perspective, it is useful to recall that the Indian economy grew at a rate of 3.5% per annum during 1951–52 to 1979–80, 5.3% during 1980–81 to 1994–95, and about 7% during 1995–96 to 2006–2007.[4] A rate of growth of 8.7% or the 9% targeted by the 11th Plan is quite different from the 5.3% of the 1980s and the 7% of the late 1990s as it may be close to the maximum sustainable growth potential of the Indian economy. There have been only 16 countries[5] in history whose per capita income growth has averaged 7.5% for a decade or more.[6] Of these, only four countries were able to sustain 7.5% average growth for two decades and only two (Japan and China) for three decades. Thus the macro-economic challenge in generating GDP growth of 9% or more or equivalently per capita GDP growth of 7.5% or more, may be quite different from those seen earlier during the period of relatively moderate growth rates.

There are two inter-related macro-economic challenges we face in maintaining high growth on a sustained basis.[7] These relate to capital inflows and inflation. Though the merchandise trade deficit has risen over the last three years to over 7% of GDP at market prices in 2006–2007, the total (goods and services) trade deficit has stabilized at around 3% of GDP in the last two years. As net factor incomes (including remittances) constitute about 2% of GDP, this has left a current account deficit of a little over 1% of GDP. Capital inflows have spurted to around 4% of GDP, far in excess of the current account financing requirements, leading to large accumulation of reserves. If the growth momentum of the economy is maintained during the 11th Plan, the capital inflows are likely to exceed current account financing requirements leading to pressures for appreciation of the currency and/or to monetary pressures on prices. We have to distinguish between equity flows (e.g. FDI and FII) in which growth expectations are a major driver and debt flows (e.g. ECB, government securities, commercial paper) that are primarily driven by interest differentials and exchange rate movements. An important challenge is to modulate the latter through financial and fiscal measures instead of using physical controls.[8]

On the real side, the relatively closed and controlled nature of international trade in agriculture is likely to result in domestic demand–supply imbalances that will lead to spurts in inflation.[9] Given the difficulty of trading-off farmers' interests against those of poor and middle-class consumers, this puts intense political pressure for quick fix solutions that make rational macro-management more difficult. A sustainable macro-management strategy therefore has to take account of these non-economic constraints. On the external side the rising price of oil is another challenge that complicates macro-management. Unless price signals are transmitted to users they have no incentive to invest in costlier energy-efficient equipment and consumer durables. The only long-term solution, that of increased efficiency in the use of energy, will be hampered and development of alternative domestic sources will be stymied.

There are also well-known constraints on the real side such as infrastructure (particularly electricity)[10] as well as emerging bottlenecks such as the shortage of educated/skilled manpower that are linked to the maintenance and possible increase in the rate of growth. These issues will be addressed by the 11th Plan. In this paper we address the problems that can disrupt growth by upsetting the macro-economic balances and have therefore to be addressed as part of fiscal, financial, and monetary policy.

A strategy for macro-management must have the following elements (with sections in which they are addressed in parentheses):

(1) Excess capital inflows reduce the costs and risks of external sector reforms and raise the opportunity cost of financial sector underdevelopment. We must therefore use this opportunity to (i) eliminate all controls and restrictions on purchase of goods and services and on outflow of capital. (ii) Accelerate financial market reforms (Sections 6.1, 6.2, 6.3.1, and 9).
(2) The impact of capital inflows depends on the extent to which they are motivated by growth opportunities or by interest differentials. We must therefore remove all policy distortions and market distortions that keep these differentials from narrowing. Fiscal deficit target will have to be adjusted downward (Sections 6.3.2 and 8).
(3) The critical macro-policy choice raised by excess capital flows is between nominal appreciation and sterilization. To improve the trade-off, policy changes needed to reduce the costs to society of both nominal appreciation and of sterilization must be identified. This will raise the overall benefit–cost ratio for capital inflows and allow us to continue the process of capital account liberalization on the inflow side (Section 7).

2. Theory and empirics

The conventional wisdom (based on neo-classical real economy and monetarist theory) is summarized in the following analysis.[11] With an open capital account and a fixed exchange rate it is impossible to have monetary independence. Thus according to this analysis, capital inflows will inevitably result in real appreciation, only the method by which this happens can differ. We can either let the nominal exchange rate appreciate as it will if the central bank does not buy foreign exchange or hold the nominal exchange rate fixed by accumulating reserves and let monetary expansion and consequent (inevitable) inflation result in a real appreciation. This is sometimes referred to as the 'trinity' or 'tri-lemma'.

On the other extreme are empirical analysts who point to the growth experience of many countries including China to posit that an undervalued exchange or a fixed exchange rate in the face of a sustained positive balance on current plus (exogenous) capital account is a driver of economic growth.[12] A number of studies done in the context of the Balassa–Samuelson effect show that, even in developed countries, the (bilateral) real exchange rate can have a long run impact on relative growth rates.[13]

The indigenous view, which guided our management of the surge in capital inflows following the liberalization of foreign direct investment (FDI) and equity inflows in the 1990s, is as follows:[14] though the rational expectations model provides useful insights for monetary management, its assumption that growth is exogenously determined by deep underlying factors is questionable for developing economies lying well inside the global production possibility/technology frontier. The process of catch-up growth that such economies are undergoing is highly diverse and variable and dependent on government policy and programmes (positive and negative).[15] As long as there is excess labour resources in the economy and no other binding input constraints in the form of 'public or quasi-public goods' such as choked highways, a rise in earnings/inflows can raise saving, investments, and technical change in the economy leading to higher growth.[16] The initial impact of the inflow of capital must be to **reduce** the cost of capital, that is, to both reduce the interest rate on borrowing/ debt and lower the cost of equity (perhaps to different degrees depending on the perceived opportunities and nature of the financial market). This in turn will lead to an increase in investment, as long as more structures and machinery can be constructed and/or machinery can be imported (i.e. as long as there is less than 100% crowding out of existing investment). The only issue is whether this increased investment leads to a sustained increase in the growth rate (for at least the duration of the capital inflows and perhaps a few years thereafter). The conventional answer is an unambiguous 'no'. Our answer is that it depends on the growth potential of the economy, though admittedly very difficult to determine, is a judgment that governments and their advisors are routinely called on to make.

Therefore, contrary to conventional wisdom, some accumulation of reserves, appropriately sterilized, can restrain inflation and the consequent real appreciation. In such circumstances a modestly undervalued exchange rate can aid the growth process without undue cost in terms of inflation.[17] Once the growth acceleration stops and growth plateaus at a higher level, the economy may start to approximate the conventional full employment model on which the 'trinity' analysis is based.[18]

The conventional model assumes the existence of complete and integrated markets, particularly financial markets. Given the dualistic nature of most developing countries (formal/organized and informal/unorganized), the model can at most be assumed to apply to the formal sector. The two-way interaction of this sector with the informal sector will however affect the results of policy changes in ways not envisioned or accounted for in the model.[19] Further, in an economy with an open capital account, a complete and integrated financial market implies interest parity between domestic and global interest rates. If this parity does not hold because of policy distortions or natural causes, we would expect the conclusions and recommendations of the model to be modified.

Policy distortions can and have, led to imperfect or non-existent markets for private-good infrastructure such as electricity as well as to other services such as education skills that will affect growth and inflation. Any realistic policy analysis must account for these imperfections and their impact on inflation and growth outcomes.

The conventional model gives little guidance on issues related to asset price inflation [20] The shortage of supply of 'urban land' is likely to be a major determinant of asset price inflation in India. It is important to be clear about what we mean by 'urban land!' 'Urban land' is distinguished from 'village land' by the presence of critical public and quasi-public goods. The most basic distinction between the two (from the start of urban history *à la* Mohenjo-Daro), is the former's planned layout.

A city is divided into parts, sub-parts, and plots, by roads of varying sizes and is in turn inter-connected and integrated by them. Overlaid on it or underlying it or tucked away from sight, are water drains, sewers, water mains, water and sewage treatment plants, garbage collection and disposal systems, and channels for utilities. Some form of public transport system is also essential for cities above a certain size/spread.[21] In virtually every state of the country the supply of 'urban land' (so defined) has been woefully inadequate because it has been made the responsibility of either monopolistic agencies or powerless, untrained planning departments (or both).[22] This along with bad policies, such as expropriatory rent control laws, has resulted both in astronomical land/real estate prices for the limited 'urban land' available in the market and in slums wherever non-marketed land was available in or near the cities. Increasing the supply of 'urban land' will therefore be an important instrument in the control of inflation, as real estate is an important input into most services.

3. Growth trend

Statistical analysis stretching over the seven post-independence decades shows two statistically significant breaks in the rate of growth of the economy (Table 1 and Figure 2). One break occurred in the early 1980s (dummy variable D80+) following a policy shift away from excessive and oppressive controls and restrictions towards gradual but persistent decontrol. The second break occurred in the mid-1990s following deeper and more broad-based reforms of the early 1990s, which put the economy on a gradually accelerating growth path (time dummy Year 94+).[23] The results of the growth regression, which also takes account of the impact of monsoon rainfall variations (drain), are as follows:

$$\text{GdpGr} = 0.035 + 0.02\,\text{D80} + 0.002\,\text{Year94} + 0.188\,\text{drain} - 0.093\,\text{drain}(-1).$$

Details are given in Table 1 and the same is depicted in Figure 1.

If we use the estimated equation to project growth rates for the 11th Plan (assuming normal rainfall in every year), then we obtain an average growth rate of 8.7% per annum during this period. The 9th Plan's target of an average growth rate of 9% is very realistic to us though it was criticized for being too modest at the time of release of the approach paper. It is, however, 1.2% points higher than the achievement of about 7.8% per annum during the 10th Plan and is consistent with historical Plan targeting at a couple of per cent above the previous Plan achievement.

Table 1.   Statistical details of GDP growth trend equation.

	Dependent Variable = GDP growth rate				
Independent variable =>	Intercept	D80+	Year 94+	drain	drain(-1)
Coefficient =	0.035	0.020	0.002	0.188	−0.093
Standard deviation =	0.004	0.006	0.001	0.029	0.029
t-statistic =	9.2	3.2	2.2	6.4	−3.2
P-Value =	0.000	0.002	0.032	0.000	0.003
R^2(adj) = 0.59 (se = 0.020)	Period: 1951–52 to 2006–2007			F = 21	

All variables (except year 94+) are significant at the 1% (5%) level.

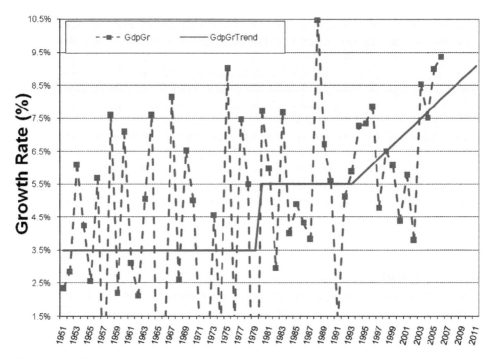

Figure 1.   GDP growth rates and fitted time trends (showing the historical breaks).

Given the Plan's efforts to fill the gaps in supply of public (roads, urban planning/land, public health, agriculture R&D) and quasi-public goods (basic education, electricity transmission – distribution, dams – canals) an augmentation of the statistical trend by 0.3% per annum is quite credible. Thus our analysis/ projection is quite different from that of most analysts, who assert/suggest that the trend growth rate is around 7% (or when pressed up to 8%) and the higher average growth of 9.2% in the last two years is all due to cyclical factors such as an upswing of world growth/trade cycle and excess liquidity/high monetary growth.[24] The appearance of cyclicality since the 1990s can be explained as follows: the 1994–95 to 1996–97 spurt and the 1997–98 to 2002–2003 slowdown may be due to the fact that quantitative restrictions (QRs) on capital goods and intermediate goods were eliminated in the first burst of reforms while those on consumer goods were eliminated during 1997–98 to 1999–2000. This resulted in a sharp rise in effective protection for consumer durables followed by an even sharper fall, possibly resulting in a boom–bust cycle in items with significant economies of scale such as automobiles and major consumer durables.

There are two potentially significant reasons for large capital inflows. One is profitable medium- to long-term investment opportunities arising from the growth potential of the economy and the other is short-term arbitrage opportunities arising from policy distortions. Let us consider each in turn. Clearly the Indian growth performance and growth potential has attracted significant amounts of equity flows and (more recently) FDI. The fact that these flows are far in excess of the current account deficit despite two years of over 9% growth suggests that investors expect opportunities for profitable investment to continue to grow. This implies that either growth will accelerate further or the expectations will prove too optimistic and capital inflows will slow down over time and eventually reach a more balanced level or both. In any case such an equilibrium is unlikely to be established over the 11th Plan period and may take 10–15 years, given the renewed attractiveness of the Indian economy for Japanese and oil-rich Gulf investors.

In the second case, there is a need to remove distortions that create arbitrage opportunities, because even short-term flows can continue for years as long as distortions persist. Together these two cases require a comprehensive strategy of macro-management.

4. Inflation convergence

The issue of excess demand arising from capital inflows or any other source cannot be analysed objectively without a price index suitable for this purpose. Globally, the consumer price index (CPI) is used for measuring the inflation trend for the purpose of macro-economic monitoring and management. Unfortunately, in India we do not have an aggregate CPI appropriate for use as an indicator of aggregate prices and demand pressures. The sectional CPIs such as those for urban non-manual and blue-collar workers and for rural and agriculture labour may serve a useful purpose for calculating real wages of these sub-groups, but are very inadequate for getting a handle on aggregate excess demand pressures. We have therefore conventionally used the wholesale price index which is more comprehensive and also available on a weekly basis, for monitoring. Clearly its weakness lies in excluding prices of retail and other services that are part of the basket of the hypothetical average consumer.

For our current purpose, the best and most comprehensive price index available is the implicit price deflator for private final consumption expenditure from the GDP accounts. The fact that it is only available on an annual or quarterly basis is not a serious handicap, as our purpose is to determine the trend in inflation and gap between Indian and global inflation. Figure 2 shows the inflation rate as measured by this indicator along with the US inflation rate as measured by personal consumption

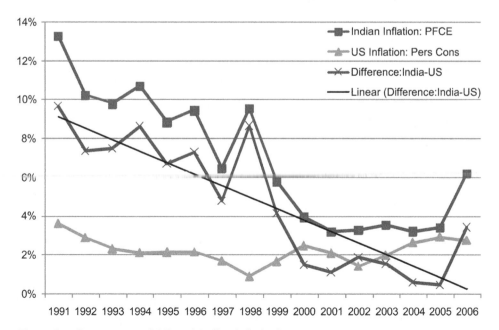

Figure 2.   Convergence of US and Indian inflation?

deflator from the GDP accounts, along with the difference between the two inflation rates.

Figure 2 shows that Indian inflation has been on a down trend since 1991, and this is reflected in the clear down trend in the gap/difference between the Indian and US inflation rates. The reasons for this are also clear, one of the most important and most successful elements of the 1990s reform has been the reduction in protection. Quantitative restrictions have been eliminated and non-agricultural tariffs have declined from a 'peak rate' of around 150% in 1991 to 10% in 2007–2008. Though most of the QRs on agricultural imports have been eliminated, average agricultural tariffs remain high relative to comparator countries with a few rates as high as 100%.

The trend line suggests that, with a continuing reduction in tariffs there is a credible possibility of eliminating the historical gap between US and Indian inflation. The sudden rise in the inflation gap in 2006 is however a warning and a source of concern; this gap seems to be linked to the global rise in food prices.[25] Given the much higher share of food in the consumption basket of the average Indian consumer,[26] the inflation gap can open even if Indian food inflation is identical to (or lower than) the global food inflation as long as it is (much) higher than for non-food consumer goods. An elimination of the inflation gap is therefore dependent on the international trade policy and internal marketing policy for agricultural products. We expect the inflation gap to narrow during 2007, but to remain above the trend line in the figure, which projects a nil gap.

5. Interest parity

With a completely open capital account, risk-free interest rates should converge. Bhatt and Virmani (2005) provided evidence to show convergence toward short-term (3-month/91-day) uncovered interest parity during 1991–92 to 2003–2004. Figure 3 depicts the nominal interest rate on three-month US Treasury bills and Indian 91-day Treasury bills and the gap between them since the equity market opening of

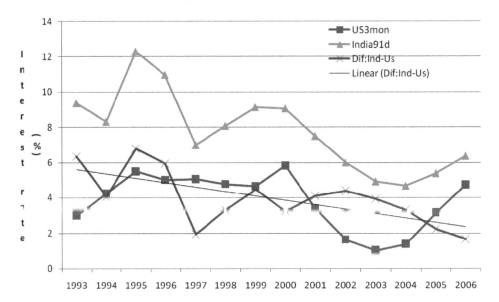

Figure 3.   Interest rates on US three-month and Indian 91-day Treasury bills.

1992. The similarity in the pattern of annual average variation illustrates this conclusion (Figure 3). Further, the interest rate differential has been on a clear down trend, falling from an average of over 6% in 1993 to below 2% in 2006.

The speed of convergence between one-year US government securities and Indian 364-day Treasury bills seems to have been much faster (Figure 4). The pattern of variation of the annual averages of the two rates is similar while the gap has been on a clear down trend. The nominal interest differential has declined from an average of about 7.5% in 1992 to an average of less than 2% in 2006.

Comparing these trends with the trend in annual inflation (Figure 2), it seems that inflation convergence has been much faster than the convergence in nominal interest rates and consequently in real interest rates. This is consistent with our earlier observation about market imperfections and distortions in capital/credit markets.

The comparative progress of interest convergence in the short- and medium-term ends of the market can be seen more clearly in Figure 5 which depicts the three-month and one-year interest differentials along with their trend rates. The interest gap at the short end of the market has been marginally higher than that at the medium end from 2002 to 2005. Similarly, the convergence has been much slower at the short end than at the medium end. This again suggests the presence of imperfections in the capital/credit market.

6.   External policy

The basic macro-management challenge is to maximize the benefits of greater globalization and financial market integration, while minimizing the costs of excess inflows. The greatest potential benefit of capital inflows into India is to make available risk capital and investment funds (a) to entrepreneurs to whom this would

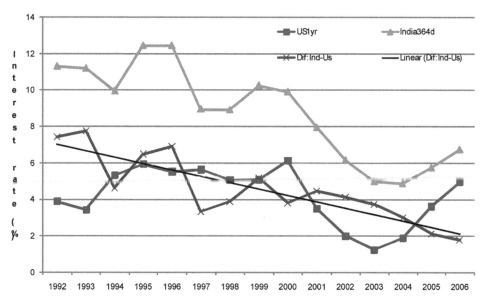

Figure 4.   Interest rates – one-year US government securities and 364-day Indian Treasury bills.

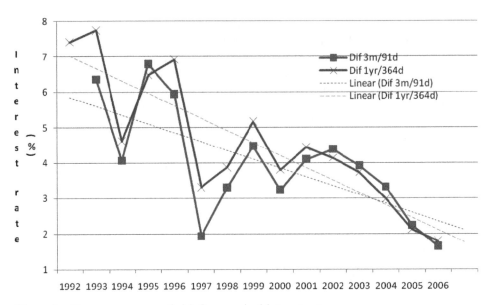

Figure 5.   Slow convergence of risk-free nominal interest rates.

not have been available otherwise and (b) at a lower cost than it would otherwise have been available. This happens and is happening in India through competition and technical change in the financial services industry, the development of new markets, and the introduction of new products. This in turn has a direct and indirect impact on economic growth. As long as net inflows and Current Account Deficit (CAD) are more or less in balance the only potential cost is a sudden outflow ('Asian crises') that has been successfully managed by many different countries including India in the past.[27] Having prepared macro-strategy papers after the Mexican, Asian, and Russian crises, at a time when both our reserves and experience was a fraction of what it is today, I have complete confidence that we can mange such outflow spikes in the future.[28]

If the medium- to long-term capital inflows are in excess of the long-term current account deficit, as they appear to be today, the cost is in the form of an appreciation of the real exchange rate with its effect on net exports of goods and services and on inflation. The first step must be to re-examine the entire policy framework to identify and remove any policy distortions that are promoting this imbalance.

6.1.   Trade policy

With a current account deficit of 1–1.5% of GDP a rise in the merchandise trade deficit or the overall goods and services deficit is not a threat to Balance of Payments (BOP) equilibrium. There are a number of policy measures that will simultaneously improve the efficiency and competitiveness of the Indian economy and increase its capacity for higher growth. They will also ensure that short-term bottlenecks in domestic supply do not result in inflation spurts. These policy measures are a more efficient means of raising the CAD, compared to a capital inflow driven appreciation of the currency and can to some extent reduce the pressure on the currency to appreciate.

6.1.1. Imports

With a peak non-agriculture tariff of 10% and a simple average (at 8 digit) of 9.1% we have now (2007–2008) reached the tariffs prevailing in ASEAN countries with relatively higher tariff levels in this category. Studies have shown that industry and services have responded splendidly to the reduction of tariffs.[29] Further gains in efficiency and competitiveness can be obtained through a reduction to OECD levels (or mid-range of ASEAN levels). We should target a uniform import duty on all non-agricultural commodities that will put us on par with OECD countries in terms of protective tariffs by 2009–2010. With a Central VAT and State VAT(s) in place by then, it would be possible to provide a level playing field to producers competing with imports as well as to exporters, by fully offsetting all indirect domestic taxes incorporated in exports.

Agricultural tariffs, at a simple (8 digit) average of 36.8%, remain relatively high. This is due to livelihood issues that are present in India, but not in middle income or higher income OECD countries. These tariffs also need to be reduced to reap the advantages of global competition, but at a much slower pace (but not glacial pace).[30] We could target a reduction of all agricultural tariffs above some rate X to this rate by 2009–2010. Trade facilitation measures should also be accelerated.

6.1.2. Exports

Services taxes and excise duties should be integrated into a Central VAT regime with full offset for exporters and full imposition of this Central VAT (CENVAT) on all imports.[31] Till such time as this happens there should be a mechanism for providing service tax offset to exporters, in a manner that is administratively sustainable keeping in view the possibility of evasion. The importance of this is heightened during a period in which the real effective exchange rate has appreciated (36-country REER). This will make it easier to have two-way movement in the exchange rate as part of a managed float.

6.2. Movement of persons

Though the export of business services is rightly feted, training and certification systems for thousands of technical skills and hundreds of specialized skills do not exist in India. A model visa regime should be set up for movement of skilled persons into India, so as to expand the skill set available in India, address potential skill constraints in the Indian economy expeditiously and smoothly, and make India a true knowledge power. This is important not only for skills used directly in industry and services, but also for the critical task of educating the educators and training the trainers, where the shortages are likely to be even more acute. Our bilateral and multilateral efforts to increase the flow of skilled professionals to developed countries will then also have greater credibility as the model law can be propagated to OECD countries. In addition, this will moderate the imbalance in labour remittances (net private remittances in BOP accounts).

6.3. Capital flows

With excess capital inflows hitting 3% of GDP and gross FDI exceeding $20 billion, there is no need to continue encouraging more debt and portfolio inflows. There is greater need to facilitate outflows, as gross inflows of capital can be partly offset by greater outflows of capital. The focus should be on those measures that increase freedom for the common citizen and/or improve the efficiency of doing business without increasing volatility. Similarly, any systemic biases towards capital inflow should now be removed as they are no longer needed. Going further, it can be argued that excess capital inflows now impose a cost on the economy (an externality) that needs to be corrected through an appropriate tax.

6.3.1. *Outflows*

Different analysts at different times argue that (a) freeing of outflows will actually encourage greater inflows and (b) that freedom of capital inflows will increase the probability of surges in capital outflows. Though these arguments are prima facie contradictory, each has a rationale for a specific context and policy framework that prevailed in the country about which examples are given. It is thus important to be clear about our own domestic and international situation today and the policy framework that we have, in weighing these possibilities. In our situation (current and foreseeable) of sustained growth, large capital inflows, and downward flexibility in exchange rates (b) is highly unlikely and easily manageable through monetary policy and exchange rate flexibility.[32] In the case of (a) the distinction between legal and illegal inflows is very important. A freeing of legal capital outflows by nationals is likely to shift some capital outflows from the illegal to legal channels thus increasing the latter. The opening of legal outflow channels can in principle also encourage the repatriation of assets held abroad illegally – however, given a decade and a half of liberalization, most if not all of this has already happened. Thus in our judgment, the overall effect of complete liberalization of capital outflows by domestic companies, organizations, and citizens will be very small net flows, but a considerable increase in economic freedom and potential efficiency gains. Such freedom must of course be subject to reasonable safeguards relating to national security and terrorism, and reporting requirements relating to tax evasion and money laundering. As a matter of abundant caution, remittances above a certain level could require advance intimation to the Reserve Bank of India (RBI), that is, when it is being planned. The larger the proposed/anticipated remittance the earlier it must be reported.[33]

As an intermediate step towards complete liberalization of outflows two categories of outflows should be freed from all controls/limits. These are outward Indian FDI and export of project services. Till such time as outflows are completely decontrolled a number of specific liberalization steps can be taken. Examples are given as follows.

All citizens should in principle be allowed to hold unlimited amounts of foreign currency (cash).[34] Any conditions imposed on rupee cash holdings by tax authorities as anti-evasion measures can also apply to holding of US dollar bills and other currency.[35] Carrying of currency across the border will continue to be regulated as it is in other countries. Thus, for example, air travellers would continue to be required to declare physical transport of any currency, including rupees, above a certain value. This change, would lead to a small increase in the stock of private foreign exchange holdings and a commensurate reduction in the public/RBI stock.

Restrictions/controls on opening of foreign bank accounts (including in foreign branches of Indian banks) by Indian citizens should be removed.[36] Controls/

restrictions on payment of interest on Exchange Earners Foreign Currency Accounts (EEFC) accounts can also be lifted so as to facilitate exports and imports.[37]

Rules, regulations, and procedures for foreign investment by Indian citizens and companies must also be simplified so that there is a readjustment of India's holding of foreign securities from Government/RBI towards private agents. For instance, they must be allowed to purchase hedge products and trade on recognized futures and forward markets in commodities etc. without restrictions.[38] For this purpose domestic financial intermediaries must be free to advise citizens about investment possibilities in other countries.

6.3.2. Inflows

All monetary requirements should be reviewed to eliminate differential reserve requirements that favour inflow of Non-Resident Indians (NRI) or other debt into Indian banks. We must also consider turning the tables by imposing higher reserve requirements on foreign borrowing by banks. It is possible to adjust this additional reserve requirement so as to eliminate the excess advantage of foreign borrowing and thus eliminate the need for borrowing bans and/or rationing. For instance, with a global interest rate of 6% and a domestic interest rate of 8%, a 25% (additional) reserve requirement can equalize the advantage of borrowing abroad and thus be a more efficient substitute for a ban on foreign borrowing by domestic banks.

This is also an appropriate time to review the rules for interest rates on NRI accounts and to eliminate those that allow payment of higher rupee interest rates on NRI accounts than on normal domestic accounts.

Similarly, any differential taxation that favours foreign creditors and investors (including NRIs) must be eliminated. We used to apply an accepted principle of income taxation, namely, zero tax on lending by foreign (non-resident) lenders to domestic (resident) borrowers.[39] We have since switched over from this principle to one of equal treatment of foreign and domestic residents on interest income earned in India, by imposing an income tax and a withholding tax as is done in the USA.[40]

6.3.2.1. Interest parity and taxation.

Till interest parity is established an important issue is that of taxation of interest paid on external commercial borrowing (ECB). The uncovered interest parity condition can be used as a guide to derive the rate of tax on interest paid on ECB consistent with a stable exchange rate. The interest parity condition is

$$(1 + (1 + x)I_w) = (1 + I_d)E_t/E_0$$

where I_w is the interest rate on ECB, x is the tax rate on this interest,[41] I_d the domestic interest rate on borrowing of equal risk and tenure, and E_t/E_0 the expected depreciation of the rupee–dollar/foreign currency rate. If the expected depreciation is zero, then the interest parity condition reduces to

$$(1 + x)I_w = I_d.$$

This yields the interest tax rate consistent with a stable global financial market equilibrium.[42] For instance, if the foreign interest rate is 6% and the equivalent domestic rate is 8%, then the interest tax rate $x = 1/3$ or 33%. This rate is almost equal to the marginal tax rate on interest income received by a resident. If there is an expectation of a continuing appreciation of the rupee the required tax rate would be higher. However, if the expectation is only temporary then the rate calculated above may be sufficient given the intangible transaction costs of borrowing from abroad.

The tax should in principle apply to all foreign borrowing. Short-term credit of tenure less than one year could be subject to a minimum interest tax calculated as the absolute amount that would be paid if it was borrowed for a full year. Thus if the borrowing is for six months at an annual rate of 6%, the tax liability would be equal to 2% of the loan even though the interest paid is about 3% of the loan amount. The effective tax rate in this case is 2/3rd and would rise progressively with shortening of tenure.[43] It is important to recall and reiterate at this point, that the tax becomes zero if the interest parity condition is established.

If such a tax can be effectively imposed on all ECB it will reduce if not eliminate the arbitrage opportunity arising from changes in interest rates resulting from monetary policy and temporary spikes in the exchange rate.[44] We can then decontrol all medium- and long-term ECB (say of a tenure of three years and above). There can also be an announcement of progressive reduction of the minimum tenure to one year over the next three to five years.

Such a tax can be justified to counter negative externalities arising from excessive capital inflows, as long as the interest parity condition does not prevail. This tax differs from the 'Tobin Tax' in that the latter was to be levied on all capital transactions, while the former is restricted to debt flows only. Recall that one reason for restricting the tax to debt alone is imperfection in and fragmentation of capital markets that do not allow interest rates and returns on riskless assets to equalize. Note also that the earlier experience of Chile and other countries in imposing some form of (explicit or implicit) capital inflow differs from the Indian situation in one important respect. Here, the tax is supposed to replace an existing QR on ECB, which has been in place for decades, not as in Chile and other countries as a substitute for another market-based policy.

Given the practical difficulties involved in the introduction of further taxation, additional reserve requirements on debt inflows and auction of borrowing rights can be considered as means of implementing such an implicit tax.

6.3.2.2. Auction of ECB rights. An alternative more flexible way of achieving the same objective would be to auction the right to undertake external commercial borrowing. The auction could be held on a quarterly or monthly basis with the annual ceiling appropriately divided into quarterly or monthly tranches. The bid variable could be the unit price per rupee crore of borrowing by Indian residents from foreign residents (all legal entities so defined). This has the added advantage that the auction cost per annum declines with term of the borrowing thus giving an incentive to long-term borrowing/debt. The ECB transaction would have to be registered (as currently) within a specified time period (three to six months) after the auction.

The sub-limits on foreign institutional investor (FII) investment in government securities and commercial debt securities need to be removed, if elimination of the interest differential is to be expedited. If found operationally feasible, we can impose a condition that the right (purchased through auction) lasts only till the time the securities are sold in the market (i.e. it is a right to gross (not net) borrowing within the specified period and not a stock holding right with implied trading rights). That is, new rights have to be purchased every time a security is purchased from the market.

This system would also allow us to reduce the minimum term to one year (say) once the system is functioning smoothly.

6.3.3. FII debt limits and cost of sterilization

No additional tax is required on portfolio flows, as it is already taxed on par with domestic portfolio investment. The necessity of eliminating the favourable treatment of portfolio capital routed through Mauritius remains. Appropriate changes in rules and procedures need to continue to eliminate the possibility of round tripping and tax avoidance.

Elimination of limits on FII investment in government securities and in private bonds can play a vital role in eliminating the interest gap between Indian and global financial markets and in establishing interest parity. Though inflows on this account are currently below the limit, this is because a serious player requires a minimum scale of operation (MES) to undertake debt business as a profitable long-term opportunity. Unless the limits are set well above the MES there is tremendous policy uncertainty about future limits, which add to the market risk of developing a completely new market. Once these limits are eliminated, serious players are likely to enter and develop the market on a long-term basis and thus increase FII flows into the debt market. The increased demand for government securities can help eliminate the interest gap between OECD government securities and Indian government securities and thus reduce the costs of sterilization. Greater FII investment in private bonds will help deepen and widen the market and eventually provide medium-sized firms better access to capital.[45]

6.3.3.1. Hybrid products.
Foreign Currency Convertible Bonds (FCCB) constitute debt till they are converted into equity. This is how they are treated domestically. The same principle should be applied to FCCBs issued abroad or when held by foreigners/non-residents. This means that they must be subject to rules similar to those applied to ECB (e.g. aggregate or individual limits). During the past year it was discovered that some companies were using optionally convertible debentures and other variations of these products and classifying these as equity. This has rightly been stopped.

Similarly preference shares can be converted into debt by imposing call/put options (directly or indirectly). To ensure that such instruments, normally treated as equity, do not become vehicles for evading existing restrictions on debt (as long as they remain in place), an undertaking must be given by those issuing such shares to foreign investors.[46] Both they and the lenders would then be liable to penalty if evasion is discovered subsequently.

6.3.3.2. Participatory notes (PNs).
Concern has been expressed in the past by the RBI and others on the lack of customer knowledge when participatory notes are used by FIIs (20 out of 882, but encompassing 35% of total FII inflow). Currently, foreigners can directly invest in India only by getting registered as a foreign institutional investor (FII) or by opening a sub-account with a registered FII. The rules for both require that the source of funds be broad based, prominent examples of which are mutual funds, insurance companies, and employee pension fund. This

means that private equity funds (with a limited number of investors) and endowment funds and high net worth individuals (including Persons of Indian Origin (PIOs)) are excluded from the market and have found indirect ways such as PNs to invest in the market. Allowing direct access will improve transparency and regulatory oversight and allow imposition of tighter controls on PNs without giving rise to accusations of anti-reform action. We should allow foreigners residing in countries with good legal systems and well-regulated markets to invest in India through domestic institutional investors (DIIs) and Securities and Exchange Board of India (SEBI) registered portfolio managers. It will be the duty of these DIIs and portfolio managers to apply 'Know Your Customer' norms for opening new accounts (KYC norms) similar to those applied by banks and report to the regulatory authorities.[47] In other words, FII should be incorporated in and become a sub-set of foreign investor (FI) regulations.

To the extent that registered FIIs and FII sub-account holders use PNs as a tax avoidance measure (by transferring tax liability to lower tax jurisdictions), a ban on PNs will eliminate the tax bias in favour of equity inflows. Such a correction is highly desirable.[48]

6.3.4. Mutual funds and venture capital funds (VCFs)

In the context of taxation a mutual fund (MF) is a pass through vehicle whose earnings should only be taxed in the hands of the MF investor (and any profits of the MF manager). Mutual fund earnings arise from company dividends, interest on debt, and capital gains on equity. To the extent that companies pay dividend tax, this component of a mutual fund's return should not be taxed in the hands of the receiver. However, any MF earnings from interest received and capital gains actualized should be appropriately taxed in the hands of the domestic receiver (and withholding tax on the foreign receiver). Any anomalies in this regard need to be corrected. This can easily be done if the MF calculates and states on its payout slips what proportion of earnings came from corporate dividends, short- and long-term capital gains, and other income such as interest, rents, and profits. Then the taxpayer would have to apportion these earnings among the different categories and pay the appropriate tax for each category, when filing returns. Other solutions can also be considered, which simplify monitoring of potential tax evasion and make it necessary for foreign receivers of dividends from Indian companies to formally file for a refund if they are entitled to do so under a double tax agreement.

The MF would in turn, as a pass through vehicle, calculate the proportion of earnings from dividends and pass a proportionate tax benefit to the MF investors. In general the dividend statement of the mutual fund (or any other investment agent) should specify the proportion of income received in the form of corporate dividends, short- and long-term capital gains, and other income (interest, rent, etc. on which corporate tax has not been paid).

A genuine VCF, in addition to being a pass through vehicle should provide special procedures to facilitate high risk or very uncertain entrepreneurial activities and incentives for the same in line with global best practice (USA, Ireland, Israel, South Korea). These incentives should in general be the same for foreign and domestic investors and not biased in favour of the former. The keywords here are 'very un-certain' and 'high risk'.[49] The latter means that these are novel activities, for which there is no historical information to calculate the probability of success/failure. Though it is not easy to operationalize these terms, one has to ascertain and adapt global best practice to Indian conditions, particularly the abysmal enforcement of laws.

7. Monetary management

In the conventional rational expectation model an exogenous increase in capital inflows (positive capital shock) must result in a real appreciation, either through a nominal appreciation or through higher inflation.[50] This in turn must result in a rebalancing of the economy from tradables (relative shrinkage) to non-tradables (relative expansion) without affecting the size of the economy or its growth rate. If the capital account is open, then the interest rate is determined by and fixed relative to the global interest rate. Consequently there are no direct affects on investment and growth of this inflow of foreign capital into the economy.

We assume that the bulk of flows into the Indian economy at this point in time are driven by medium- to long-term growth expectations (economy, corporate sector, etc.) not by short-term arbitrage opportunities (interest differentials cum appreciation expectations).[51] An imperfect indicator is the proportion of net equity in total inflows.[52] The inflow of FDI, equity, and venture capital into an emerging economy characterized by expectation of sustained growth, can in our view, change the level of investment, the efficiency of intermediation, and the productivity of capital and consequently the rate of growth of the economy. To the extent that this happens the assumptions of the conventional model are incorrect and therefore the implications for monetary and exchange rate management must be modified.[53] For capital inflows driven by interest differentials, reform of financial markets (debt, banking, credit, inflow rules) and a reduction in the fiscal deficit are essential for correcting the differential and eliminating such flows.[54]

Capital markets in emerging economies are typically underdeveloped and fragmented. Thus the relatively free flow of foreign capital into and out of the economy (which arguably holds for India) may not imply that all interest rates meet the interest parity condition.[55] Further, greater inflows of capital, as they are accompanied by special skills and knowledge, could accelerate the monetization of the economy by broadening and deepening the degree of financial intermediation.[56]

7.1. Exchange management

It has been our policy since 1992 to allow foreign exchange markets to respond to permanent adverse changes in the BOP situation but to ensure that this happens in an orderly manner. On the other hand, temporary shocks are to be dealt with through appropriate monetary and exchange rate interventions. Given the cacophony of public debate and strong disagreements among experts on the issue of managing large capital inflows, the paper tries to articulate policy for managing medium- to long-term excess flows of capital.

There is a fair degree of consensus that in a market economy (i.e. where foreign trade is not explicitly or surreptitiously managed through subsidies) a real appreciation of the exchange rate has (a) a negative effect on exports and a positive effect on imports[57] and (b) reduces the size of the tradable sector relative to the non-tradable sector. The precise impact will differ for different countries depending on a number of factors including the elasticity of demand and supply and the extent of pass through. There is no such consensus on the affect of the exchange rate on economic growth, whether through its effect on foreign trade or through the effect on the tradable sector (particularly modern manufacturing) or through other channels. Broadly, the theorists tend to discount any such effects, while the empiricists tend to find some effect of exchange rate under/overvaluation on growth.

7.1.1. *Exchange rate and growth*

Our research on economic growth in India has shown that an appreciation of the real exchange rate, defined as the price of tradable goods relative to the price of non-tradable services (ReXr) has a negative effect on growth.[58] The effect of changes in the real effective exchange rate (REER) on growth was not however, found to be statistically significant, once the ReXr is accounted for.[59] The difference probably arises because the ReXr is the net result of the interaction of the exchange rate, quantity controls, and tariff rates.[60] One of the channels for this effect is the impact of the REER on net exports of goods and services, with a depreciation increasing the effective demand in the economy.[61] The positive effect of such an increase depends critically on the capacity of the economy for acceleration in real economic growth. Such a possibility is clearly greater when the economy is growing at 5% than when it is growing at 9%.[62] There are, however, indirect gains from a higher level of exports and imports even when the net balance of goods and services trade does not change much. These gains arise from the effect of greater competition and competitive access to technology, capital goods, and ideas. There is therefore, we believe, merit in moderating the appreciation of the rupee (as measured by the 36-country REER), arising from excessive capital inflows (net inflow in excess of current account deficit if any).[63]

7.1.2. *Exchange rate and reserves*

One way to do this is to mirror the policy approach that has been adopted for negative trends and shocks. That is, to allow managed appreciation of the rupee in response to medium-term trends but moderate the short-term positive shocks through appropriate exchange rate policy. Some would say that this is what RBI/Government has been doing till 2006–2007 and that the approach should be continued. Others argue that there was too little flexibility during 2004–2005 to 2006–2007 and that this flexibility has increased in 2007–2008 and that the latter is more suggestive of a flexible approach. Another, more formal operational version that has been suggested in similar contexts is for the Central Bank to set a symmetric band of 5–10% within which it does not intervene in the market. Intervention is then used only if the exchange rate moves out of the band. The band is also adjusted on a rolling/moving average basis if the exchange rate hits the band and stays there.

Whatever the version that is adopted, it should be complemented by an explicit policy for investment of reserves. All additions to reserves that are an outcome of this policy would either be (a) put in a separate fund or (b) treated as part of a separate reserve tranche. The objectives and risk parameters for such a tranche/fund would be somewhat different from the existing reserves.[64] The (ultimate) objective would be to earn a rate of return equal to the interest rate on Indian government securities purchased for the purpose of sterilizing these reserves plus targeted appreciation. This fund/tranche could only be invested in specified countries and specified categories/lists of securities with an investment grade rating. If successful, such a strategy would eliminate the cost of sterilization that has so exercised a number of observers/analysts.

A depreciation of the US dollar against major currencies generates a partial appreciation of the rupee as measured by the REER 36-country trade/export weighted (REER36), even if there is no change in capital inflows and/or purchases by the RBI. A view would have to be taken on whether to treat it similarly to or differently from a change in rupee value vis-à-vis all currencies.

7.2. Money supply

The sterilization operations have to be meshed with the monetary management and inflation targets.

7.2.1. Inflation and money

It is now conventional wisdom that lags between monetary growth and inflation are long and variable.[65] Thus sound empirical research is needed to determine these links. Our very preliminary research finds a link between money (M1) growth and WPI inflation:

$$\text{GrWpi} = 0.049 - 0.645\,\text{GrGdpfc} + 0.436\,\text{GrM1}$$
$$(1.7) \quad (-2.5)^{**} \qquad\qquad (2.5)^{**} \qquad\qquad\qquad (1)$$
$$R^2 = 0.28, \quad R^2(\text{adj}) = 0.23$$

$$\text{GrWpi} = 0.057 - 0.627\,\text{GrGdpfc} + 0.4546\,\text{GrM1} - 0.0385\,\text{GrNrfea}$$
$$(2.1)^{**} \quad (-2.6)^{**} \qquad\qquad (2.9)^{**} \qquad\qquad (-2.6)^{**} \qquad\qquad (2)$$
$$R^2 = 0.40, \quad R^2(\text{adj}) = 0.36$$

where GrX stands for growth rate of X, WPI is the wholesale price index, Gdpfc is the GDP at factor cost, M1 is the money supply and Nrfea is net foreign exchange assets of the RBI. Two facts stand out. One that the explanatory power of both equations is limited. This means that there is a substantial element of inflation that is not explained by monetary factors. Second the coefficients of GDP and money supply are different from one, contrary to the simplified quantity theory of money.[66]

These or similar/better equations can be used to determine a monetary target consistent with targeted inflation and projected growth rate. This in turn can be translated into a targeted change in the monetary base using a multiplier. For instance, if we use Equation (1) and target an inflation of less than 5%, with a projected GDP growth rate of 9% the targeted M1 growth rate is 13.5%. Assuming an M1 multiplier of 1.4 and assuming that the NDA will not grow this yields a targeted growth in RBI's net foreign exchange assets (Nrfea) of 10%.[67]

Thus any growth of the RBI's net foreign exchange assets above this level would have to be sterilized. Sterilization would also have to be increased if the growth in NDA is positive or the GDP growth falls short of 9% (from Equation (1) or (2)).

During 2004–2005 to 2006–2007 RBI purchases of foreign exchange and the sterilization of these reserves (both) averaged about 1.7% of GDP. On average about 60% of the sterilization was done through an increase in CRR and the rest through Market Stabilization Scheme (MSS). During the first half of 2007–2008, RBI purchases have already reached about 3.4% of GDP and sterilization about 2.4% of annual GDP.[68] The increase in CRR represents a reversal of the long-term objectives of policy and RBI has stated that it is a short-term reversal of the long-term objective. Therefore, increasing reliance will have to be placed on MSS and/or open market operations for sterilization in the future. This also makes it urgent to decontrol investment in government securities and commercial paper, by potential domestic and foreign investors, so that interest can fall and converge to corresponding global rates and eliminate sterilization costs.[69]

7.2.2. *Interest rates*

The approach outlined above has implications for the use of interest rate as an instrument of monetary management. Once the limits of GDP growth acceleration are reached the tri-lemma of monetary policy becomes applicable. This paper suggests that we break this tri-lemma by the use of an additional instrument, a fiscal instrument, the explicit or implicit tax on interest on foreign debt. This is used to eliminate arbitrage possibilities by equating after-tax interest rates in India and abroad. If this tax is held constant (or changed only in response to foreign interest rates) then domestic interest rates cannot be changed at will without recreating the problem. If the RBI wishes to continue to use interest rate signals to change domestic interest rates, then the interest parity will have to be restored by changing the tax on foreign interest payments. As frequent changes in the tax rate may not be possible, the interest rate cannot be used as a frequent signalling device and sterilization operations would become the main instrument for controlling the monetary situation. With the risk-free interest rate anchored to the global rate (as it must be under an open capital account) RBI may have to make more active use of prudential norms to signal its views on euphoric asset price-based lending.

If the right to ECB is auctioned, however, the market price for this privilege will adjust to offset the interest rate changes. For instance, with a positive interest gap, a tightening of monetary policy (whether through interest rate signals or otherwise) would lead to a rise in the auction price of ECB rights.

In either case the width of the interest rate band around the global interest rate rates (and the corresponding tax rate/auction price) is limited by the need to minimize the incentive for tax evasion and/or the incentive to substitute equity inflows for debt flows.

If investment by financial intermediaries (domestic and foreign) is completely decontrolled, we believe that the interest rates will converge over time and eliminate the need for such a tax.

7.2.2.1. *Administered interest rates.* For banks and other financial intermediaries to function effectively within such a flexible financial market, any remnants of administered rates must be eliminated. This will mean making small saving rates and interest rates on government pension funds, market related. Several committees have deliberated on this issue and suggested that they be related to interest rate on government Treasury bills and government securities and/or bank deposit rates.

8. Fiscal deficit

A further reduction of the fiscal deficit can widen the space for monetary policy effectiveness. In the long term a lower fiscal deficit will result in a reduction in the real domestic long-term interest rate of the economy and thus brings it closer to the world long-term rates (USA, Japan, EU).[70] In the short term it can reduce the excess demand pressure created by the inflow of foreign funds. Most high growth South East Asian economies had a fiscal surplus during most of their high growth period. Even in the short term, a lower fiscal deficit will mean a reduced supply of government securities and for any given demand structure a higher price for government securities and Treasury bills, that is, a lower interest rate. This will directly reduce the interest gap with the USA, Japan, etc. We should target a reduction in the consolidated general government fiscal deficit to 3% by 2013, with 1.5% each for the Centre and States, from the existing (2008–2009) target of 6% (3% each for the Centre and States).[71] A further reduction should be considered thereafter.[72]

9. Financial market development

A coherent and consistent framework of monetary management will allow us to accelerate the development of financial markets. There is an urgent need for developing competitive, open, and well-regulated markets for (a) long-term debt, (b) rupee futures and forwards, and (c) interest rate/credit risk products, so that economic agents can hedge their exposure in an efficient market with low transaction costs.[73] By promoting the developments of these markets in India it will also generate financial skills and jobs in India. Such learning by doing in the financial sector is an essential foundation for the export of financial services in the future.[74]

The lesson that we draw from the recent global financial crisis (sub-prime mortgages, ABS, ABCPs, CDOs, SIVs, etc.) is not that we should slow or stop financial innovation but that regulatory forbearance and accommodating accounting standards are inappropriate. We must apply (at least initially) stringent transparency conditions and strict accounting standards to fancy new products that few people in the economy really understand and initially regulate them fairly strictly. Conversely we must always be prepared to loosen the strict regulations once the market participants are fully cognizant of all the implications of these new products so that the market can spread and grow rapidly to the benefit of relatively less well-endowed participants.

10. Conclusion

This paper lays out a consistent framework for monetary management in the context of excess capital inflows. Among the important features of this framework are:

(1) A change in the emphasis of capital inflow policy from a positive to a neutral stance on equity inflows and a negative stance on debt inflows.
(2) A reduction of the gap between Indian and foreign interest rates so as to reduce the incentive for debt inflows and reduce the cost of sterilization.

(3) A continuation/acceleration of our autonomous, widely acclaimed, and highly beneficial reductions in tariff rates.

(4) A faster opening of the capital account to resident companies, entrepreneurs, and citizens in terms of capital outflows.

(5) A rational trade-off between nominal appreciation and sterilization coupled with a flexible exchange rate policy and clear mandate for sterilization.

A shared perception of this policy framework and its broad approach will ensure that the government helps market agents reduce and manage the uncertainty arising from external and domestic shocks through development of markets for risk and sound regulation.

Acknowledgement

The views expressed in this paper are those of the author and do not necessarily reflect those of the Ministry of Finance or the Government of India.

Notes

1. The initial draft of this paper was completed in August 2007, so some of the subsequent policy changes are reflected in the footnotes rather than in the text. It was revised and updated in January 2008.
2. Details in Section 3.
3. With policy and institutional reforms this trend may accelerate!
4. These are underlying rates derived from a statistical analysis that accounts for rainfall fluctuations.
5. Among medium–large countries. In addition there were five small and five tiny countries.
6. Our per capita GDP growth would be approximately 7.5% if GDP grows at 9%.
7. Besides the numerous real side challenges (public goods infrastructure, skills and education, credible rule of law, public service delivery mechanisms, institutional reform).
8. A 1974 MOF paper first wrote about moving from physical to financial controls and the Dagli committee added its weight to this move in the late 1970s. Thirty years later we should not have to argue about the merits of the latter under normal conditions, that is, except in an emergency or crisis such as our BOP crises in 1990–91 and the Asian crisis of 1997–98.
9. These must be and are expected to be, addressed as part of the 11th Plan.
10. Virmani (2007) provides a somewhat unconventional view of what types of infrastructure are important.
11. Rational expectations model. See Bery, Lal, and Pant (2003) and Shah and Patnaik (2007) for application to India.
12. See Razin and Collins (1997) and Bhalla (2002, 2005, 2006).
13. See, for example, Faria and Leon-Ledesma (2000).
14. In Virmani (1998).
15. With major inconsistencies between the assumptions and implications of the neo-classical growth model and its implications. Again this does not mean that the insights of this model are not useful!
16. This cannot happen in the monetarist model because the economy is already at full employment. Alternatively/equivalently the real side of the economy is driven by real factors that are independent of monetary developments/shocks and monetary policies.
17. Illustrative calculations showed that this is what happened in 1993–94.
18. This is perhaps what happened in much of South East Asia during the 1990s!
19. For instance, a policy-induced rise in interest rates will result in both higher capital inflows and a transfer of savings/capital from the informal segment to the formal segment of the economy.
20. Whence the phrase 'irrational exuberance'.

21. Parking space for private transport is also an essential element of modern urban land use, though the mix of private and public transport can vary from one city to another and even within a city.

22. In modern cities land can also be expanded vertically, by re-defining floor space indices and changing municipal by-laws, and providing bigger sewers, water mains, and parking spaces.

23. Virmani (2005a, 2006a) explain this paradox – 'slower reforms immediate acceleration' vs. 'major reforms gradual but sustained acceleration'.

24. Note that this is quite different from the effects of rainfall which is accounted for in our estimates but not in the estimates (and projections) of others.

25. Energy prices are also a source of concern, but have not so far been reflected in domestic prices because of incomplete pass through. The demand effects through the fiscal have also been moderated by physical controls on prices that have the effect of taxing oil company profits (additional tax on).

26. Relative to the average US, EU, or Japanese consumer.

27. Soon after the BOP crises of 1990 had been successfully dealt with in 1991–92, the Ministry of Finance freed equity inflows through FIIs. This resulted in an unprecedented equity inflow into India from September 1993 to October 1994 of about $6 billion or 2% of GDP for this 12-month period. This was followed by the Asian crises of 1997 and the Russian crises of 1998. The strategy developed during 1997 was used successfully to manage the outflows that resulted from the crises. See Virmani (2003) or Virmani (2001b) for analysis of external sector reforms.

28. Through monetary measures and flexible exchange rate management. Looking into the future, fiscal consolidation (reduction of fiscal deficit) in a period of high growth creates fiscal space that can be used to run a counter-cyclical fiscal policy which further reduces the cost of large capital outflows.

29. See, for instance, Virmani et al. (2004) or Virmani (2006b).

30. This could be accelerated if the developed countries eliminate subsidies on agriculture. The latter in turn would be facilitated by increased demand for bio-fuels that have led to temporary increase in global prices.

31. Virmani (2001a) or Virmani (2002).

32. As per the experience acquired in handling earlier episodes of potential and actual outflows, such as the Mexican, Asian, and Russian crises.

33. This should not be confused with the reporting requirements under the Money Laundering Act or anti-terrorist legislation. The two should be kept strictly separate.

34. Currently residents can hold up to $2000/- in cash.

35. For instance, there can be an overall cash holding limit with residents free to hold a mix of rupees and foreign currency. This can be tailored to meet legitimate money laundering concerns.

36. Currently residents can open RFC accounts with money gifted to them by family members and other legitimate remittances.

37. Recently interest was allowed to be paid on such accounts up to a maximum balance of US$1 million.

38. Currently companies are not allowed to undertake 'naked margin trading'. If this restriction is removed, Indian financial institutions can start specializing in such trading and offer these products to a wider array of small–medium companies in India who are engaged in international trade.

39. We had argued for this principle in the early 1990s when the objective was to raise all private capital flows.

40. For instance, interest (or other forms of income) on US debt held by foreigners is taxed in the USA. Dividends paid by most companies are also similarly taxable.

41. Subsidy if negative.

42. In the conventional monetarist model, interest parity is guaranteed in the absence of capital controls. In empirical work ad hoc risk premiums have often to be assumed to explain divergence form these conditions for all but the most developed economies (USA, EMU, UK).

43. However, there may be practical difficulties in implementing such a format.

44. If the source country has a credit type taxation of foreign income or a tax treaty that effectively eliminates the (additional) tax liability implied in the current withholding tax,

then other methods become necessary. Indirect taxation though zero interest CRR requirements on capital inflows can be explored.

45. The direct effect is merely to transfer some of the debt inflow from the ECB to the domestic bond market, this itself has beneficial long-term effects.

46. There are suspicions in the markets that this has happened in the real estate sector after ECB to it was restricted.

47. All payment from the investor to the DFI or portfolio manager would have to be made from a recognized/regulated bank in a legally/regulatory clean country (e.g. any OECD member country bank).

48. Surjit Bhalla has pointed out that off-shore use of derivatives allows foreign investors to avoid payment of 33% tax that local residents have to pay.

49. Not 'technology intensive', 'high tech', and 'knowledge based'.

50. The converse is supposed to happen if capital flows out (negative shock).

51. And that this is likely remains true in the next 5–10 years in terms of either the proportion of flows or the ratio to GDP.

52. Sophisticated financial contracts may be used to disguise debt flows as equity in some cases.

53. Unlike in developed economies this phase can last a couple of decades in fast growing emerging economies.

54. Short and long term, respectively.

55. Bhatt and Virmani (2005) showed the existence of uncovered interest parity (UIP) in the money markets for three-month Treasury bills (USA and India).

56. Incorrect assumptions and simplistic application of developed country lessons can also have negative effects such as euphoria and panic à la Asian crisis.

57. Virmani (1991) showed that earlier results were flawed because market sectors (e.g. manufactured goods) were not dis-aggregated from controlled sectors (e.g. agriculture and petroleum oil). Only the former can be expected to respond freely to price signals.

58. Virmani (2005b, 2006b).

59. In a comparative framework (in contrast to our single country analysis) Faria and Leon-Ledesma (2000) show for a set of four developed countries (USA, UK, Germany, Japan) that even though (bilateral) purchasing power parity (PPP) seems to prevail in the long run, the (bilateral) real exchange rate seems to have a long run impact on relative growth rates (thus contradicting the theory underlying PPP).

60. Thus a reduction in QRs and tariffs, resulting in the reduction in effective tariffs can offset part of the appreciation of the REER.

61. Excessive focus on the rupee–US dollar rate or even the 5/6-country REER is inappropriate as they give partial and sometimes a completely misleading picture.

62. On the other hand if the economy is growing faster because it is more productive/efficient, then exports may respond more strongly to exchange rate changes.

63. Which is driven by expectations of returns in a fast growing (relatively) newly opened economy.

64. If capital inflows continue and reserves continue to grow at the current pace it will not be long before reserves double. In that case we may have to create another tranche or fund managed by an investment corporation that could invest in equity and below investment grade paper.

65. For Europe according to one expert this is between one and a half and three years.

66. Lagged values of these variables are not found to be significant. M3 is either not statistically significant or the explanatory power of the equation is lower.

67. Please note that these are merely illustrative calculations.

68. During the first half of 2007–2008 the ratio is 30:70, though the ratio for the whole year can be different.

69. This is a key assumption of the monetarist/rational expectation model. Without it some of the conclusions and recommendations of the model are not valid.

70. Chapter 3 of the WEO of October 2007 also shows that a reduction in the fiscal deficit reduces the costs of subsequent reversal of capital flows.

71. This would also bring us into equivalence with the EU which has a 3% fiscal deficit limit under the Maastricht treaty. Note that the current target is double that of the EU.

72. A fiscal surplus can also contribute to an increase in a nation's global wealth holdings. The most prominent example is China.
73. This requires the presence of speculators with diverse expectations.
74. *A la* regional or global financial centre.

References

Bery, Suman, Deepak Lal, and Pant Devendra Kumar. 2003. The real exchange rate, fiscal deficits and capital flows – India: 1981–2000. *Economic and Political Weekly* XXXVIII, no. 47, November 22.

Bhalla, Surjit S. 2002. Trade, growth and poverty: Re-examining the linkages. Presented at World Bank–ADB, Fourth Asia Development Forum, November, Seoul, Korea.

Bhalla, Surjit S. 2005. India–China: Diverging to converge. Presented at CESifo Economic Studies Conference on Understanding the Chinese Economy, June, Ifo Institute, Munich, Germany.

Bhalla, Surjit S. 2006. Second among equals: The middle class kingdoms of India and China. Executive Summary, Peterson Institute of International Economics, June.

Bhatt, Vipul, and Arvind Virmani. 2005. Global integration of India's money market: Interest rate parity in India. Working Paper No. 164, ICRIER, July.

Faria, Joao Ricardo, and Miguel Leon-Ledesma. 2000. Testing the Balassa–Samuelson effect: Implications for growth and PPP, September. www.kent.ac.uk/economics/papers/papers-pdf/2000/0008.pdf.

Razin, Ofair, and Susan M. Collins. 1997. Real exchange rate misalignments and growth. NBER Working Paper No. 6174, September.

Shah, Ajay, and Ila Patnaik. 2007. India's experience with capital flows: The elusive quest for a sustainable current account deficit. Chapter 13 of *Capital controls and capital flows in emerging economies: Policies, practices and consequences*, ed. Sebastian Edwards, 609–43. Chicago: The University of Chicago Press.

Virmani, Arvind. 1998. Macro-management of economic growth with underemployed labor and technological inertia. ADB/World Bank Senior Policy Seminar on 'Managing Global Financial Integration in Asia', March 10–12, Manila, Philippines.

Virmani, Arvind. 1991. Demand and supply factors in India's trade. *Economic and Political Weekly* 2, no. 6. February 9, 1991.

Virmani, Arvind. 2001a. Central value added tax: CENVAT. *Economic and Political Weekly* XXXVI, no. 8, February 24–March 2: 630–2.

Virmani, Arvind. 2001b. India's 1990–91 crisis: Reforms, myths and paradoxes. Planning Commission Working Paper No. 4/2001-PC, December. http://www.planningcommission.nic.in/reports/wrkpapers/wp_cris9091.pdf.

Virmani, Arvind. 2002. Towards a competitive economy: VAT and customs duty reform. Planning Commission Working Paper No. 4/2002-PC, April. http://www.planningcommission.nic.in/reports/wrkpapers/wp_vat.pdf.

Virmani, Arvind. 2003. India's external reforms: Modest globalisation significant gains. *Economic and Political Weekly*, no. 32, August 9–15: 3373–90.

Virmani, Arvind. 2005a. India's economic growth history: Fluctuations trends, break points and phases. Occasional Policy Paper, January. http://www.icrier.org/Growth05_Policy1.pdf.

Virmani, Arvind. 2005b. Policy regimes, growth and poverty in India. Lessons of government failure and entrepreneurial success! Working Paper No. 170, ICRIER, October. http://www.icrier.org/WP170GrPov9.pdf.

Virmani, Arvind. 2006a. The dynamics of competition: Phasing of domestic and external liberalisation in India. Working Paper No. 4/2006-PC, Planning Commission, April. http://planningcommission.nic.in/reports/wrkpapers/rpwpf.htm.

Virmani, Arvind. 2006b. *Propelling India from socialist stagnation to global power: Growth process*, Vol. I *(Policy reform*, Vol. II*)*. New Delhi: Academic Foundation.

Virmani, Arvind. 2007. The Sudoku of growth, poverty and malnutrition: Lessons for lagging states. Working Paper No. 2/2007-PC, Planning Commission, July.

Virmani, Arvind, Goldar Bishwanath, Choorikkad Veeramani, and Vipul Bhatt. 2004. Impact of tariff reforms on Indian industry: Assessment based on a multi-sector econometric model. Working Paper No. 135, ICRIER, June. www.icrier.org/wp135.pdf.

Capital account liberalization and conduct of monetary policy: the Indian experience

Rakesh Mohan

Reserve Bank of India, Central Office, Mumbai, 400 001, India

The distinguishing feature of our overall reform process initiated in the early 1990s has been the acceleration in growth while maintaining price and financial stability even in the face of large and repeated domestic and foreign shocks. This successful outcome can be attributed, inter alia, to our calibrated and cautious approach to capital account and financial sector liberalization and our encompassing approach – multiple objectives and multiple instruments – to the conduct of monetary policy. For emerging market economies like India, monetary policy and exchange rate regimes have necessarily to be operated as fuzzy or intermediate regimes not obeying the almost received wisdom of purist approaches. The judgement on the legitimacy of such a regime must be based on their efficacy as revealed by the outcomes. On this count, India's macroeconomic, monetary and financial managers can justifiably claim a reasonable degree of success: economic growth is high and accelerating; inflation has shifted to lower sustainable levels; savings and investments are growing; financial markets have been growing and developing in an orderly manner; the health of the banking system has improved continuously and is approaching best practice standards; the external account is healthy in the presence of robust trade growth in both goods and services; increasing capital flows indicate growing international confidence in the Indian economy; and the Indian exchange rate has been flexible in both directions providing for reasonable market determination, in the presence of central bank forex interventions. As we ascend to a higher growth path, and as we have fuller capital account convertibility, we will face newer challenges and will have to continue to adapt. The key point is that with greater capital account openness, we have to develop markets such that market participants, financial and non financial, are enabled to cope better with market fluctuations. As we do this, we need to be cognizant of the vast range of capabilities of different market participants in as diverse a country as India: from subsistence farmers to the most sophisticated financial market practitioners.

1. Overall approach

The distinguishing feature of our overall reform process initiated in the early 1990s has been the accomplishment of high economic growth in an environment of macroeconomic and financial stability. In fact, we have achieved acceleration in growth while maintaining price and financial stability.

During this period, apart from all the other reforms, we have achieved current account convertibility, and also opened the capital account to a substantial extent. With this growing openness, we have not been insulated from exogenous shocks. These shocks, global as well as domestic, included a series of financial crises in Asia, Brazil, Russia and Mexico, in the 1990s and other events such as 9/11 terrorist attacks in the US, border tensions, sanctions imposed in the aftermath of nuclear tests, political uncertainties, changes in the government, and the current oil shock. Nonetheless, stability could be maintained in financial markets. Indeed, inflation has been contained since the late-1990s to an average of around 5%, distinctly lower than that of around 7–8% per annum over the previous four decades. Simultaneously, the health of the financial sector has recorded very significant improvement.

The story of Indian reforms is by now well-documented (e.g. Ahluwalia 2002); nevertheless, what is less appreciated is that India achieved this acceleration in growth while maintaining price and financial stability. With increased deregulation of financial markets and increased integration of the global economy, the 1990s were turbulent for global financial markets: 63 countries suffered from systemic banking crises in that decade, much higher than 45 in the 1980s. Among countries that experienced such crises, the direct cost of reconstructing the financial system was typically very high: for example, recapitalization of banks had cost 55% of gross domestic product (GDP) in Argentina, 42% in Thailand, 35% in South Korea and 10% in Turkey. There were high indirect costs of lost opportunities and slow economic growth in addition (McKinsey & Company 2005). It is therefore particularly noteworthy that India could pursue its process of financial deregulation and opening of the economy without suffering financial crises during this turbulent period in world financial markets. The cost of recapitalization of public sector banks at less than 1% of GDP is therefore low in comparison. Whereas we can be legitimately gratified with this record, we now need to focus on the new issues that need to be addressed for the next phase of financial development, particularly in the context of fuller capital account convertibility and increasing integration of financial markets.

That the current annual GDP growth of around 8.5% to 9% can be achieved in India with a level of gross domestic investment in the range of 30% to % over the past four years suggests that the economy is functioning quite efficiently. Thus our policy of gradual and sequenced reform cannot be said to have been at the cost of growth or efficiency. We need to ensure that we maintain this level of efficiency and attempt to improve on it further. As the Indian economy continues on such a growth path and attempts to accelerate it, new demands are being placed on the financial system.

In examining the conduct of monetary policy in India in the presence of continuing and gradual capital account liberalization, a key lesson is that this process has to be viewed in the context of the overall reform process. As an economy undergoes the transition from a closed to an open economy, first on the current account and then on the capital account, the interest of financial stability is served by simultaneous action on a number of different fronts. The framework of monetary policy itself has to undergo a change from the previous direct methods of control of monetary aggregates to indirect methods imparting signals through the market.

For such a change to be effective the monetary policy transmission process has to be strengthened through development of all financial markets, and the building of market micro-infrastructure. On the external front, the transition from a fixed or pegged exchange rate to a market determined one itself needs careful assessment of the efficiency of the foreign exchange market, the capabilities of market players and evaluation of effects of exchange rate volatility. The operation of financial markets and the degree of vulnerability that an economy becomes exposed to with greater opening is itself influenced significantly by fiscal conditions. Hence the efficacy of monetary policy, efficiency of financial markets, and external vulnerability are closely linked to the practice of prudent fiscal policy. Finally, for efficient monetary policy transmission, and depth, liquidity and efficiency of financial markets, financial intermediaries themselves have to be strengthened. It is in view of all these inter-linkages that I have chosen to provide a brief overview of developments in each of these areas as they have evolved over the past decade and a half in India.

2. Process of setting out monetary policy objectives

2.1. General objectives

Traditionally, central banks pursue the twin objectives of price stability and growth or employment. In pursuing the basic objectives, central banks also need to keep in view considerations of orderly financial markets and financial stability. Needless to say, the objectives of monetary policy are interrelated and have trade-offs as well. The preamble to the Reserve Bank of India Act 1934 sets out the Bank's objectives as 'to regulate the issue of Bank notes and the keeping of reserves with a view to securing monetary stability in India and generally to operate the currency and credit system of the country to its advantage'. Although there is no explicit mandate for price stability, as is the current trend in many countries, the objectives of monetary policy in India have evolved as those of maintaining price stability and ensuring adequate flow of credit to the productive sectors of the economy. In essence, monetary policy aims to maintain a judicious balance between price stability and economic growth. The relative emphasis between price stability and economic growth is governed by the prevailing circumstances at a particular time and is spelt out from time to time in the policy announcements of the Reserve Bank.

Considerations of financial stability have assumed greater importance in recent years in view of the increasing openness of the Indian economy, financial integration and the possibility of cross border contagion. As we observed the severe costs of financial instability elsewhere, financial stability has ascended the hierarchy of monetary policy objectives since the second half of the 1990s. Strong synergies and complementarities are observed between price stability and financial stability in India. Accordingly, we believe that regulation, supervision and development of the financial system remain within the legitimate ambit of monetary policy broadly interpreted.

2.2. Framework

Until 1997–98 monetary policy in India used to be conducted with broad money (M3) as an intermediate target. The aim was to regulate money supply consistent with the expected growth of the economy and the projected level of inflation. The targeted monetary expansion used to be set on the basis of estimates of these two crucial parameters. In practice, the monetary targeting framework was used in a flexible manner with feedback from developments in the real sector.

In the wake of financial sector reforms and opening up of the economy in the 1990s, appropriateness of the monetary targeting framework was questioned with the changing inter-relationship between money, output and prices. Accordingly, the Reserve Bank switched over in 1998–99 to a multiple indicator approach. With this approach, interest rates or rates of return in different markets (money, capital and government securities markets), along with data on currency, credit extended by banks and financial institutions, fiscal position, trade flows, capital flows, inflation rate, exchange rate, refinancing and transactions in foreign exchange available on high-frequency basis, are all examined along with output in framing monetary policy.

The specific features of the Indian economy, including its socio-economic characteristics predicate the investing of the monetary authority with multiple objectives for some time to come. While it could be desirable in the interest of clarity and transparency to stack up the objectives in a hierarchy, the jury is still out on the merits of public announcement of the policy weights assigned to each objective. Flexibility in the setting of monetary policy should override consideration of transparency so that public indication of weighting patterns associated with objectives should not solidify into a binding rule. Moreover, continuous monitoring of the underlying macroeconomic and financial conditions for monetary policy purposes will necessitate a continuous re-balancing of weights assigned to various objectives. In a pragmatic sense, therefore, it should suffice for the monetary authority to indicate the main objectives and an ordinal ranking, at best, to reflect the reading of underlying developments.

A single objective for monetary policy, as is usually advocated, particularly in an inflation targeting framework, is a luxury that India cannot afford, at least over the medium term. The cause of monetary policy is not lost, however; analytically, it can be shown that even if one of the multiple objectives is nominal among others that may be real, it can serve as the quintessential nominal anchor and enable monetary policy to work. This view is supported by a pragmatic and influential strand in the literature which questions the recent proliferation of inflation targeting as a monetary policy framework (Friedman 2000; McCallum 1981). As regards inflation targeting, as the monetary policy regime fulfilling the single mandate advocacy, the jury is still out. Even though there has been an increase in the number of central banks adopting inflation targeting since the early 1990s, a number of central banks, notably the Federal Reserve, retain multiple objectives. I am not a monetary scholar, but I do feel that, given the current domestic and international complexities, we need to continue with a flexible framework for monetary policy. The least we need in the current circumstances is a less simplistic approach.

In India, we have not favoured the adoption of inflation targeting, while keeping the attainment of low inflation as a central objective of monetary policy, along with that of high and sustained growth that is so important for a developing economy. Apart from the legitimate concern regarding growth as a key objective, there are other factors that suggest that inflation targeting may not be appropriate for India. First, unlike many other developing countries we have had a record of moderate inflation, with double digit inflation being the exception, and largely socially unacceptable. Second, adoption of inflation targeting requires the existence of an efficient monetary transmission mechanism through the operation of efficient financial markets and absence of interest rate distortions. In India, although the money market, government debt and forex market have indeed developed in recent years, they still have some way to go, whereas the corporate debt market is still to develop. Though interest rate deregulation has largely been accomplished, some administered interest rates still persist. Third, inflationary pressures still often emanate from significant supply shocks related to the effect of the monsoon on agriculture, where monetary policy action may have little role. Finally, in an economy as large as that of India, with various regional differences, and continued existence of market imperfections in factor and product markets between regions, the choice of a universally acceptable measure of inflation is also difficult (Mohan 2006b).

It is important to recognize the reality of multiple objectives of monetary policy in India. Nonetheless, it needs to be appreciated that relative to the past, we need to communicate better on the objective of price stability and as firmly as possible, *albeit* without necessarily a precise numerical objective. Indeed, why should a monetary policy invested with multiple objectives choose to quantify only one – the inflation rate? Indeed, setting such a precise numerical objective for inflation runs the risk of loss of central bank credibility in the context of the dominance of supply side shocks emanating from sources such as monsoon failure and administered pricing of various agricultural commodities and petroleum products. Whereas the share of agriculture in GDP has been declining and is now less than 20%, the sector continues to be extremely important since the majority of the population remains dependent on agriculture. Therefore, setting precise numerical targets for inflation is fraught with the risk of loss of reputation across a large constituency.

Nevertheless, as the Indian economy becomes increasingly open with fuller capital account convertibility, the objective of progressively bringing inflation down to near international levels and maintaining price stability assumes greater importance. The experience of successfully bringing down inflation from persistent higher levels since the late 1990s to around 5% in recent years has already brought down inflation expectations significantly.

As we place greater emphasis on low inflation and price stability, we also need to improve communication with respect to the understanding of inflation. At present, headline inflation in India is indicated by the weekly release of the All India Wholesale Price Index (WPI). Most countries use the consumer price index (CPI) instead. The CPI is difficult to use in India because of the existence of four indexes of CPI, each reflecting the consumption basket of different sets of consumers in urban and rural areas.

An appropriate inflation indicator should (i) reflect price changes of constituent items accurately and (ii) provide some understanding of headline inflation. Whereas it is feasible to construct an economy wide consumer price index on the lines of the harmonized consumer price index (HICP) adopted in the UK and the Euro Area, it is not clear how useful it would be as an indicator of the general price level, given the widely differing consumption baskets as between rich and poor, between rural and urban areas and even between regions in India. In fact, a measure of producer prices to which the WPI is akin, is likely to be more representative and familiar across the country, since these prices are more likely to be uniform across the country. Accordingly, the commodity/services based price index should be seen as useful more as an indicator/information variable than as defining the inflation objective. Moreover, the WPI is available on a weekly basis, with a two week lag, whereas the CPI indices are only available on monthly basis, and with a two month lag.

Monetary policy should be more explicitly associated with managing inflation expectations rather than current inflation. Accordingly, the guiding criterion for inclusion of a variable in the inflation indicators panel should be the information content on future inflation. An important sub-set would be real sector indicators of future inflation such as variability of output around trend/potential, capacity utilization, inventory, corporate performance, industrial/ investment expectations and other indicators of aggregate demand. We have initiated greater quantitative technical work in these areas over the last couple of years to better inform our monetary policy making with a forward looking approach.

The Reserve Bank has also initiated inflation expectation surveys so that we can have some direct indicators of changing inflation expectations of the public. These quarterly surveys are still in the pilot testing stage so their results are not yet in the public domain. But the initial results look promising.

The more complex is the mandate for the central bank, the greater is the necessity of communication (Mohan 2005). The Reserve Bank of India (RBI) clearly has complex objectives. Apart from pursuing monetary policy, financial stability is one of the overriding concerns of the RBI. Within the objective of monetary policy, both control of inflation and providing adequate credit to the productive sectors of the economy so as to foster growth are equally important. This apart, the Reserve Bank acts as a banking regulator, public debt manager, government debt market regulator and currency issuer. Faced with such multiple tasks and complex mandate, there is an utmost necessity of clearer communication on the part of the Reserve Bank.

A significant step towards transparency of monetary policy implementation is the formation of various Technical Advisory Committees (TACs) in the Reserve Bank, with representatives from market participants, other regulators and experts. In line with the international best practices and with a view to further strengthening the consultative process in monetary policy, the Reserve Bank, in July 2005, set up a Technical Advisory Committee on Monetary Policy (TACMP) with external experts in the areas of monetary economics, central banking, financial markets and public finance. The Committee meets at least once in a quarter, reviews macroeconomic and monetary developments and advises the Reserve Bank on the stance of monetary policy. The Committee has contributed to enriching the inputs and processes of monetary policy setting in India. Whether any further institutional changes are necessary, however, remains an open question.

3. Development of monetary policy instruments and transmission process

Consistent with the structural changes in the monetary policy framework, improvements in the channels of transmission emerged early on as a concurrent objective in order to enhance policy effectiveness. Monetary policy clearly cannot work without adequate monetary transmission and the appropriate monetary transmission cannot take place without efficient price discovery of interest rates and exchange rates in the overall functioning of financial markets and their integration. Therefore, the corresponding development of the money market, government securities market and the foreign exchange market became necessary. Accordingly, from the 1990s, the RBI simultaneously undertook the development of the domestic financial market spectrum, sequenced into the process of deregulation of interest rates, the withdrawal of statutory pre-emptions, the qualitative improvement in monetary–fiscal coordination and the progressive liberalization of the exchange and payments regime, including the institution of a market oriented exchange rate policy. The development of financial markets in India encompassed the introduction of new market segments, new instruments and a sharper focus on regulatory oversight.

We have made a carefully calibrated transition from an administered interest rate regime to one of market determined interest rates over a period of time, while minimizing disruption and preserving financial stability. This approach also provided market participants adequate time to adjust to the new regime.

The growing market orientation of monetary policy has tilted the choice of instruments decisively from direct to more indirect and market-based monetary policy measures. Until the early 1990s, statutory pre-emptions in the form of cash reserve ratio (CRR) and statutory liquidity ratio (SLR) requirements locked away nearly 65% of bank deposits, severely eroding the profitability of the financial system and effectiveness of monetary policy. The SLR was brought down from 38.5% of net demand and time liabilities (NDTL) in early 1992 to 25% in October 1997. The CRR had been reduced progressively from 15% in 1991 to 4.5% in 2003, before it had to be increased again in steps to 6.5% in the current monetary tightening phase. Monetary manoeuvrability has now been strengthened further with removal of the erstwhile floor of 3% and ceiling of 20% in CRR through a statutory amendment. The statutory minimum SLR of 25% has also been removed to provide for greater flexibility in the RBI's monetary policy operations.

The key policy development that has enabled a more independent monetary policy environment was the discontinuation of automatic monetization of the government's fiscal deficit since April 1997 through an agreement between the government and the Reserve Bank of India in September 1994, marking a unique milestone in monetary–fiscal coordination. Another important institutional change was the freeing of the RBI's balance sheet from the burden of exchange guarantees accumulated in the pre-reform era. Subsequently, enactment of the Fiscal Responsibility and Budget Management Act 2003 has strengthened the institutional mechanism further: from April 2006 onwards, the Reserve Bank is no longer permitted to subscribe to government securities in the primary market. This step completes the transition to a fully market based system for government securities. Looking ahead, consequent to the recommendations of the Twelfth Finance Commission, the central government has now ceased to raise resources on behalf of state governments, which now have to access the market directly. Thus, state governments' capability in raising resources will be market determined and based on their own financial health. For ensuring a smooth transition, institutional processes are being revamped towards greater integration in monetary operations.

Given the pivotal role of the money market in transmission, efforts initiated in the late 1980s were intensified over the full spectrum. Following the withdrawal of the ceiling on inter-bank money market rates in 1989, several financial innovations in terms of money market instruments such as certificate of deposits, commercial paper and money market mutual funds were introduced in phases. Barriers to entry were gradually eased by increasing the number of players and relaxing the issuance and subscription norms in respect of money market instruments, thus fostering better price discovery. In order to improve monetary transmission and also on prudential considerations, steps were initiated in 1999 to turn the call money market into a pure inter-bank market and, simultaneously, to develop a repo market outside the official window for providing a stable collateralized funding alternative, particularly to non-banks who were phased out of the call segment, and banks. The Collateralized Borrowing and Lending Obligation (CBLO), a repo instrument developed by the Clearing Corporation of India Limited (CCIL) for its members, with the CCIL acting as a central counter-party for borrowers and lenders, was permitted as a money market instrument in 2002. With the development of market repo and CBLO segments, the call money market has been transformed into a pure inter-bank market, including primary dealers, from August 2005. A recent noteworthy development is the substantial migration of money market activity from the uncollateralized call money segment to the collateralized market repo and CBLO markets. Thus, uncollateralized overnight transactions are now limited to banks and primary dealers in the interest of financial stability. Technological upgrading has accompanied the development of the money market. Efforts are currently underway to introduce screen-based negotiated quote-driven dealings in call/notice and term money markets. Information on overnight rates and volumes would be disseminated by the RBI in order to enable market participants to assess the liquidity conditions in an efficient and transparent manner.

The government securities market was moved to an auction-based system in 1992 to obtain better price discovery and to impart greater transparency in operations. This was a major institutional change, which, along with the freeing of the money and foreign exchange market and the phasing out of automatic monetization of fiscal deficits, created a conducive environment for the progressive deregulation that was to follow. The setting up of well capitalized primary dealers (PDs) for dealing in government securities followed in 1995, backed up by the introduction of Delivery *versus* Payment (DvP) for government securities, adoption of new techniques of floatation, introduction of new instruments, particularly treasury bills of varying maturities and repos on all central government dated securities and treasury bills of all maturities by April 1997.

Since April 1992, the entire central government borrowing programme in dated securities has been conducted through auctions. In 2005, the Reserve Bank put in place an anonymous order matching system to improve price discovery, and settlement procedures for mitigating risks. To further activate trading and improve the depth of the securities market, the introduction of a 'when issued' market has also been announced recently. All these measures have brought about significant changes and a new treasury culture is developing, contributing to the formation of the term structure of interest rates. The demand for government securities is now driven more by considerations of effective management of liquidity rather than by statutory liquidity requirements.

The Indian foreign exchange market has been widened and deepened with the transition to a market-determined exchange rate system in March 1993 and the subsequent liberalization of restrictions on various external transactions leading up to current account convertibility under Article VIII of the Articles of Agreement of the International Monetary Fund in 1994. Since the mid-1990s, banks and other authorized entities have been accorded significant freedom to operate in the market. Banks have been allowed freedom to fix their trading limits and to borrow and invest funds in the overseas markets up to specified limits. They have been allowed to use derivative products for hedging risks and asset-liability management purposes. Similarly, corporates have been given flexibility to book forward cover based on past turnover and are allowed to use a variety of instruments like interest rates and currency swaps, caps/collars and forward rate agreements. The swap market for hedging longer-term exposure has developed substantially in recent years. A number of steps have also been taken to liberalize the capital account covering foreign direct investment, portfolio investment, outward investment including direct investment as well as depository receipt and convertible bonds, opening of Indian corporate offices abroad and the like. In recent years, the Reserve Bank has delegated exchange control procedures to banks and authorized dealers to such an extent that there is hardly any need to approach the Reserve Bank for any approval. These reforms are being reflected in vibrancy in activity in various segments of the foreign exchange market with the daily turnover over US$ 28 billion (as at the end of April 2007).

A key area of emphasis in the development of financial markets in India is the provision of the appropriate technological infrastructure for trading, clearing, payment and settlement. Since the late 1990s, the establishment of a modern, robust payments and settlement system consistent with international best practices has emerged as an important objective of the RBI. A three-pronged strategy of consolidation, development and integration has been pursued in this regard. Consolidation revolves around strengthening the existing payment system by providing the latest levels of technology. The developmental dimension includes real time gross settlement, centralized funds management, securities settlement and structured electronic financial messaging. Other key elements in the technological content of market development are electronic clearing (introduced in 1994), electronic finds transfer (1996), quick funds transfers with centralized settlement in Mumbai (2003), negotiated dealing system (NDS), screen based order matching system (2002) for electronic reporting of trades and online dissemination system and submission of bids for primary issuance of government securities and a Clearing Corporation of India Ltd., promoted by banks, financial institutions and primary dealers for clearing and settlement of trades in foreign exchange, government securities and other debt instruments, commenced operations in April 2001. The CCIL acts as a central counterparty (CCP) to all transactions and guarantees settlement of trades executed through its rules and regulations eliminating counterparty risks in adherence to international best practices. Oversight over the payments and settlement system is vested in a National Payments Council, and Board for Payment and Settlement Systems established within the RBI.

As may be seen from this brief description of the various measures that had to be taken to develop the market and institutional framework for efficient monetary policy transmission, development of markets is an arduous and time consuming activity that requires conscious policy making and implementation. Markets do not develop and function overnight: they have to be created, nurtured and monitored on a continuous basis before they start functioning autonomously. Efficient transmission of monetary impulses clearly needs integration of markets.

3.1. *Issues*

Interest rate deregulation is essential to help smooth the transmission channels of monetary policy and to enhance the signalling effects of policy changes. Whereas considerable progress has been made in this direction, full deregulation is constrained by the need for various policy interventions in the context of a still developing economy. The government had nationalized most of the banking system in 1969 in order to ensure the spread of banking throughout the country. Whereas new private sector banks have now been introduced since the mid-1990s, public sector banks still account for 70% of banking assets. These banks need to continue to perform various public policy activities, particularly in the area of agriculture, small and medium enterprises, and the cause of overall financial inclusion. This can also include a certain degree of credit allocation and interest rate directions. Hence, monetary transmission can get muted at the margin.

The government also fixes certain administered interest rates on a number of small saving schemes and on provident funds, along with providing certain tax incentives, in the absence of well developed social security systems. As banks have to compete for funds with small saving schemes, the rates offered on long term deposits mobilized by banks sometimes have to be set at levels higher than would have obtained under competitive market conditions. In fact, this has been observed to be a factor contributing to downward stickiness of lending rates, which has some implications for the effectiveness of monetary policy. This is a reality that we have to appreciate and live with given the absence of social security coverage and adequate safety nets in the country. These small savings schemes administered by the government through the wide reach of post offices, and some through commercial banks, provide small savers access to tax savings instruments that are seen as safe and stable. Whereas they do have some impact in terms of blunting monetary transmission mechanisms, they can perhaps be seen as contributing to overall financial stability. Benchmarking these administered interest rates to market determined rates has been proposed from time to time. Whereas some rationalization in schemes has indeed been done, more progress will depend on the emergence of better social security and pension systems, and perhaps easier access to marketable sovereign instruments.

While the government securities market is fairly well developed now, the corporate debt market remains to be developed for facilitating monetary signalling across various market segments. We understand, however, that it has been difficult to develop the corporate bond market in most countries. Almost half the world's corporate bond market is in the US, and another 15% in Japan. Among other countries, while the UK has a long standing bond market, the European bond market has only begun to really develop after European monetary integration and introduction of the Euro. Among developing countries, it is perhaps only South Korea that has a reasonably well developed bond market.

In the absence of a well developed corporate debt market, the demand for debt instruments has largely concentrated on government securities with the attendant implications for the yield curve and, in turn, for monetary transmission. The secondary market for corporate debt has suffered from a lack of market making resulting in poor liquidity. Corporates continue to prefer private placements to public issues for raising resources in view of ease of procedures and lower costs.

There is a need for development of mortgage-backed securities, credit default swaps, bond insurance institutions for credit enhancement, abridgment of disclosure requirements for listed companies, credit information bureaus, rating requirements for unlisted companies, real time reporting of primary and secondary trading, and eventual retail access to the bond market by non-profit institutions and small corporates. A concerted effort is now being made to set up the institutional and technological structure that would enable the corporate debt market to operate. Furthermore, the on-going reforms in the area of social security coupled with the emergence of pension and provident funds are expected to increase the demand for long term debt instruments. In the process, the investor base for government securities would be broadened, extending the monetary transmission across new players and participants.

For monetary policy to be more effective, the monetary transmission process has to be improved on a continuous basis so that price discovery is better. In this endeavour, we need to keep developing the various financial markets, increase their connection with credit markets, remove distortions in the market and reverse the current tendency to move back to administered interest rates.

4. Development of financial markets

There has been a great deal of progress in developing the money market, government securities market and forex market. With greater capital account openness, we need to develop them further to enable market participants to absorb greater volatility and shocks. Each of these markets needs to be deeper. In the context of progress towards further capital account convertibility, the market participants are going to be faced with increased risks on multiple accounts: volatility in capital flows, volatility in asset prices, increased contagion and state of ability of legacy institutions in managing risks.

4.1. Money market

The money market remains fragmented with different segments giving rise to different overnight rates. The call money market, which remains an uncollateralized market, has now become a pure inter-bank market among banks and primary dealers with the withdrawal of non-banks. Alongside, primarily for non-bank participants at the shorter end, there is the market repo outside the repo market under the liquidity adjustment facility. This is a collateralized segment of the money market. The CBLO market, operated by the CCIL among its members is yet another collateralized money market instrument. With the decision to move gradually towards a pure inter-bank call/term money market, there is a need to remove the operational/regulatory constraints in the repo market. One of the perceived hurdles in the development of the repo market is the inability to rollover contracts. To enable continuous access to funds from the repo market, rollover of repos has been allowed with migration to DvP III.

The issue remains what further developments are needed in terms of eligible collaterals, membership, etc. to integrate the different segments of the money market so that the money market as a whole is enabled to cope better with market fluctuations in the run-up to fuller capital account convertibility. An important gap in developing the money market is that term money market is still to emerge and hence, the evolution of yield curve remains inadequate. We need to explore what is to be done to build this market with further opening of capital account.

4.2. Interest rate derivatives

The need for a well developed interest rate derivatives market cannot be overemphasized in providing effective hedging tools for interest rate risks present in the balance sheet and in facilitating trading based on two-way view on interest rates, which is not possible in the underlying cash market in the absence of short selling. Deregulation of interest rates, which helped in making financial market operations efficient and cost effective, has brought to the fore a wide array of risks faced by market participants. To manage and control these risks, several instruments such as forward rate agreements (FRA) and interest rate swaps (IRS) were introduced in July 1999, which could provide effective hedges against interest rate risks. Further, in June 2003, the Reserve Bank of India had issued guidelines to banks/primary dealers/Financial Institutions (FIs) for transacting in exchange traded interest rate futures, which were introduced on the exchanges. There has also been a sharp increase in the volume of transactions in the Over the Counter (OTC) products. Though there has been a significant increase in the number and amount of contracts, participation in the markets continues to remain limited mainly to select foreign and private sector banks and PDs. In fact, PDs are expected to be market makers in this segment. Since some difficulties have been experienced in the operation of the exchange traded interest rate futures market, we are now in the process of reviewing the structure so that it can become an active market for interest rate discovery and hedging.

Despite the growing volumes in the OTC derivatives market, as is the case globally, there had been some apprehensions regarding the appropriate legal backing for these instruments. This issue has now been addressed with an appropriate amendment to the Reserve Bank of India Act. OTC derivatives are now clearly legally valid, even if they are not traded on any recognized stock exchange. Exchange traded derivatives have their own role to play in the debt market – but by their very nature they have to be standardized products. OTC derivatives, on the other hand, can be customized to the requirements of the trading entities. Thus, both OTC and exchange traded derivatives are essential for market development.

A central counter party based clearing arrangement for OTC derivatives would reduce counterparty risk and extend the benefits of netting. Accordingly, in order to strengthen the OTC derivatives market and to mitigate the risks involved, a clearing arrangement for the OTC interest rate derivatives also need to be considered. This measure would strengthen the OTC interest rate derivatives market, and provide greater transparency as needed through adequate reporting requirements.

While everywhere in the world most trading is in the OTC segment, there is no reason why we cannot innovate and have electronic based, order matched trading to have a wider reach and also thereby enhance liquidity in the market. Work is now afoot to provide for an exchange traded system for corporate bonds.

As we make arrangements for the operation of better markets for interest rate discovery, trading and hedging instruments, I would like to stress the need and importance of sound and adequate risk management practices by market participants in the derivatives market. International experience teaches us the need for greater care in handling these instruments. I would expect that the market players not only put in place an appropriate risk management policy and procedures for these products, but would also give equal importance to the skills development of their human resources to handle these instruments and to appreciate the underlying risks. As interest rate derivatives grow an area which requires attention relates to accounting and disclosures. The relevant standards need to be comprehensive and benchmarked to international standards.

4.2.1. Government securities market

Following the enactment of the Fiscal Responsibility and Budget Management Act 2003, from April 2006 onwards, the Reserve Bank is no longer permitted to subscribe to government securities in the primary market. In order to ensure a smooth transition to the new regime, restructuring of current institutional processes has already been initiated (Mohan 2006a). These steps are helping to achieve the desired integration in the conduct of monetary operations.

In the new milieu, the Reserve Bank may need to carry out greater open market operations (OMO) in the secondary market. Such operations could be qualitatively different from its Liquidity Adjustment Facility (LAF) or Market Stabilization Scheme (MSS) operations, which are guided by considerations of liquidity management primarily at the shorter end. The issue is what should be the determining factor for such secondary market operations. Generally, by controlling the short term interest rate while letting markets determine the rest of the yield curve, the central bank attempts to transmit monetary policy impulses across the yield curve. The sovereign yield curve in turn influences the lending and deposit rates in the economy. Once bank lending gets affected, interest rates impact real variables such as consumption and investment, which in turn impact output and inflation levels. However, the government securities market is yet to emerge fully as a deep and liquid market across different maturities. Given such a state, in the interest of monetary transmission, there is a case for secondary market operation across the yield and maturity spectrum in the government securities market and more so, in the context of RBI's withdrawal from the primary market.

Efforts are being made to improve the retail holding of government securities since the government securities market still lacks in depth and is dominated by banks and financial institutions often exhibiting uni-directional perceptions about liquidity. To attract retail participation in the government securities market, one of the foremost tasks ahead is to create an environment that provides a safe and secure investment avenue for small investors with adequate returns and liquidity. In this context, the RBI is emphasizing the provision of a demat holding facility for non-institutional retail/small investors for risk mitigation in scrip losses or settlement of deals in the secondary market. Non-competitive bidding has also been introduced since January 2002 for direct access to the primary issues for non-sophisticated investors.

As part of its constant endeavour to improve the facilities for trading and settlement in the government securities market, the Reserve Bank had formally launched, on 1 August 2005, an electronic order matching trading module for government securities on its negotiated dealing system (NDS-OM in short). The NDS-OM is an additional facility available to the participants and the participants continue to have the option of using the current reporting and trading platform of the NDS. While the NDS-OM now accounts for a significant share of the total traded volume in government securities, the countrywide, anonymous, screen based, order driven system for trading in government securities introduced in the stock exchanges (NSE, BSE and OTCEI) in January 2003 has continued to suffer from very poor trading volumes, which need to be looked into for revival.

4.3. Corporate debt market

In order to activate the corporate debt market, the government had appointed an expert committee (the Chairman was R.H. Patil) to provide directions on how this is to be done (Government of India 2005). A key point that I would like to emphasize is that learning from the experience of developing the government securities market, we need to proceed in a measured manner with well thought out appropriate sequencing for developing the corporate debt market. Financial market development involves action on a number of fronts with the key objective, obviously, being to enable the most efficient allocation of resources to the most productive uses and efficient intermediation from savers to investors. In other words, banking development, equity market development, and debt market development all go hand in hand. And within the debt market, an efficient government securities market is essential for price discovery and for providing reliable benchmarks to price corporate bonds off the credit risk free yield curve.

The key problem is that for a corporate bond market to function, we need a large number of issuers, a large number of investors and issues of a large size. It may be noted that each of the problems mentioned in respect of corporate bonds has been addressed in the context of development of the government securities market. That goes to show that the problems are not insurmountable but only that it takes some time to resolve. But we have just begun and work is now in progress. It is true that the government securities market took a long time to develop, despite being much simpler. The corporate debt market being much more complex would require some extra effort to move ahead. In short, we have a long way to go but we have to make a determined effort.

5. Exchange rate policy

Our exchange rate policy in recent years has been guided by the broad principles of careful monitoring and management of exchange rates with flexibility, without a fixed target or a pre-announced target or a band, coupled with the ability to intervene if and when necessary, while allowing the underlying demand and supply conditions to determine the exchange rate movements over a period in an orderly way. Subject to this predominant objective, the exchange rate policy is guided by the need to reduce excess volatility, prevent the emergence of destabilizing speculative activities, help maintain adequate level of reserves, and develop an orderly foreign exchange market.

The Indian market, like other developing countries' markets, is not yet very deep and broad, and can sometimes be characterized by uneven flow of demand and supply over different periods. In this situation the Reserve Bank of India has been prepared to make sales and purchases of foreign currency in order to even out lumpy demand and supply in the relatively thin forex market and to smooth jerky movements. However, such intervention is not governed by a predetermined target or band around the exchange rate. As the foreign exchange exposure of the Indian economy expands, the role of such uneven demands can be seen to reduce.

With this approach, we have achieved flexibility along with stability in the external sector. Increased earnings from exports of services and remittances coupled with enhanced foreign investment inflows have provided strength to the external sector. Reflecting the strong growth prospects of the Indian economy, the country has received large investment inflows, both direct and portfolio, since 1993–94 as compared with negligible levels until the early 1990s. Total foreign investment flows (direct and portfolio) increased from US$ 111 million in 1990–91 to US$ 24,748 million in 2006–2007. Over the same period current account deficits remained modest – averaging 1% of GDP since 1991–92 and in fact recorded small surpluses during 2001–2004. With capital flows remaining in excess of the current financing requirements, the overall balance of payments recorded persistent surpluses leading to an increase in reserves, which have now reached US$ 199,179 million at end-March 2007. The emergence of foreign exchange surplus lending to continuing and large accretion to reserves since the mid-1990s has been a novel experience for India after experiencing chronic balance of payment problems for almost four decades. These surpluses began to arise after the opening of the current account, reduction in trade protection, and partial opening of the capital account from the early to mid-1990s.

India's integration with the world economy is also getting stronger, with implications for the conduct of exchange rate policies in the future. Trade in goods (i.e., exports plus imports) as a proportion of GDP increased from 14.6% in 1990–91 to 32.5% in 2005–2006; while gross current account receipts and payments as a percentage of GDP increased from 19.4% to 50.2% over the same period, reflecting the buoyant growth in Indian trade in services. The trade deficit is also as high as 6.4% of GDP. Correspondingly, in the capital account, gross flows (total inflows *plus* outflows) have more than doubled as a proportion of GDP: from 12.1% in 1990–91 to 32.4% (US$ 260 billion) in 2005–2006. Thus, the Indian economy is today substantially exposed to the international economy and arguably more open than even the United States in terms of these metrics.

5.1. *Issues*

5.1.1. *Dutch disease*

In recent years, the growth in current payments has been accompanied by healthy growth in current receipts – in both goods and services, thus providing for some confidence in the sustainability of current trade patterns and financial stability. Current receipts pay for up to about 90% of current payments. Within current receipts, merchandise exports are being rapidly exceeded in terms of growth rates by software earnings, currently at 2.9% of GDP. Besides, private transfer receipts, comprising mainly remittances from Indians working abroad, seemed to have acquired a permanent character and have risen steadily to constitute around 3% of GDP in recent years, impervious to exchange rate movements. These factors have strengthened the capability of the Indian economy to sustain higher current account deficits (CADs) than in the past. Net capital flows have thus regularly exceeded the CAD requirements by a fair measure, enabling large accretions to the reserves.

The large inflow of remittances and major and sustained spurt in software exports coupled with capital inflows have the potential for possible overvaluation of the currency and the resultant erosion of long term competitiveness of other traditional and goods sectors – popularly known as the Dutch disease. Given the fact that more people are in the goods sector, the human aspects of the exchange rate management should not be lost sight of. Therefore, Dutch disease syndrome has so far been managed by way of reserves build-up and sterilization, the former preventing excessive nominal appreciation and the latter preventing higher inflation. However, the issue remains how long, and to what extent, such an exchange rate management strategy would work given the fact that we are faced with large and continuing capital flows apart from strengthening current receipts on account of remittances and software exports. This issue has assumed increased importance over the last year with increased capital flows arising from the higher sustained growth performance of the economy and significant enhancement of international confidence in the Indian economy.

5.1.2. *Liquidity management*

Volatility in capital flows and hence in liquidity has marked the period during 2001–2007 and posed considerable problems in liquidity and exchange rate management. Sharp shifts in capital flows can be explained as partly frictional and arising from seasonal and transient factors, partly cyclical and associated with the pick up in growth momentum and the induced demand for bank credit, and partly led by growth expectation. Moreover, the absorption of external savings is also dependent on the stage of a business cycle that a country may be going through. Further, the stage of business cycle and the timing of capital flows may not coincide. The early years of this decade were characterized by low industrial growth and hence the absorptive capacity of the country was constrained. In an expansionary phase, the current account widens and the potential for greater absorption manifests itself.

The volatile capital flows have warranted appropriate monetary operations to obviate wide fluctuations in market rates and ensure reasonable stability consistent with the monetary policy stance. In fact, the Indian experience illustrates the tight link between external sector management and domestic monetary management. What may be small movements in capital flows for the rest of the world can translate into large domestic liquidity movements distorting market exchange and interest rates in a developing country. Just as foreign exchange reserves can act as a shock absorber, on the external front, we had to look for a parallel liquidity shock absorber for domestic monetary management.

In this context, a new instrument, called the MSS has evolved as a useful instrument of monetary policy to sustain open market operations. The MSS was made operational from April 2004. Under this scheme, which is meant exclusively for liquidity management, the Reserve Bank has been empowered to issue government treasury bills and medium duration dated securities for the purpose of liquidity absorption. The scheme works by impounding the proceeds of auctions of treasury bills and government securities in a separate identifiable MSS cash account maintained and operated by the RBI. The amounts credited into the MSS cash account are appropriated only for the purpose of redemption and/or buy back of the treasury bills and/or dated securities issued under the MSS. MSS securities are indistinguishable from normal treasury bills and government dated securities in the hands of the lender. The payments for interest and discount on MSS securities are not made from the MSS account, but shown in the Union budget and other related documents transparently as distinct components under separate sub-heads. The introduction of MSS has succeeded, in principle, in restoring LAF to its intended function of daily liquidity management. Since its introduction in April 2004, the MSS has served as a very useful instrument for medium term monetary and liquidity management. It has been unwound in times of low capital flows and greater liquidity needs and built up when excess capital flows could lead to excess domestic liquidity. In principle, the MSS is designed to sterilize excess capital flows that are deemed to be durable or semi-durable. In practice this is difficult to discern ex-ante: hence the range of MSS instruments in terms of their duration can effectively modulate the sterilization on an *ex-post* basis.

Our strategy of introducing this new MSS instrument to manage excess capital flows and reduce volatility in the exchange rate reflects the overall issue of global capital flows that many developing countries are facing, particularly in Asia. Net private flows (equity + debt) have increased from an average of about US$ 180 billion over the five year period 1998–2002, to about US$ 650 billion in 2006, amounting to about 5% of their GDP (World Bank 2007). Absorption of such a volume of flows would imply a corresponding current account deficit of about 5% of GDP. What should be the approach to exchange rate determination in such circumstances? To what extent is the current account balance a good guide to evaluation of the appropriate level of an exchange rate? To what extent should the capital account influence the exchange rate? What are the implications of large current account deficits for the real economy? Are they sustainable and, if not, what are the implications for financial stability in developing countries? In India's case, as mentioned, we have almost always had a modest current account deficit though, because of remittances and service exports, the trade deficit has widened significantly in recent years. These are the issues that we have to deal with as we negotiate fuller capital account convertibility, but I believe these are wider questions that are engaging most countries in Asia.

Going forward there will be a continuous need to adapt the strategy of liquidity management as well as exchange rate management for effective monetary management and short term interest rate smoothening. The key questions we continue to face are what should be the instruments and modes of management of liquidity in the interest of growth and financial stability and how much should capital flows affect exchange rate. These issues become even more relevant under a freer regime of capital flows. Global developments are expected to have an increasing role in determining the conduct of monetary and exchange rate policies in our countries. In an environment of global convergence, retaining independence of monetary policy may become increasingly difficult, calling for hard choices in terms of goals and instruments.

6. Fiscal situation and Fiscal Responsibility and Budget Management Act

6.1. Some progress

Public finances have exhibited a mixed trend in the reforms period. After witnessing some correction until 1996–97, public finances underwent deterioration, reflecting a variety of factors such as the decline in tax revenues (as percentage to GDP) in consonance with the cyclical downturn of economic activity, as well as the effects of the 5th Pay Commission award. Indeed, the combined fiscal deficit of the centre (Central Government) and states was higher in 2001–2002 than that in 1990–91. Since 2002–2003 onwards, public finances have witnessed a significant improvement, reflecting both policy efforts at fiscal consolidation as well as the upturn in economic activity (see Table 1). A noteworthy development at the federal level is the transformation of state level sales taxes into value added tax (VAT), which has introduced a large measure of rationality and uniformity in the state tax system. The state sales tax system had also suffered from great complexity in terms of multiplicity of rates and special provisions. A vital feature of this tax reform has been the consultative process among all the states as mediated by the central government, which then resulted in this consensus for massive reform.

Table 1. Combined deficit indicators: centre and states.

			(As % of GDP)
Year	Fiscal deficit	Revenue deficit	Primary deficit
2001–2002	10.0	7.0	3.7
2002–2003	9.6	6.6	3.1
2003–2004	8.5	5.8	2.1
2004–2005	7.5	3.7	1.4
2005–2006	7.4	3.1	1.6
2006–2007	6.4	2.2	0.8

Source: Reserve Bank of India.

6.1.1. Issues

Notwithstanding the recent correction, combined public debt remains high (almost 79% of GDP at the end March 2006). The latest most significant measure taken is the introduction of the Fiscal Responsibility and Budget Management Act (FRBM) in 2004, which enjoins the government to eliminate its revenue deficit and reduce its fiscal deficit to 3% of GDP by 2009. Similar acts have been passed by most state governments (25 states so far). So fiscal responsibility has now become part of our legislative commitments. However, together they amount to a total deficit of about 6% of GDP, which is considered high by global standards.

After the award of the 5th Pay Commission in 1997, public finances had come under strain and hence public savings had become negative. Now the growth process has clearly recovered and we seem to be on a sustainable path of annual GDP growth in excess of 8.5%. The 8.5% plus growth would itself place demand for higher government wages and the 6th Pay Commission yet to come, complicating the fiscal consolidation process.

Achieving the FRBM target of zero revenue deficit by 2008–2009 requires continued focus on containing expenditures, increasing tax revenues and reducing tax exemptions. Revenue augmentation would critically depend upon improvement in tax/GDP ratio as non-tax revenue is set to decline in the coming years. In this context, the reversal of the declining trend in tax/GDP ratio is welcome. This increasing trend needs to be maintained through further widening of the tax base and curtailment in tax exemptions. It is in this context that the erosion of the tax base on account of various exemptions poses a cause for concern.

With the attainment of a sustainable higher growth path in excess of 8.5% annual real GDP growth, the prospects for continued fiscal consolidation have improved. Tax revenues have become buoyant with continuing healthy growth in corporate profits and personal incomes. Furthermore, the introduction of the VAT system at the state level provides further ground for optimism. What we will need to guard against are the usual demands for exemptions that contribute to erosion of the tax base.

An important point to note in relation to the Indian fiscal situation is that, despite the long term persistence of high fiscal deficits by any standards, India has not been subject to banking or financial market turbulence. Our fiscal parameters have not been too different from some of the countries that have experienced the most turbulence, such as Turkey and Argentina. In fact, it is because of our inadequate fiscal performance that India did not have investment grade rating until earlier this year. The main reasons why India has been able to maintain financial stability in the presence of such fiscal stress is that almost all the sovereign debt has been domestic, except for bilateral and multilateral external borrowing, which itself has been small proportionately. India has eschewed sovereign borrowing in external markets, thereby insulating us from external volatility in exchange rates and interest rates. The move to increased market borrowing has also been useful in providing market signals on the cost of borrowing. Finally, coordination between monetary policy, domestic debt management, and financial sector policies in the Reserve Bank and the government has also helped in this regard.

7. Strengthening of financial sector/banks

The financial system in India, through a measured, gradual, cautious, and steady process, has undergone substantial transformation. It has been transformed into a reasonably sophisticated, diverse and resilient system through well-sequenced and coordinated policy measures aimed at making the Indian financial sector more competitive, efficient, and stable. The overall capital adequacy ratio of the banking sector as a whole has increased from 10.4% at end-March 1997 to 12.3% at end-March 2007.[1] The asset quality of the banking sector has recorded a significant improvement: the ratio of net non-performing assets to net advances has declined from 8.1% at end-March 1997 to 2% at end-March 2007 despite the tightening of Non-performing Asset (NPA) classification norms. The profitability of banks as defined by the return on assets increased from 0.7% in 1996–97 to 0.9% in 2006–2007. Intermediation cost of banks has declined from 2.9% in 1995–96 to around 2% by 2006–2007. The financial system is now robust and resilient, and is enabling accelerated economic growth in an environment of stability.

Consistent with the policy approach to benchmark the banking system to the best international standards with emphasis on gradual harmonization, in a phased manner, all foreign banks operating in India and all Indian commercial banks having foreign operations are required to start implementing Basel II with effect from 31 March 2008, while other commercial banks are required to implement Basel II by 31 March 2009.[2] Recognizing the differences in degrees of sophistication and development of the banking system, it has been decided that the banks will initially adopt the standardized approach for credit risk and the basic indicator approach for operational risk. After adequate skills are developed, both by the banks and also by the supervisors, some of the banks may be allowed to migrate to the internal rating based (IRB) approach. Although implementation of Basel II will require more capital for banks in India, the cushion available in the system – at present, the capital to risk assets ratio (CRAR) is over 12% – provides some comfort. In order to provide banks greater flexibility and avenues for meeting the capital requirements, the Reserve Bank has issued policy guidelines enabling issuance of several instruments by the banks *viz.*, innovative perpetual debt instruments, perpetual non-cumulative preference shares, redeemable cumulative preference shares and hybrid debt instruments.

The Reserve Bank founded the Board for Financial Supervision (BFS) in 1994 to upgrade its practice of financial supervision of banks. In the course of time, development finance institutions, specialized term-lending institutions, non-banking financial companies (NBFCs), urban cooperative banks and primary dealers have all been brought under the supervision of the BFS. A set of prudential norms for the commercial banking sector had been instituted as early as 1994 with regard to capital adequacy, income recognition and asset classification, provisioning, exposure norms and more recently, in respect of their investment portfolio. With the aim of regulatory convergence for entities involved in similar activities, prudential regulation and supervision norms were also introduced in phases for Development Finance Institutions (DFIs), NBFCs, cooperative banks and PDs.

In tandem with the gradual opening up of the economy, the regulatory and supervisory framework was spruced up comprising of a three-pronged strategy of regular on-site inspections, technology-driven off-site surveillance and extensive use of external auditors. As a result of improvements in the regulatory and supervisory framework, the degree of compliance with the Basel Core Principles has gradually improved. The supervisory framework has been further upgraded with the institution of a framework of risk-based supervision (RBS) for intensified monitoring of vulnerabilities. A scheme of prompt corrective action (PCA) was affected in December 2002 to undertake mandatory and discretionary intervention against troubled banks based on well-defined financial/prudential parameters. In view of the growing emergence of financial conglomerates and the possibility of systemic risks arising there from, a system of consolidated accounting has been instituted. A half-yearly review based on financial soundness indicators is being undertaken to assess the health of individual institutions and macro-prudential indicators associated with financial system soundness. The findings arising thereof are disseminated to the public through its various reports.

The bankruptcy procedures for containing the level of NPAs have been strengthened over the years. Debt recovery tribunals (DRTs) were established consequent to the passing of the Recovery of Debts Due to Banks and Financial Institutions Act, 1993. With a view to putting in place a mechanism for timely and transparent restructuring of corporate debts of viable entities facing problems, a scheme of corporate debt restructuring (CDR) was started in 2001 outside the purview of Board for Industrial and Financial Reconstruction (BIFR), DRT and other legal proceedings. Similar guidelines on debt restructuring of viable or potentially viable Small and Medium Enterprise (SME) units were issued in September 2005. To provide a significant impetus to banks to ensure sustained recovery, the Securitization and Reconstruction of Financial Assets and Enforce-ment of Security Interest (SARFAESI) Act was passed in 2002 and was subsequently amended to ensure creditor rights. With a view to increasing the options available to banks for dealing with NPAs, guidelines were also issued on sale/purchase of NPAs in July 2005. Subsequently, a few asset reconstruction companies have been registered. Thus, the bankruptcy procedures for recovery of bad debts have been streamlined over the years even though the Sick Industrial Companies Act (SICA) continues to be in vogue.

A further challenge for policy in the context of fuller capital account openness will be to preserve the financial stability of the system as greater deregulation is carried out on capital outflows and on debt inflows. This will require market development, enhancement of regulatory capacity in these areas, as well as human resource development in both financial intermediaries and non-financial entities. In consonance with the objective of enhancing efficiency and productivity of banks through greater competition – from new private sector banks and entry and expansion of several foreign banks – there has been a consistent decline in the share of public sector banks in total assets of commercial banks. Notwithstanding such transformation, the public sector banks still account for nearly 70% of assets and income. Public sector banks have also responded to the new challenges of competition, as reflected in their increased share in the overall profit of the banking sector. This suggests that, with operational flexibility, public sector banks are competing relatively effectively with private sector and foreign banks. Public sector bank managements are now probably more attuned to the market consequences of their activities (Mohan 2006a). But it is also they who face the most difficult challenges in human resource development. They will have to invest very heavily in skill enhancement at all levels: at the top level for new strategic goal setting; at the middle level for implementing these goals; and at the cutting edge lower levels for delivering the new service modes. Wide disparities exist within the banking sector as far as technological capabilities are concerned: the percentage of 'computer literate' employees as a percentage of total staff in 2000 was around 20% in public sector banks compared with 100% in new private banks and around 90% in foreign banks (Reserve Bank of India 2002). Data reported by the RBI suggests that nearly 71% of branches of public sector banks are fully computerized. However, computerization needs to go beyond the mere 'arithmeticals', to borrow a term from the Report of the Committee on Banking Sector Reforms (Government of India 2008), and instead, needs to be leveraged optimally to achieve and maintain high service and efficiency standards. Given the average age of 45 years *plus* for employees in the public sector banks, they will also face new recruitment challenges in the face of adverse compensation structures in comparison with the freer private sector.

The issue of mixed ownership as an institutional structure where the government has a controlling interest is a salient feature of bank governance in India. Such aspects of corporate governance in public sector banks is important, not only because public sector banks dominate the banking industry, but also because it is likely that they would continue to remain in banking business. To the extent that there is public ownership of public sector banks, the multiple objectives of the government as owner and the complex principal-agent relationships needs to be taken on board. Over the reform period, more and more public sector banks have begun to get listed on the stock exchange, which, in its wake, has led to greater market discipline and, concomitantly, to an improvement in their governance aspects as well. The broad based and diversified ownership of public sector banks has brought about a qualitative difference in their functioning, since there is induction of private shareholding as well as attendant issues of shareholder's value, as reflected by the market capitalization, board representation and interests of minority share-holders. Given the increased technical complexity of most business activities including banking and the rapid pace of change in financial markets and practices, public sector banks would need to devise imaginative ways of responding to the evolving challenges within the context of mixed ownership.

Another aspect of greater capital market openness concerns the presence of foreign banks in India. The government and Reserve Bank outlined a roadmap on foreign investment in banks in India in February 2005, which provides guidelines on the extent of their presence until 2009. This roadmap is consistent with the overall guidelines issued simultaneously on ownership and governance in private sector banks in India. The presence of foreign banks in the country has been very useful in bringing greater competition in certain segments in the market. They are significant participants in investment banking and in development of the forex market. With the changes that have taken place in the United States and other countries, where the traditional barriers between banking, insurance and securities companies have been removed, the size of the largest financial conglomerates has become extremely large. Between 1995 and 2004, the size of the largest bank in the world has grown three-fold by asset size, from about US$ 0.5 trillion to US$ 1.5 trillion, about one and a half times the size of Indian GDP. This has happened through a great degree of merger activity: for example, J.P. Morgan Chase is the result of mergers among 550 banks and financial institutions. The 10 biggest commercial banks in the US now control almost half of that country's banking assets, up from 29% just 10 years ago. Hence, with fuller capital account convertibility and greater presence of foreign banks over time, a number of issues will arise. First, if these large global banks have emerged as a result of real economies of scale and scope, how will smaller national banks compete in countries like India, and will they themselves need to generate a larger international presence? Second, there is considerable discussion today on overlaps and potential conflicts between home country regulators of foreign banks and host country regulators: how will these be addressed and resolved in the years to come? Third, given that operations in one country such as India are typically small relative to the global operations of these large banks, the attention of top management devoted to any particular country is typically low. Consequently, any market or regulatory transgressions committed in one country by such a bank, which may have a significant impact on banking or financial market of that country, is likely to have negligible impact on the bank's global operations. It has been seen in recent years that even relatively strong regulatory action taken by regulators against such global banks has had negligible market or reputational impact on them in terms of their stock price or similar metrics. Thus, there is loss of regulatory effectiveness as a result of the presence of such financial conglomerates. Hence, there is inevitable tension between the benefits that such global conglomerates bring and some regulatory and market structure and competition issues that may arise.

Along with the emergence of international financial conglomerates we are also witnessing a similar growth of Indian conglomerates. As in most countries, the banking, insurance and securities companies each come under the jurisdiction of their respective regulators. A beginning has been made in organized cooperation between the regulators on the regulation of such conglomerates, with agreement on who would be the lead regulator in each case. In the United States, it is a financial holding company that is at the core of each conglomerate, with each company being its subsidiary. There is, as yet, no commonality in the financial structure of each conglomerate in India: in some the parent company is the banking company; whereas in others there is a mix of structure. For Indian conglomerates to be competitive, and for them to grow to a semblance of international size, they will need continued improvement in clarity in regulatory approach.

8. Concluding remarks

I have described at length the evolution of India's macroeconomic and monetary management over the last decade and a half to demonstrate the complexity of such management in the context of a developing economy that manages its opening up to the rest of the world in a gradual manner. Monetary policy and exchange rate regimes have necessarily to be operated as fuzzy or intermediate regimes not obeying the almost received wisdom of purist approaches. The judgement on the legitimacy of such a regime must be based on their efficacy as revealed by the outcomes. On this count, I believe that India's macroeconomic, monetary and financial managers can justifiably claim a reasonable degree of success: economic growth is high and accelerating; inflation has shifted to lower sustainable levels; savings and investments are growing; financial markets have been growing and developing in an orderly manner; the health of the banking system has improved continuously and is approaching best practice standards; the external account is healthy in the presence of robust trade growth in both goods and services; increasing capital flows indicate growing international confidence in the Indian economy; and the Indian exchange rate has been flexible in both directions providing for reasonable market determination, in the presence of central bank forex interventions.

These are the achievements of the past. As we ascend to a higher growth path, and as we have fuller capital account convertibility, we will face newer challenges and will have to continue to adapt. The key point is that with greater capital account openness, we have to develop markets such that market participants, financial and non financial, are enabled to cope better with market fluctuations. As we do this, we need to be cognizant of the vast range of capabilities of different market participants in as diverse a country as India: from subsistence farmers to the most sophisticated financial market practitioners.

Acknowledgements

Paper presented at an International Monetary Seminar organized by Banque de France on Globalization, Inflation and Financial Markets in Paris on 14 June 2007. The assistance of Sanjay Hansda, Indranil Bhattacharyya, Partha Ray and M.D. Patra in preparing the paper is gratefully acknowledged.

Notes

1. Data for 2006–2007 are unaudited and provisional.
2. They have, however, the option of implementing Basel II with effect from 31 March 2008 as well.

References

Ahluwalia, M.S. 2002. Economic reforms in India since 1991: has gradualism worked? *Journal of Economic Perspectives* 16, no. 3: 67–88.

Friedman, Benjamin. 2000. The Role of Interest Rates in Federal Reserve Policymaking. Working Paper 8047, National Bureau of Economic Research.

Government of India. 2005. *Report of High Level Expert Committee on Corporate Bonds and Securitization* (Chairman: R.H. Patil). http://finmin.nic.in/reports/index.html.

McCallum, Bennett T. 1981. Price level determinancy with an interest rate policy rule and rational expectations. *Journal of Monetary Economics* 8, no. 3: 319–29.

McKinsey & Company. 2005. *Indian Banking 2010: Towards a High Performing Sector*. Mumbai: McKinsey & Company.

Mohan, Rakesh. 2005. Communications in central banks: a perspective. *Reserve Bank of India Bulletin*, October 2005.

Mohan, Rakesh. 2006a. Recent trends in the Indian debt market and current initiatives. *Reserve Bank of India Bulletin*, April 2006.

Mohan, Rakesh. 2006b. Evolution of Central Banking in India. Lecture delivered at the seminar organized by the London School of Economics and the National Institute of Bank Management at Mumbai on January 24. *Reserve Bank of India Bulletin*, June 2006.

Reserve Bank of India. 2002. *Report on Trends and Progress of Banking in India, 2001–2002*. Mumbai: Reserve Bank of India.

World Bank. 2007. *Global Development Finance*. Washington, DC: World Bank.

Coming of age – a comparative study of emerging foreign exchange markets

Jamal Mecklai and Anis Shaikh

Mecklai Financial Services Limited, Mumbai, India

We developed a market maturity index as a composite of the relative liquidity index (which was used historically to measure market maturity) and a market sophistication index, constructed by analyzing market volume and transaction data. We also constructed a risk management index using volatility and V2 (volatility of the volatility) to measure ease of risk management. Five (out of 14) emerging markets we studied – India, Brazil, Malaysia, Turkey and Poland – improved their risk management index scores from 2007 to 2009, suggesting increasing maturity. On the other hand, South Africa, Taiwan and South Korea, all markets that had seemed reasonably mature in 2007, performed extremely poorly from a risk management perspective in 2009, suggesting that their original high market maturity index scores were probably not very stable.

Background

The global foreign exchange (FX) market has emerged relatively unscathed by the 'worst financial crisis since the Great Depression'. Other than a few cases of banks suffering losses as a result of settlement risk – when, for instance, one of the German Landesbanks delivered Euro (expecting US dollars in return) to Lehman Brothers on the morning it went bankrupt – there have been no defaults in the FX market.

Volatility has risen across the board, to be sure, as has the volatility of the volatility, which has made risk management much more difficult. Despite this, the FX markets, both those that are fully mature and, to a lesser extent, those that are emerging, have continued to do their job, enabling users to hedge risk and take positions at reasonable cost.

The Indian FX market

As a rule of thumb, the maturity of a FX market can be measured by the ratio of the daily volume traded to the country's underlying foreign trade (imports + exports). By that measure, India ranked third, behind Russia and South Africa, of 14 emerging markets we studied (see Figure 1), using Bank for International Settlements (BIS) data for transaction volumes and World Trade Organisation (WTO) data for trade volumes. (Since the BIS survey is conducted only once every three years, this data is from April 2007.) China and Brazil were far behind, with

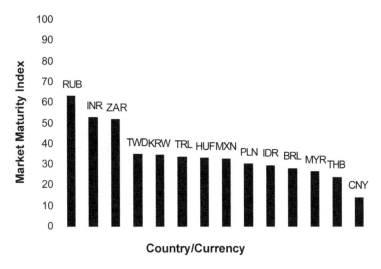

Figure 1. Market Maturity Index (2007).

China ranking last. In fact, total Chinese Yuan (CNY) traded volumes were only about 25% of Indian Rupee (INR) traded volumes.

Of course, the Chinese market has opened up considerably since then, and will likely have climbed a few notches. But the Indian market has been the real killer – the fastest-growing FX market of the 54 covered by the BIS. Daily volumes rose from US$34 billion in April 2007 to US$53 billion in April 2008, before falling to US$44 billion in April 2009. Despite this dramatic growth, there is still a lot of work to be done before the INR market could be considered highly liquid – we note that in 2007 its trade-adjusted liquidity was less than 40% of the US market.

Of course, and despite the continuing constraints on the capital account, the Indian market has matured in several other ways. There is increasing breadth of participation, and a substantial increase in the volume of options and other derivatives being traded; the offshore non-deliverable forwards (NDF) market has also grown in liquidity and depth. Most importantly, two-way movements in the price of the rupee are now a matter of course, confirming that our domestic FX market is certainly coming of age.

The market maturity index (MMI)

Highly mature markets, like US Dollar (USD), Euro (EUR), British Pound (GBP), Swiss Franc (CHF) and Japanese Yen (JPY), all have excellent liquidity, and a broad array of different types of users. They enable pricing and transacting of long tenor (up to 30 years) products, and a wide variety of hedging instruments at a low cost.

Recognizing that a simple ratio of traded volumes to underlying trade is too simplistic to measure the highly complex markets of today, we developed a market maturity index (MMI), which incorporates a range of other variables – cross border transaction volumes, domestic volumes traded by non-financial players (real sector players), volumes traded domestically by investment entities (hedge funds and the like), and volumes of derivatives transacted.

The MMI consists of two indices, each of which has equal weight. The first is the relative liquidity index (the classic model), and the second is a market sophistication index, which is constructed by analyzing market volume and transaction data – how much is being transacted, who is transacting, what kinds of products are being used, etc. We believe the MMI enables a more tailored way of looking at different elements of maturity and can assist in providing direction to regulation. A detailed explanation of how the MMI is constructed is given below.

We selected a sample of 14 currency markets for the study: seven Asian emerging market currencies (China, India, Indonesia, Malaysia, South Korea, Taiwan and Thailand), and seven other emerging market currencies (Brazil, Hungary, Mexico, Poland, Russia, South Africa and Turkey), using, again, BIS data from 2007.

Methodology – market maturity index

The market maturity index is composed of two separate indices. The first is the relative liquidity index, the classic tool used to estimate market maturity, which is calculated as the ratio of the total traded volume in a particular currency to the total underlying trade (imports + exports) of the currency's country.

The second, which could be called a market sophistication index, is actually a combination of four sub-indices.

Globalization sub-index

This is calculated as the ratio of cross-border FX turnover to the total volume traded in that currency. It gives a measure of the ease with which on-shore parties can access the global market.

Real sector sub-index

This is calculated as the total turnover undertaken by non-financial, non-bank entities – i.e., companies with trade and capital exposures – divided by the total volume of underlying trade (imports + exports). It provides a measure of both the ease with which companies can access the FX market, and, of course, the sophistication of such users.

Investor activity sub-index

This is calculated as the ratio of non-dealer, non-real sector turnover to total domestic FX turnover. It is a proxy for capital mobility or portfolio flows as it captures FX hedging and trading activity of institutional investors, hedge funds, and non-dealing financial institutions with FX assets and liabilities.

Derivative use sub-index

This is calculated as the total volume of FX forwards, options and currency swaps divided by the total domestic volume. This ratio measures a deeper layer of sophistication to the FX market. A well-developed OTC derivatives market allows participants considerably greater flexibility in managing their exposures.

All the indices and sub-indices are scaled to 100, using the US market as the benchmark.

Results and analysis

The study shows that Russia was by far the most mature market in terms of its MMI (see Table 1). The Indian market, which came in second on the MMI, has the highest market sophistication index. The South African market, which was also highly liquid, came in third, with an MMI score very close to India's.

Taiwan, South Korea, Turkey, Hungary and Mexico were more or less at the same level of maturity. Each of them had very similar MMI scores, which were about 20 points behind India and South Africa. In general, most of the markets had similar rankings on both market liquidity and sophistication – however, South Korea and Turkey were somewhat conflicted. South Korea had a strong rating on liquidity (4th), but was much weaker (10th) on market sophistication. Conversely, Turkey had a very poor liquidity rating (13th) but an excellent market sophistication rank (2nd).

Poland, Indonesia and Brazil were close behind these, with Indonesia, surprisingly, showing the best market sophistication of the three. Malaysia and Thailand were down the scale, even though Thailand scored reasonably well on the relative liquidity index. China, unsurprisingly, was in the cellar.

A closer look at the components of the MMI provides a lot of more interesting information, and, as mentioned earlier, can provide signals for regulatory focus.

We note, for instance, that India (together with Turkey) had the highest possible score on the Derivatives Use sub-index.[1] Anecdotally, we know that 2007 was a year of huge derivative volumes, which has subsided substantially since. Thus, this component of India's MMI score will certainly be lower today.

More important, however, is the fact that India's score on the investor activity sub-index was extremely low – indeed it was the second lowest (to Thailand) of all 14 markets. While this activity has also most certainly picked up, this reading indicates that Reserve Bank of India (RBI) needs to do more to increase market access for the investment community.

Again, India's score on the globalization sub-index is also relatively low – it ranks sixth from the bottom ahead only of China, Brazil, South Korea, Malaysia and Thailand. This may well have to do with the conservative approach of the banking regulator that limited the cross-border activity of domestic banks, which, given the trauma of the past couple of years, may not be such a bad thing.

On the flip side, India scored second highest (to Russia) on the real sector sub-index, confirming considerable anecdotal evidence that Indian companies are extremely savvy and pro-active in hedging their risk.

Interestingly, except in these two countries, and, to a smaller extent, South Africa, Taiwan and South Korea, the corporate sector appears to have very limited play in the FX market in most countries. In particular, countries like Mexico, Hungary, Poland and Turkey, which are very highly globalized but still score very low on the real sector sub-index, could likely see a strong increase in market maturity if the corporate sector is more effectively educated in risk management.

Correlating MMI with risk management

Of course, the ultimate test of maturity of a market is how well it enables users to manage their risk. In a well-developed market, volatility stays reasonably steady over the medium term, which makes managing risk relatively easy. In less mature markets, the volatility itself is very volatile – it jumps around, sometimes because of

Table 1. MMI and its sub-indices.

	MMI	Relative liquidity index	Market sophistication index	Globalization sub-index	Real sector sub-index	Investor activity sub-index	Derivatives use sub-index
Brazil	28.06	9.48	46.64	36.94	9.13	100	40.47
China	14.27	2.29	26.65	3.52	0.01	100	1.46
Hungary	33.35	18.38	48.32	100	12.04	65.06	16.19
India	53.23	38.6	67.85	65.25	77.11	25.05	100
Indonesia	29.74	7.21	52.26	58.68	17.19	43.66	89.52
Malaysia	26.95	5.4	48.5	63.2	5.57	83.49	41.75
Mexico	32.86	14.9	50.83	100	9.16	81.61	12.55
Poland	30.53	14.87	46.19	100	16.86	31.65	36.27
Russia	53.43	66.49	60.38	95.23	91.34	47.35	7.59
South Africa	52.28	51.43	53.09	100	44.06	42.52	25.53
South Korea	34.82	22.89	46.74	62.88	23.27	29.79	71.04
Taiwan	35.41	16.4	54.42	89.42	24.85	40.88	62.53
Thailand	24.03	10.27	37.78	63.93	14.73	26.75	45.73
Turkey	33.82	6.6	61.04	100	2.34	41.82	100

lack of liquidity and sometimes as a result of stop–start central bank intervention. This makes risk management much more difficult.

In trying to assess the effectiveness of different markets for risk management, it is clear that volatility alone does not tell the complete tale. For instance, while the average volatility of EUR/USD, a highly mature market, was 6.97% during 2006–07, there were less mature markets that had higher volatility – e.g. Hungary (11.5%), South Africa (15.3%), Brazil (11.8%) – and some where the volatility was lower – e.g. Taiwan (4%), Russia (3.5%), India (4.1%).

In most instances, currencies with lower volatility have greater capital controls and aggressive central banks – many of these were in Asia. Countries with higher volatility usually have more open capital accounts and/or thinner markets.

To understand more fully how volatility relates to market maturity we need to look beyond the simple volatility to its first derivative, the volatility of the volatility (V2). This provides an assessment of how difficult it is to use a market for risk management – if the volatility jumps around too much (i.e. V2 is very high), even buying options can result in opportunity losses. Clearly, the more mature a market, the lower will be the volatility of its volatility.

In 2007, the EUR/USD market had the lowest V2 (17.8%). At the other end of the scale were the Indonesian rupiah at 38% and the Turkish lira at 40%. Note, again, that there is no correlation between volatility and V2. For instance, the Brazilian real had high volatility (11.8%) and a high V2 (31%); on the other hand, the Indian rupee had low volatility (4.1%) but a high V2 (33%). Thus, simply looking either at volatility or at V2 does not give the complete picture.

To be able to use this volatility data meaningfully, we constructed a risk management index incorporating both the volatility (representing the cost of using the market for risk management) and the volatility of the volatility (representing the difficulty of using that market). The index sets at zero for a fully mature market – we used EUR/USD – and the index value measures the difficulty of risk management.

We found that, from an ease of risk management perspective, the best markets (in 2007) were quite different from the ones deemed most mature according to the MMI. South Korea and Taiwan topped the list, with Hungary and Russia close behind. Risk management in the Indian market was relatively difficult – it ranked seventh of the 14 emerging markets, in terms of relative ease of risk management.

By 2009, with global volatility up sharply, risk management has become more difficult across the board. Interestingly, while the volatility of EUR/USD rose sharply (from 6.97% to 17.67%), V2 remained virtually unchanged (17.8% in 2007 and 18.02% in 2009), indicating a very high degree of stability in ease of risk management – a hallmark, in our view, of a successful and mature market.

Perhaps showing the instability of less mature markets, we found that our sample of emerging markets showed considerable and diverse movements in their risk management indices between 2007 and 2009. India improved its perfor-mance dramatically – its risk management index came down substantially, from 17.71 to 9.98 – making it the best performer of the 14 emerging markets (see Table 2).

While there is clearly no strong correlation between the risk management index and the MMI, they both assess the maturity of the market from different standpoints. Thus, we could conclude that markets that have shown an improvement

Table 2.   Risk management index.

	2007		2009		
	Rank	Score	Rank	Score	Change
Brazil	8	18.28	3	12.82	+++
China	13	23.31	13	27.85	−
Hungary	3	7.44	7	18.06	− − −
India	7	17.71	1	9.98	+++
Indonesia	12	20.56	9	19.08	+
Malaysia	10	19.92	5	14.36	+++
Mexico	9	19.78	10	21.97	−
Poland	6	17.46	4	13.37	++
Russia	4	7.97	2	11.62	− −
South Africa	5	12.77	12	26.56	− − − −
South Korea	1	3.84	14	27.98	− − − − −
Taiwan	2	6.28	8	18.54	− − −
Thailand	11	20.04	6	17.18	++
Turkey	14	31.35	11	23.19	+++

in their respective risk management index scores would also have matured on an MMI basis. This would suggest that, other than India, markets in Poland, Brazil, Malaysia, Thailand and Indonesia have all increased in maturity over the past two years. Rather surprisingly, South Africa and South Korea, both markets that had seemed reasonably mature in 2007, performed extremely poorly from a risk management perspective in 2009.

Methodology – risk management index

We started with the assumption that the EUR/USD market is perfect from a risk management standpoint – the consistency of V2 over the wide range of volatilities seen from 2007 (7%) to 2009 (17%) suggests that this is a reasonable assumption.

We constructed the risk management index as follows.

Say, the V and V2 are the volatility and volatility of volatility of a market, and E and E2 are the volatility and volatility of the EUR/USD market; we first create a volatility index.

$$\text{If } V > E, \text{ volatility index} = V + (V2 - E2)$$

$$\text{If } V < E, \text{ volatility index} = V - (V2 - E2)$$

Thus, if a market has high volatility (relative to EUR), the difference between its V2 and that of EUR is added to the volatility, pushing it farther away from EUR volatility; so, too, if a market has low volatility, the difference in V2, again, pushes it further away from EUR volatility (see Figure 2)

To create the risk management index, we subtract E (EUR volatility) from the volatility index (bring the risk management index of EUR to zero), and take the absolute value of this difference to be able to compare markets on both sides of the volatility spectrum.

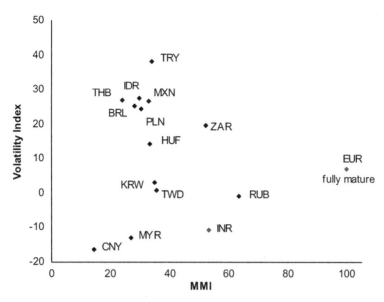

Figure 2.   Volatility index versus MMI (2007).

Conclusions

Russia, India and South Africa were the most mature FX markets of the 14 emerging markets we studied, according to the market maturity index (MMI) we developed using data from the last (2007) BIS survey of central banks. China was in last place.

A key output of market maturity is ease of risk management and we constructed a risk management index to measure this. There was relatively little correlation between this index and the MMI. While Russia and South Africa remained in the top five using this measure, India performed quite badly in 2007, ranking only seventh and quite far behind the leaders.

Of course, as we are anecdotally aware, the Indian market has developed quite considerably since 2007, both in liquidity and sophistication. In parallel, its risk management index has also improved. In 2008–09, when risk management has been particularly difficult in all markets (including the fully developed FX markets, like EUR/USD), India ranked top of all the emerging markets in the study.

South Africa, Taiwan and South Korea, all markets that had seemed reasonably mature in 2007, performed extremely poorly from a risk management perspective in 2009 when market conditions became more severe. On the other hand, four markets (other than India) – Brazil, Malaysia, Turkey and Poland – improved their risk management index score quite substantially by 2009, suggesting that these markets would likely also have seen an improvement in their MMI.

Note

1. It may be significant that most countries in Asia, including those, like Thailand, which had a very low overall MMI, had high ratings on derivatives use. Contrariwise, there were countries, like Russia and South Africa, which had extremely high MMI scores, where derivatives use was relatively modest.

Indian financial institutions: healthy amid global crises

Shyamala Gopinath

Deputy Governor, Reserve Bank of India

What began as a sub-prime crisis in the US housing mortgage sector in the second half of 2007 has turned successively into a global banking crisis, global financial crisis and now a global economic crisis. With the spread of the contagion from the financial to the real sector, it is now expected that global recession will be more protracted and the recovery path fairly long. As the global crisis persists with no turnaround in sight, banks around the world, including those in India, are taking earnest measures with a view to crisis resolution. As the much touted decoupling theory has failed the test in today's globalized world, India too is weathering the negative impact of the crisis. There is, however, an important difference between the crisis in the advanced countries and the developments in India. While in the advanced countries the contagion traversed from the financial to the real sector, in India the slowdown in the real sector is affecting the financial sector, which in turn, has a second-order impact on the real sector.

Impact of the crisis on India/the Indian financial system

India has by-and-large been spared of global financial contagion due to the sub-prime turmoil for a variety of reasons. India's growth process has been largely domestic demand driven and its reliance on foreign savings has remained around 1.5% in recent periods. It also has a comfortable level of foreign exchange reserves. The credit derivatives market is in an embryonic stage, the originate-to-distribute model in India is not comparable to the ones prevailing in advanced markets, there are restrictions on investments by residents in such products issued abroad and regulatory guidelines on securitization do not permit immediate profit recognition. Financial stability in India has been achieved through perseverance of prudential policies which prevent institutions from excessive risk taking, and financial markets from becoming extremely volatile and turbulent.

Even so, India is experiencing the knock-on effects of the global crisis, through the monetary, financial and real channels – all of which are coming on top of the already expected cyclical moderation in growth. The financial markets – equity market, money market, foreign exchange market and credit market – have faced increasing pressure due to the 'substitution effect' of: (i) the drying up of overseas financing for Indian banks and Indian corporates in the form of trade credit as well as external commercial borrowings; (ii) constraints in raising funds in a bearish domestic capital market; and (iii) decline in the internal accruals of the corporates. These factors compounded the pressure on the domestic credit market. Simultaneously, the reversal of capital flows, caused by the global de-leveraging process, has put pressure on India's foreign exchange market. The sharp fluctuation in the overnight money market rates in October 2008 and the depreciation of the rupee reflected the combined impact of the global credit crunch and the de-leveraging process underway.

The Indian banking system has not been directly exposed to the sub-prime mortgage assets and has very limited indirect exposure to the US mortgage market or to the failed institutions and stressed assets. Indian banks, both in the public sector and in the private sector, are financially sound, well capitalized and well regulated. The average capital to risk-weighted assets ratio (CRAR) for the Indian banking system, as at end-March 2008, was 13% (September 2008 was 12.5%) as against the regulatory minimum of 9% and the Basel norm of 8%. Foreign subsidiaries and foreign branches of Indian banks have, however, suffered some market-to-market losses on financial instruments due to the general widening of credit spreads. These losses are modest relative to the size of their business for which adequate provisioning has been made. Indian banks including public sector banks have been affected only peripherally as they did not have direct exposure to sub-prime assets. Overall, these banks' exposure, especially to Lehman Brothers Holding Inc., which has filed for bankruptcy, is not significant and banks are reported to have made adequate provisions.

Health of the Indian financial system

Owing to the various initiatives taken since the early 1990s, the Indian financial system has displayed resilience to withstand shocks. The commercial banking system in India has become strong, sound and competitive following the various measures taken to bring it in line with the global best practices.

The health of Indian banking is apparent from the fact that net profits of Scheduled Commercial Banks (SCB) showed a significant increase of 36.9% during 2007–2008 as compared with 26.9% in the previous year, in spite of the larger increase in provisions and contingencies. Despite an upturn in the interest rate cycle in the period up to August 2008, SCBs have been able to maintain their return on assets (RoA). A significant improvement in the asset quality is reflected in the decline in gross and net non-performing assests (NPA) ratios, which are now comparable with the international standards. The strong capital position of the banking sector, which is significantly above the regulatory requirement of 9%, has provided them with the much needed cushion to withstand shocks and other emerging risks. The Indian banking system is on a sound footing compared to its counterparts in other countries in terms of various financial and soundness indicators such as RoA, non-performing loans (NPLs) ratio and capital levels (Table 1). The NPA levels of the banking sector have reduced to 2.3% at end-March 2008 as against the global range of 0.3% to 13.2% in 2008. The provisioning to NPL ratio of Indian banks was 52.4% at the end-March 2008, as against the global range of 26% to 187%.

Table 1. Benchmarking of Indian banking sector, 2008 (in %).

Country	Return on assets	Gross NPL to gross adv.	CRAR	Provisions to NPL	Capital to assets
India	1.0	2.3	13.0	52.4	6.3
Emerging markets					
Argentina	1.7	2.8	16.8	122.3	12.6
Brazil	2.8	2.9	18.1	181.7	9.5
Mexico	2.9	2.1	16.0	184.0	14.1
Korea	0.9	0.8	12.0	183.8	8.8
S. Africa	1.4*	1.4*	12.8*	–	7.9*
Developed countries					
US	0.6	1.7	12.8	88.9	10.2
UK	0.4*	0.9*	12.6*	54.6∧	8.9∧
Japan	0.3	1.4	12.3	26.4	4.3
Canada	0.3	0.9	12.3	36.7	5.3
Australia	1.0*	0.3	10.5	128.6	4.1
Memo item: Global range					
Minimum	0.2	0.3	10.0	26.4	3.5
	(Montenegro)	(Australia)	(Sweden)	(Japan)	(Netherlands)
Maximum	4.2	13.2	28.7	187.5	22.7
	(Moldova)	(Bangladesh)	(Moldova)	(Chile)	(Armenia)

Notes: –: Not available. *: Data pertains to 2007. ∧: Data pertains to 2006.
Source: 'Report of the Trend and Progress of Banking in India', Reserve Bank of India, December 2008.

The CRAR of 56 banks was over 12%, of 21 banks was between 10% and 12%, while those of the remaining two banks was between 9% and 10%. The CRAR of Indian banks was comparable with most emerging markets and developed economies. The global range of CRAR in 2008 varied between 10% and 28.7%. A capital to asset ratio is another simple measure of soundness of a bank. The lower the ratio, the higher is the leverage and greater vulnerability of a bank. Globally the ratio varied between 3.5% to 22.7% in 2008, while Indian banks' capital to assets ratio at 6.3% suggested a lower degree of leverage and higher stability.

Key elements of RBI regulatory framework

The multi-pronged approach followed for strengthening and developing financial institutions, markets, payment systems and infrastructure has had a positive impact on the Indian financial system. The assessment of developments during 2007–2008 and 2008–2009 so far suggests that financial institutions, especially SCBs, are on a sound footing. There are a number of reasons why the Indian financial system is healthy in the midst of the global financial crisis.

Capital adequacy framework

The recent crisis has clearly pointed out the procyclicality of capital regulations including the Basel II risk sensitive capital measures and several international fora are now emphasizing the need for countercyclical capital regulations. What this means is that capital requirements decrease in boom times but rise in downturns as credit quality declines. In India during periods of rapid credit growth, particularly in certain sensitive sectors, the RBI increased risk weights to build capital buffers in the event of future unexpected losses in these sectors. For instance, a higher risk weight of 125% was introduced in 2004 as a temporary countercyclical measure for consumer loan and credit cards receivables which exhibited strong growth. In view of the rapid expansion of credit to commercial real estate, the risk weight was increased from 100% to 125% and then to 150% in 2006.

In November 2008, on a review it was decided, as a countercyclical measure, to reduce the risk weights on unrated corporate and commercial real estate exposures to 100%.

Provisioning norms

Given the procyclicality of the provisioning norms and since unusually high credit growth in a sensitive sector can be seen as a precursor to higher default rates in future, as a countercyclical prudential measure, the general provisioning requirement on standard advances for residential housing loan beyond Rs.20 lakh had been progressively increased from 0.25% to 1%, while that on standard advances in the commercial real estate sector, personal loans including outstanding credit card receivables, loans and advances qualifying as capital market exposure and sys-tematically important non-deposit taking non-banking finance companies (NBFC-ND-SI) was progressively increased from 0.25% to 2%.

Recently in view of the downturn the provisions were reduced to 0.4 percent. However, banks are not allowed to write back the provisions.

Approach to liquidity risk management

As the current global financial crisis has shown, liquidity risks can rise manifold during a crisis and can pose serious downside risks to macroeconomic and financial stability. The Reserve Bank of India (RBI) had already put in place steps to mitigate liquidity risks at the very short-end, risks at the systemic level and at the institution level as well. Some of the important measures by the Reserve Bank in this regard include, first, restricting the overnight unsecured market for funds to banks and Primary Dealers (PD) as well as limits on the borrowing and lending operations of these entities in the overnight inter-bank call money market. Second, large reliance by banks on borrowed funds can exacerbate vulnerability to external shocks. This has been brought out quite strikingly in the ongoing financial crisis in the global financial markets. Accordingly, in order to encourage greater reliance on stable sources of funding, the Reserve Bank has imposed prudential limits on banks on their purchased inter-bank liabilities and these limits are linked to their net worth. Furthermore, the incremental credit–deposit ratio of banks is also monitored by the Reserve Bank since this ratio indicates the extent to which banks are funding credit with borrowings from wholesale markets (now known as purchased funds). Third, asset-liability management guidelines for dealing with overall asset-liability mismatches take into account both on and off balance sheet items. Finally, guidelines on securitization of standard assets have laid down a detailed policy on provision of liquidity support to Special Purpose Vehicles (SPVs).

Composition and quality of liquid assets

This crisis has again demonstrated the risks of treating any asset which is marketable as liquid. It is difficult to arrive at the optimal liquidity ratio as much depends on the composition of assets and liabilities and the extent of maturity transformation and leverage. However, it is now recognized that there is a need to insist that a part of the liquid assets should be in the form of risk free government securities. In that sense, the Statutory Liquidity Ratio (SLR) in India has ensured that the banks hold a certain proportion of the liabilities in credit risk free government securities. This has also introduced some counter cyclicality in earnings since in downturns the government securities portfolio provide assured income and also capital gains. It helps banks maintain a diversified portfolio which contributes to financial stability.

Securitization

The RBI guidelines on securitization of standard assets had laid down detailed policy on provision of liquidity support to Special Purpose Vehicles. While the policy enabled a liquidity facility, by the originator or a third party, to help smoothen the timing differences faced by the SPV between the receipt of cash flows from the underlying assets and the payments to be made to investors, it was subject to certain conditions to ensure that the liquidity support was only temporary and got invoked to meet cash flow mismatches. Any commitment to provide such liquidity facility is to be treated as an off-balance sheet item and attracts 100% credit conversion factor as well as 100% risk weight. The liquidity support was specifically prohibited for the purposes of: (i) providing credit enhancement; (ii) covering losses of the SPV; (iii) serving as a permanent revolving funding; and (iv) covering any losses incurred in the underlying pool of exposures prior to a draw down.

Off balance sheet exposures

In order to further strengthen capital requirements, the credit conversion factors, risk weights and provisioning requirements for specific off-balance sheet items including derivatives have been reviewed and increased. These are more stringent than the Basel guidelines. Furthermore, in India, complex structures like synthetic securitization have not been permitted so far.

Non-banking financial intermediaries

An additional feature of recent prudential actions by the Reserve Bank relate to the tightening of regulation and supervision of NBFCs, so that regulatory arbitrage between these companies and the banking system is minimized. The overarching principle is that banks should not use an NBFC as a delivery vehicle for seeking regulatory arbitrage opportunities or to circumvent bank regulation(s) and that the activities of NBFCs do not undermine banking regulations. Thus, capital adequacy ratios and prudential limits to single/group exposures in the case of NBFCs have been built into the regulatory framework. The regulatory interventions are graded, higher in deposit-taking NBFCs and lower in non-deposit-taking NBFCs. Thus, excessive leverage in this sector has been contained.

Likely impact of macroeconomic developments on asset quality

The not so favourable macroeconomic climate in the near term is expected to impact on the Indian financial sector. The present environment could affect the asset quality of the Indian financial system. Nevertheless, the overall impact is not expected to be significant and banks should be able to maintain overall good asset quality. These expectations follow from the following two observations.

(1) Structurally, India's financial sector is stable and healthy. The indicators of financial strength such as capital adequacy and ratio of non-performing assets for our commercial banks are robust. The CRAR of SCBs as at end-June 2008 was a healthy 12.74% which provides a sufficient additional cushion to absorb unexpected losses. Further, the capital requirements for Indian banks are presently higher at 9% of risk weighted assets as against 8% internationally, with tier 1 capital at minimum of 6%. The net NPA level of banks was 1.1% as at end-March 2008. The analysis done in the Report on Currency and Finance, Reserve Bank of India, September 2008 reveals that the Indian banking system which is the backbone of our financial system is stable and we do not have periods of extreme volatility in earnings/business followed by steep downturns.

(2) It is expected that the credit risk management by banks including the appraisal standards and risk pricing would show improvement. Banks are also empowered to restructure the troubled and distressed accounts, if considered viable, so that problems arising on account of economic downturns or sector specific problems are addressed at the institutional and industry (corporate debt restructuring) level. Some provisions in this regard for exposures to commercial real estate and second restructuring done for certain sectors were announced by the Reserve Bank in December 2008. Prudential guidelines on restructuring of advances by banks have been reviewed and fresh guidelines on the subject have been issued in August 2008 and January 2009. These will ensure that banks deal with potential stress assets in a timely manner and ensure continued flow of credit.

However, the NPAs of banks on an incremental basis could come under pressure in the near future on account of the high growth in credit in the last few years and factors such as softening of real estate prices. Hence, the provisioning requirement may also go up. Nevertheless, the profitability of Indian banks is not expected to be affected significantly. The slowing down of the economy would have implications for maintaining CRAR under Basel II for two reasons. Firstly, credit rating of borrowers normally deteriorates during the downswing. Secondly, banks find it difficult to raise capital from the market. However, as most banks maintain CRAR at significantly higher levels than the stipulated level, they should be able to meet the stipulated level in next couple of years.

Challenges ahead

While the financial system on the whole is quite robust which augurs well for financial stability, there is a need to be aware of some downside risks in certain areas that could have a bearing on the health of the financial sector in the near future. The major challenges facing the banking system in the country, particularly in the wake of the global financial crisis include the following:

(1) *Maintaining credit flow*

As stated in the RBI statement of 2 January 2009, there is evidence of economic activity slowing down. Industrial activity has decelerated and the services sector, which has been an engine of growth during the last five years, has also been slowing down. In these circumstances it would be a major challenge for the banks to ensure healthy flow of credit to the productive sectors of the economy. Economic growth, even in normal times, requires efficient financial intermediation. An economic downturn, therefore, requires even more efficient financial intermediation – and this is a major challenge that the banking community has to address. There is a need to ensure a steady credit flow to the real sector of the economy in order to sustain demand even while maintaining credit quality. There are two aspects to lending *viz.*, availability and cost of credit. While the availability of credit should not be an issue, the cost of credit seems to be an issue at the current juncture due to the high weighted-average cost of funds because of high interest rates on deposits and concerns about credit quality, which makes the banks risk averse, particularly in lending to certain segments. However, as credit demand seems to be slackening, the reduced funding demand should enable banks to reduce the interest rates on deposits and thereby reduce the overall cost of funds. In addition, the deceleration of headline inflation should enable a reduction in nominal interest rates of banks. These developments in turn, would facilitate lending at lower interest rates, making fresh lending more viable and at least partly obviating the risk aversion of the banks.

(2) *Relaxing regulatory norms*

There has been a sustained demand from various quarters for exercising regulatory forbearance in regard to extant prudential regulations applicable to the banking sector. As stated earlier, a part of countercyclical package, the Reserve Bank has made several changes to the current prudential norms. There are demands for further regulatory forbearance such as relaxing the asset classification norms by increasing the period of delinquency beyond the current norm of 90 days, after which the loan asset is required to be classified as non-performing. Such forbearance will not be in the interest of the banking system and we should be wary of doing anything that militates against preserving the soundness of our banks and tweaking basic prudential norms.

The Reserve Bank has been closely following the developments in international financial regulation and supervision. One of the early reports was the action plan devised by the Financial Stability Forum (FSF) for implementation by the countries affected by the recent financial turbulence. The Reserve Bank has already put in place regulatory guidelines covering many of the aspects highlighted in the policy recommendation by the FSF. In certain cases, actions have to be considered as work-in-progress. Recently the G-30 has released a very comprehensive report on financial reform. In the short to medium term, the approach is to keep a close watch on the unfolding macro-financial conditions – both domestic and international – with a view to taking corrective measures as and when required.

Although India remains vulnerable to global financial and economic develop-ments, the measures taken so far have eased the liquidity and credit flow situation considerably. While the package of macroeconomic and prudential measures taken to help the economy/banks deal with the effect of the financial market turmoil has had some positive effect, challenges still remain as global uncertainties continue to persist. As neither macroeconomic management nor prudential regulations can be static, the Reserve Bank takes and will continue to take appropriate measures as the situation unfolds. Also, in managing the impact of the global crisis, the Reserve Bank has been mindful that no policy initiative is totally costless. Managing the delicate balance between costs and benefits has been one of the major challenges.

Learning from crises

Usha Thorat

Reserve Bank of India, Central Office Mumbai 400 001, Mumbai, India

Instead of learning from crises the same mistakes seem to get repeated. Therefore recollecting and extracting lessons from crises is essential. Key potential lessons are in anticipation, pre-emptive action, crisis management, and prevention. The paper details the internal and external shocks that hit India's financial system in the post-reform period and the regulatory lessons that were learnt and implemented as a consequence.

Introduction

The late John Kenneth Galbraith, Harvard Economics Professor Emeritus, attributed the longevity of his book *The Great Crash 1929* – published in 1955 and never since out of print – to the tendency of history to threaten a repeat. 'Each time it has been about to pass from bookstores,' he wrote in a later foreword, 'another speculative episode – another bubble or the ensuing misfortune – has stirred interest in the history of this, the great modern case of boom and collapse, which led on to an unforgiving depression.' So here we are again. The financial crisis that has engulfed credit markets over the recent period has pushed the old Keynesian economist's book back into the Amazon charts.

'Bad distribution of income' is the first of five weaknesses of the US economy that Galbraith cites in his definitive work on the stock market collapse. Though Galbraith says it was 5%, not 3%, of Americans who received one-third of personal income in 1929, he says this well-heeled group played a crucial role in the crash. 'The collapse in securities values affected in the first instance the wealthy and the well-to-do. But in the world of 1929 this was a vital group. The members disposed of a large proportion of the consumer income; they were the source of the lion's share of personal savings and investment.'

History has an eerie way of repeating itself and memory of the pain of busts, according to Galbraith, is perhaps the best regulator.

In the latest best seller *The Ascent of Money*, Niall Ferguson has also highlighted the fact that the income of the median household in US has scarcely changed since 1980, increasing by just 7% in the last 18 years while their borrowings multiplied several times and made what seemed a sub prime mortgage crisis to a full blown global financial crisis.

In the current global crisis, no country has been spared, be it big or small, developing or developed, relatively insulated or more open. The shock has impacted both the financial and real sectors although it was financial sector led. In India, the impact though significant, has not been to the same extent as in other parts. This is partly attributed to the curbs India still has on the capital account, but mainly to the dominance of domestic expenditure – consumption and investment – and high savings rate, leading to a balanced macro economy, having small current account deficits. Nevertheless, the impact has been felt by the domestic credit equity and foreign exchange (forex) markets leading to slowing down in the growth rate and employment generation. Still, the country is the second fastest growing economy in the world with over 6% growth projected for 2009.

As Galbraith recalled it is amazing how the same mistakes get repeated. Hence I think we owe it to the system to recollect and recount lessons from crises. The key lessons are how to anticipate and take pre-emptive action and equally important, once you are in the middle of a crisis, how to respond effectively *viz.* crisis management. Post-crisis, the critical issues are how do we put in systems and buffers that can cushion the impact of economic cycles and booms and busts that are so typical of market driven systems.

During the journey I have traversed in the Reserve Bank of India (RBI), I have been witness to many crisis situations of differing dimensions, especially since 1991. Delving into the past I feel veteran enough to share these experiences and draw lessons.

The balance of payments (BOP) crisis of 1991

This was a major crisis in the country. In mid-1991, the foreign exchange reserves of the country were down to 11 days imports, even what little reserves that remained were not unencumbered. While the crisis was triggered by increase in oil prices and the Gulf War, the underlying factors were the macro imbalance in the form of unmanageable current account and fiscal deficits. External debt servicing as a proportion of current receipts increased from 10.2% in 1980–81 to 35.3% of current receipts in 1990–91. The responses included curbing imports through a system of administrative controls for large value letters of credit, giving incentives for exports, pledging of gold reserves with the Bank of England and Bank of Japan, devaluation of the Indian rupee, issuing attractive bonds in foreign currency to non-resident Indians, encouraging return flow of capital, an amnesty scheme through gold bonds, borrowing from multilateral institutions, etc., and so on. The long term response included major reforms in trade industry foreign investment fiscal and financial sector paving the way for development of equity, forex money and government securities markets. There were fundamental changes in monetary management consequent upon stoppage of automatic monetization of the government deficit and switch over to an auction based market borrowing for meeting the fiscal deficits.

Many valuable lessons were learnt from the crisis:

- exchange rates should not be overvalued for long periods;
- providing exchange guarantees by the central bank or government are best avoided;
- on the external account, liberalizing equity flows first is a better option followed by commercial credit and longer term debt, while limiting the access to foreign debt by the financial sector;

- central bank funding of the government in the primary market should not be resorted to;
- excessively high remuneration on reserve requirements erodes monetary control;
- financial sector repression – excessive interest controls and credit rationing – is deleterious to growth;
- a strong financial sector requires prudential regulation and effective supervision;
- removing or reducing entry barriers to facilitate more competition; and
- co-ordinated action by the government and the central bank with a well knit professional team working together greatly facilitates the process.

The securities irregularities of 1992

The irregularities reflected speculative buying in the stock market funded by bank liquidity through repurchase transactions in government securities and bonds, facilitated by a nexus between brokers and banks. In part this reflected a way of earning higher yields in an otherwise administered interest rate structure. Such transactions were done against bank receipts where there were no underlying government securities. The events that led to these irregularities could be attributed to weaknesses and lack of transparency in the market infrastructure for government securities, excess liquidity with public sector undertakings, nexus between banks and brokers and inadequate internal controls that led to bank funds flowing to the stock markets fuelling abnormal stock price increase. Poor internal controls were reflective of low levels of computerization and reliance on manual processing. Consequences resulted when a settlement failure triggered panic and the irregularities surfaced in the open. The RBI had to undertake a series of investigations to unravel the irregular transactions and fix responsibility. A Joint Parliamentary Committee (JPC) constituted to investigate into these operations required enormous resources of the management.

There were several positive fallouts of this crisis:

- acceleration of capital market reforms and introduction of screen based order matching systems with commensurate depository custody clearing and settlement arrangements that are continuously upgraded;
- institution of a delivery versus payment mechanism for settlement of trades in government securities initially in the RBI but later led to establishment of a central counterparty in the form of the Clearing Corporation Of India (CCIL) which today undertakes guaranteed settlement for government securities, repos in government securities (G Secs) and forex market trades;
- dissemination of information on all individual transactions in the government securities market on a daily basis and currently on real time basis;
- tightening of internal controls in investment transactions;
- removal of administered interest rates – currently only the savings bank deposit rate is fixed by the RBI, while all other deposit rates are deregulated;
- strengthening supervision over banks and other financial institutions and establishment of the Board for Financial Supervision (BFS) in 1994 with the primary objective of undertaking supervision of the financial sector comprising commercial banks, financial institutions and non-banking financial companies;

- recognition of the possibility of systemic risk in the absence of proper assessment of counterparty risk and well functioning securities markets with greater transparency; and
- focused attention on the role of the regulator which ensures adherence to regulations in letter and spirit and need for greater accountability.

Imbroglio caused by dealings of non-banking financial companies in 1997

Non-banking financial companies (NBFCs) have been historically subjected to a relatively lower degree of regulation vis-à-vis the banks, the higher rates of return on deposits they could offer enabled them to attract a large base of small savers and a potential threat to the stability of the financial system. Added to these was the fact that operations of NBFCs were characterized by several distinctive features *viz.* no entry barriers, no requirement for large investment in fixed assets and inventories, freedom to open branch offices, all of which led to their proliferation in an unbridled manner. A few such companies which were perceived as well-functioning, well-managed and financially healthy and consequently had a large depositor base, defaulted in repayment of deposits, leading to the realization that the extant framework was inadequate to monitor and regulate these companies. Though there were no systemic problems, confidence of the depositors in the NBFCs as a sector was eroded and the Reserve Bank faced the risk of loss of reputation. In a specific instance, the in-principle approval given by the Reserve Bank to start a bank was used by the entity to mobilize huge funds from the unsuspecting public and the payable-at-par cheques issued by the entity on a leading commercial bank resulted in a huge exposure and default to the bank because of the lag between the timing of payments and providing funds cover.

The learning points were:

- recognition of the possibility of regulatory arbitrage between the entities regulated by banks and non-banking financial companies and between the securities regulator and the bank regulator; and
- need for legal powers to regulate the activities of NBFCs, including framing of guidelines for compulsory registration, stringency in conditions for deposit-taking companies akin to banks, and applicability of prudential norms for such companies.

In the recent period, it has been noted that, even if not accepting deposits, these companies can contribute to systemic risk as they access public funds and participate in various markets (debt, equity and foreign exchange markets). Hence capital ratios and a quarterly system of reporting were introduced for large non-deposit taking NBFCs in 2007.

Asian crisis of 1997 – the first global contagion

The South-East Asian crisis started with stock market and currency crashes followed by financial crisis which spilt over to the real sector. It changed irrevocably the way Asian countries look at issues of financial stability. The Indian market was not immune and even though there was a general belief that some correction in the rupee was required, the pressure on the rupee in later part of the year required the RBI to intervene to maintain orderly conditions. Withdrawal of funds by foreign institutional investors (FIIs) hit the equity and foreign exchange markets and the sale of foreign exchange by the RBI also affected the money and bond markets. In addition to intervention, monetary and administrative measures had to be taken to stabilize markets. The impact on the domestic interest rates and liquidity was the cost to be paid for restoring stability. The government borrowing programme was managed through private placement and subsequent open market operations when the markets stabilized.

The learning points were:

- need for complementarity between macroeconomic stability and financial stability and exchange rate management for preserving competitiveness and confidence in the economy;
- need for closer supervision and regulation of banks and other financial institutions;
- during asset price booms it is important to ensure that banks' exposure to capital markets and real estate is not excessive and to understand that banks can be subject to foreign exchange risk even without any currency mismatches in their books, when their constituents have huge unhedged exposures;
- management of capital account is important for countries having chronic current account deficit (CAD) and where inflation and interest rates are persistently over global levels;
- dollarization of the domestic market or internationalization of the domestic currency can both require careful management; and
- financial stability emerged as a specific objective of policy as the cost of instability to the real sector is huge especially on the vulnerable segments of society.

Urban co-operative banks – the weak link

The tightening of regulation over the banking and NBFC sectors saw the gravitation of risk to the lightly regulated urban co-operative banks (UCBs) which were under dual regulation of the RBI and the registrar of co-operative societies. The stock market crash in 2002 triggered a payments problem and it was found that the nexus between the broker and a large UCB (Madhavpura Mercantile Co-operative Bank) led to huge exposure to the broker and the bank collapsed. The systemic implication was that hundreds of small UCBs had exposure to this bank and the collapse of these banks would have been very disruptive though confined to a small region. The Deposit Insurance and Credit Guarantee Corporation (DICGC) had to make a large payout to the collapsed bank under a restructuring package and averted the domino effect. But the Madhavpura Bank collapse led to erosion in public confidence and there were a series of UCB failures across the country. The immediate measures taken were to ban connected lending, exposure to share-brokers and inter-UCB deposits. The supervisory system – both on-site and off-site – was triggered and strengthened. In 2004, all new branch and bank expansion was stopped and a vision document was put out in 2005 which provided for a memorandum of understanding (MoU) with the state governments to work out a way for the non-disruptive exit of weak UCBs while simultaneously incentivizing the growth of strong banks. Subsequently various resolution options have been provided such as merger with or without support from DICGC, restructuring of liabilities, introduction of new capital-like instruments, and transfer of assets and liabilities. The UCB sector has seen a reduction in the number of weak banks from 725 to 496. 102 banks have gone out of the system through mergers and liquidation. DICGC has also strengthened its claim payments system to ensure that prompt relief is given to small depositors of failed banks.

The lessons learnt were:

- in dealing with a crisis arising out of interconnectedness, breathing time needs to be provided through liquidity injection;
- reduce interconnectedness within the financial system as it leads to a 'moral hazard' problem of 'too interconnected to fail';
- the most lightly regulated entity in the financial system becomes the weakest link. The system's weakest link becomes a source of reputation risk and erosion in public confidence; and
- even though under dual regulation, the bank regulator has to use its powers more effectively and take steps to resolve weak banks.

Failure of a fairly significant mid sized commercial bank in 2004

The Global Trust Bank Ltd, a private sector bank had reported substantial growth and was growing too fast. The bank's balance sheet was flawed and disclosures inadequate. Very large capital market exposures and shortfall in provisioning were the causes for downfall of the bank. The common depositor does not have the wherewithal to study bank balance sheets before making a deposit, but even the institutional investors seem to be gullible investors. It was also realized that even though insolvent, a bank can carry on without a run as long as it has adequate liquidity or access to liquidity. Interestingly, even at the time of moratorium, the bank had huge inter-bank borrowings and deposits reflecting the confidence placed by other banks and institutional investors or the moral hazard view that banks will not be allowed to fail. Auditor accountability came under focus. The problem had to be dealt with head on when all avenues and options for revival by the promoters and directors failed. Compulsory amalgamation with a public sector bank was resorted to.

This experience gave us valuable lessons of how to deal with a bank run:

- the process of resolution should be swift and decisive and preferably over the weekend;
- in a computerized system with 24/7 banking, and large retail base, the preparation for a moratorium has to be much more meticulous than in traditional banking;
- the role of media is critical and in any crisis management media management has to be given priority. We actually had to go on media to give out reassurances about the bank to stop the run;
- adequate liquidity and currency needs to be kept ready to stem a run once the resolution strategy is decided; and
- a moratorium is useful to give breathing time to put a resolution package in place but hardship requests can become tedious to handle.

Institutional factors

This decade has been one of challenges in managing capital flows both inflows and outflows. Both monetary policies and prudential policies have been used through a variety of instruments to manage the macroeconomic and financial stability challenges arising out of large capital flows, external shocks such as 9/11, political uncertainty, geo-political events, and have called for vigilance and prompt actions. While evolving policy instruments to manage these conditions such as the Market Stabilization Scheme for sterilizing the impact of inflows are important, I would like to flag a few critical institutional factors which I think are required to be encouraged and made part of the automatic trigger mechanisms in the system. I would like to turn to these.

Problem recognition – the meaning of being vigilant is to be able to constantly scan the horizon and recognize that a problem is brewing and take pre-emptive action before the problem becomes disruptive. The indicators could be asset values, excess credit growth, large unhedged exposures, continuing current account deficits financed by short term credit, weakly regulated entities in the system, opportunities for regulatory arbitrage, large leveraged positions, prolonged periods of liquidity excesses or shortages; or the tendencies of entities to leverage, especially by exploiting the inter-linkages in the financial system.

Committee approach – as part of crisis management, it is necessary to have a harmonized approach. First it is essential to have close co-ordination with the government. As in 1991, this was an important requirement in responding to the recent crisis. Putting in place an institutional mechanism and systems that can facilitate continuous dialogue and co-ordination between those in charge of monetary policy, debt management, foreign exchange management, regulation and supervision of banking entities, supervision of non-banking entities, securities markets regulation and the like is a *sine-qua-non*. Within each of these segments it is crucial to be in sync. We have a Financial Markets Committee (FMC) in the central bank consisting of senior executives responsible for monetary policy and operations, debt management and foreign exchange reserves management. The FMC meets at least once every day in the morning and emergent meetings are also convened when there are episodes of sharp volatility in equity markets, or when any of the other markets are significantly affected. Other regulatory departments including the department responsible for payment system also get involved during such times. The Committee keeps in touch with the securities regulator Securities and Exchange Board of India (SEBI), the stock exchanges, especially the clearing and settlement corporation of the exchanges, the CCIL and the like. We also have a Crisis Management Group that meets whenever a crisis is anticipated or occurs.

Inter-regulatory co-ordination – financial sector harmonization among the securities, insurance, pension fund and bank regulators is enabled through the High Level Co-ordination Committee on Financial Markets (HLCCFM). The HLCCFM is headed by the Governor of the RBI and meets as and when felt required. The Ministry of Finance provides the secretariat. Sub-committees/groups formed among SEBI, Insurance Regulatory and Development Authority (IRDA), Pension Fund Regulatory and Development Authority (PFRDA) and (RBI), meet to discuss and sort out issues relating to developments in the financial markets having implications cutting across different regulators. Institutionalized and formal approach to decision-making in a crisis has the benefit of building on the experience of the members.

Consultative approach – we have also reaped the advantages of using external experts in our policymaking. We have a Technical Advisory Committee for Monetary Policy consisting of academicians, practitioners and experts, which tenders advice to the RBI on monetary policy stance. There is also a technical advisory committee that consists of financial sector experts from areas such as banking, academics, government, stock exchanges, credit rating agencies and market representatives. This committee meets once a quarter to deliberate on developments in money, foreign exchange and government-securities markets and offers advice on policies for regulation, growth and further reforms in financial markets, including products, practices and institutional arrangements.

Capacity building – equally crucial is the need to develop people and systems to deal with scenarios and contingencies, which can be achieved only through a sustained process of capacity building. Giving exposure through participation in meetings at local and international levels, allowing officers even at fairly junior levels to be part of the dialogue process at the top levels in various co-ordination fora, enormously helps in nurturing talent. A consultative and participative approach to decision-making through the setting-up of working groups consisting of a mix of internal and external people with clearly set tasks and time-lines not only casts responsibility but also aids developing expertise. Emphasis in these groups is on harnessing collective wisdom and balanced judgment, typical of a college-like atmosphere for decision-making.

Robust infrastructure – I am referring to the development of sound market infrastructure for payments and settlement for all financial transactions as also market infrastructure for trading reporting information dissemination and clearing settlement. Central Counter Party (CCPs) for clearing and settlement of equity government securities forex and money markets are in place following the best practices laid down by International Organization of Securities Commissions (IOSCO)/Committee on Payment and Settlement Systems (CPSS). The infrastructure for electronic payments and real time gross settlements (RTGS) are now taken for granted.

Summing up

The major learning from this crisis is that globalization has meant no country is immune from the happenings in global financial markets. Also, at one level, the presence of complex and interconnected financial entities across several jurisdictions with regulators at the national level has posed huge challenges in ensuring that there is no regulatory arbitrage and that there is co-ordination amongst regulators. Even within a jurisdiction, it is recognized that all regulators have to deal with systemic risk and there is need for inter-regulatory dialogue and vigilance.

At the macro level, Asian countries and Latin American countries have learnt lessons from their own past currency and financial crises and have built up reserves and have strengthened their financial systems apart from consciously developing their financial markets. But they have been careful to ensure that their banks are not involved excessively in toxic assets or innovative transactions. Even so, the countries have had to face the consequences of falling global trade and gross domestic product (GDP) and unemployment and slowing credit growth. Macroeconomic imbalances continue though they have reduced. Savings are increasing in the Western world and consumption increasing in the East.

Ultimately, we all have to be concerned about the real sector and recognize that financial sector development is not a goal by itself but is intended to enable the growth, not just of the rich, but more importantly inclusive growth cutting across all segments of the society and regions. As regulators and central banks, it is our duty to ensure this.

Acknowledgement

Based on the 'Institute of Banking and Finance (IBF) Distinguished Speaker Series' lecture delivered by Mrs Usha Thorat Deputy Governor, Reserve Bank of India at Singapore on 12 October 2009.

Reference

Ferguson, N. 2008. *The ascent of money: a financial history of the world.* New York: Penguin Press.

The coming unwinding of global imbalances and what it means for India

Vivekanand Jayakumar

Sykes College of Business, University of Tampa, Tampa, USA

Large US current account deficits, financed mainly by East Asian countries and some OPEC members, gave rise to significant global imbalances in recent years. This paper argues that such imbalances are unsustainable going forward. Faced with lower asset valuations and tighter credit access, Americans are likely to curtail consumption and increase personal saving. The resulting decline in US imports will significantly impact export-driven Asian countries. Diminished foreign desire to finance excessive American borrowing, along with rising concerns over dollar's reserve status, will also affect global imbalances. The paper highlights the relevance of the evolving global economic landscape to India.

1. Introduction

Global imbalances, characterized by massive current account deficits in the US and correspondingly large surpluses in Japan, Germany, and more recently, in China and some Middle Eastern oil-exporters, has been a central feature of the international economy during the past decade. Recognizing the factors that gave rise to the global imbalances and determining the future sustainability of such imbalances is critically important.

This article argues that many of the factors that gave rise to significant global imbalances are in retreat, and that a radical restructuring of the basic arrangement underlying international macroeconomic relationships is likely to occur (and may in fact already be underway). We provide multiple reasons for the coming unwinding of global imbalances. The impending shift towards less profligate consumption in the US, and a corresponding improvement in the personal saving levels of American households, is emphasized in this article. We expect this shift to fundamentally affect US import levels going forward.

The relevance of structural changes in the global economy to a key emerging economy, namely India, is explored in this study. Specifically, we make the case that it is not feasible for India to replicate China's export-dependent growth strategy. This study also highlights policy options that can help India sustain high growth rates in the future, even in a global environment that is far less accommodative towards export-driven growth strategies.

The rest of the paper is organized as follows. In section 2 we provide a background on global imbalances, and in section 3 we explore the various factors that gave rise to global imbalances and discuss the sustainability of large imbalances going forward. We compare and contrast the economic development pattern of India with that of China in section 4. This is followed by a discussion highlighting the impracticality of India adopting a Chinese style export-oriented growth model in section 5. We briefly discuss some policy alternatives for sustaining future growth in India in the midst of a changing global environment and conclude in section 6.

2. Brief background on global imbalances

In order to obtain a clear sense of the sharp rise in global imbalances during the past decade, a quick review of basic international macroeconomic relations is useful. In the absence of inter-planetary trade (still only a possibility in the science fiction realm), the global economy as a whole can be considered as a closed economy. As such, total global saving (S_{glob}) should equal total global investment (I_{glob}):

$$S_{glob} = I_{glob} \tag{1}$$

But for each individual economy, i, the following condition must hold (note: S_i is national saving, I_i is domestic private investment and CA_i is the current account balance, in country i:

$$S_i = I_i + CA_i. \tag{2}$$

From Equations (1) and (2), it is clear that large current account deficits in some countries have to be offset by surpluses in others.[1] In other words, to reconcile the relationship representing the global economy as a whole (Equation (1)) with the open-economy relationship representing individual countries (Equation (2)), we need the sum of the current account balances of all the countries in the world to equal zero (see Equation (3)).

$$\sum_i CA_i = 0 \tag{3}$$

It should also be noted that, according to Equation (2), a country facing excess national saving ($S_i - I_i > 0$) will be running a current account surplus, which will be lent abroad. In the case where a country faces a current account deficit ($S_i - I_i < 0$), the country has to be a net foreign borrower.

A quick glance (see Figure 1) at trends in the current account balance of key economies from around the world clarifies the above noted open-economy concepts. While the US, UK and Spain ran massive current account deficits during much of the past decade, there was, correspondingly, a sharp increase in the current account surplus of China, NIEs (newly industrialized economies – Hong Kong, South Korea, Singapore, and Taiwan), ASEAN-5 (Indonesia, Malaysia, Philippines, Thailand, and Vietnam), Gulf Cooperation Council (Bahrain, Kuwait, Oman, Qatar, Saudi Arabia, and United Arab Emirates), Germany, and Japan.

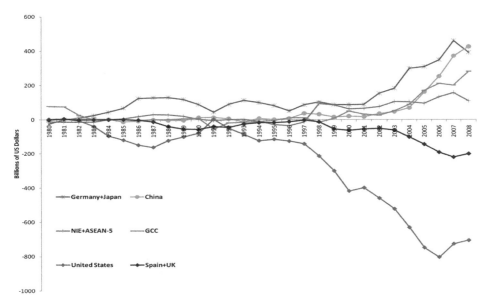

Figure 1. Current account balance (1980–2008).
Source: IMF World Economic Outlook Database, October 2009.

While Japan and Germany have long been noted for their trade surpluses and export-dependent economies, the biggest recent change in current account surpluses occurred elsewhere. Broadly speaking, the two regions that saw the most dramatic shift towards rising current account surpluses, and excess national saving ($S_i - I_i > 0$), are developing Asia (see Figure 2) and the Middle East (see Figure 3). The US, on the other hand, saw its trade and current account deficit levels explode during the past decade. Between 2000 and 2008, the magnitude of the US current account deficit reached unprecedented levels (approaching $800 billion in 2006), and this gave rise to concerns regarding global imbalances.

3. Explaining the rise (and coming decline) of global imbalances

There is considerable disagreement about the primary causes of the global imbalances and about the sustainability of large US current account deficits. In this section, we summarize the major explanations for global imbalances and discuss factors that are likely to reduce the level of imbalances in the future. We classify the explanations into four broad groups here: (a) revived Bretton Woods theory and export-led growth, (b) global saving glut hypothesis, (c) dollar standard/precautionary reserve accumulation, and (d) profligate American consumption.

3.1. Revived Bretton Woods theory and export-led growth

The international arrangement underlying key areas of the global economy during the past two decades has been christened by some as a revived Bretton Woods system (or Bretton Woods II). A mutually beneficial core–periphery relationship is a central feature of this framework. According to the proponents of revived Bretton Woods theory (Dooley, Folkerts-Landau and Garber 2003; Dooley et al. 2004, 2005), the

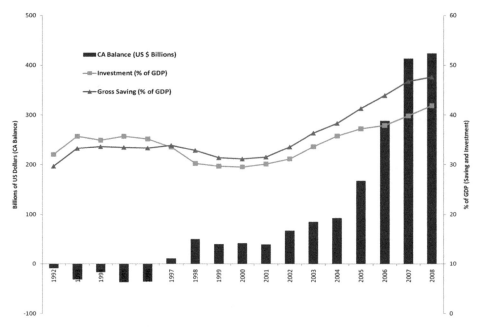

Figure 2. Developing Asia – saving, investment and current account balance.
Note: Developing Asia includes Afghanistan, Bangladesh, Bhutan, Brunei, Cambodia, China, Fiji, India, Indonesia, Kiribati, Laos, Malaysia, Maldives, Myanmar, Nepal, Pakistan, Papua New Guinea, Philippines, Samoa, Solomon Islands, Sri Lanka, Thailand, Timor-Leste, Tonga, Vanuatu, and Vietnam.
Source: IMF World Economic Outlook Database, October 2009.

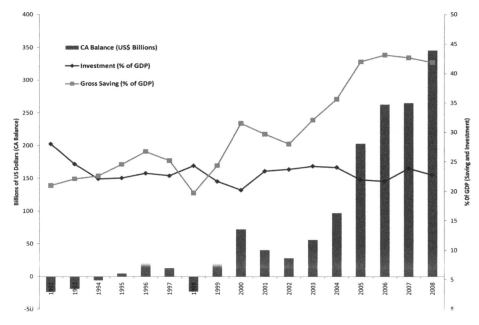

Figure 3. Middle East – saving, investment and current account balance.
Note: Middle East includes Bahrain, Egypt, Iran, Iraq, Jordan, Kuwait, Lebanon, Libya, Oman, Qatar, Saudi Arabia, Syrian, United Arab Emirates, and Yemen.
Source: IMF World Economic Outlook Database, October 2009.

past decade and a half has been characterized by an economic relationship between emerging Asia and the US that bears a striking resemblance to that between Western Europe (and Japan) and the US during the post-World War II era. Dooley et al. (2005) observe that many Asian economies 'chose the same periphery strategy as intermediate post-war Europe and Japan, undervaluing the exchange rate, managing sizeable foreign exchange interventions, imposing [capital] controls, accumulating reserves, and encouraging growth by sending goods to the competitive [centre] countries'. Large US trade deficits are considered easily manageable by supporters of the revived Bretton Woods framework. They suggest that Asian nations, desirous of a continuation of their export first strategy, will stay tied to exchange rate management policies and gladly accumulate even more dollar reserves going forward.

Eichengreen (2007) provides an excellent critique of the revived Bretton Woods theory. While acknowledging the existence of a few parallels with the original Bretton Woods system, Eichengreen (2007) underscores the following distinctions between the current era and the post-World War II era: (a) the Asian countries that dominate the current periphery are a far less cohesive group than the Western European countries that made up most of the periphery in original Bretton Woods era; (b) the emergence of the euro as a true competitor to the dollar (the original Bretton Woods era lacked a true challenger to dollar's status as the pre-eminent reserve currency; but now, the euro presents a genuine alternative to the US dollar); (c) most importantly, during the original Bretton Woods era, the US ran a current account surplus (and was the world's largest net lender), which sharply contrasts with the massive deficits experienced in recent years (currently, the US is the world's largest net debtor); and, (d) the lowering of capital controls around the world implies that private investors (who are motivated primarily by their desire for maximizing returns) have a much greater say in overseas investment decisions.

While the successful development strategies of Japan, the NIEs, ASEAN-5, and more recently China has led economists and policymakers to look upon the export-led growth model in a generally positive light, there is an underlying fallacy of composition that is often ignored. There is little doubt that individual countries (and in some cases entire regions) can and have benefited significantly from an export-led growth strategy, *but* it is impossible for *all* countries to undertake an export-led growth approach.

Coming out of the Global Credit Crisis of 2008–2009, if, as is likely, the United States decides to pursue an export-oriented recovery strategy, then the prospect for a future of export-led growth appear doubtful, not just for Japan, Germany, China, and the NIEs, but also for India down the road. In fact, Lawrence Summers (the current White House Economics Director) in a recent speech at the *Petersen Institute for International Economics* in Washington, DC, noted that in the future the US should rely on an export-oriented growth strategy (and reduce the significance of domestic consumption). In his speech, Summers (2009) proclaimed that:

> The rebuilt American economy must be more export-oriented and less consumption-oriented, more environmentally-oriented and less fossil-energy-oriented, more bio- and software-engineering-oriented and less financial-engineering-oriented, more middle-class-oriented and less oriented to income growth that disproportionately favors a very small share of the population.

Suppose that the absorption or total spending by the US is given by A^{US} and the absorption of the rest of the world by A^*. Then, by definition, 4(a) and 4(b) must hold. (Note: C^{US} denotes consumption in the US, I^{US} denotes private domestic investment in the US, G^{US} denotes government purchases in the US, Y^{US} denotes US output or gross domestic product (GDP) and N^{US} denotes US net exports; variables with a * represent rest of the world).

$$A^{US} = C^{US} + I^{US} + G^{US} = Y^{US} - N^{US} \qquad (4a)$$

and,

$$Y^{US} - A^{US} = N^{US} = -N^* = A^* - Y^* \qquad (4b)$$

Essentially, a net export improvement in the US requires a concomitant or symmetric adjustment in absorption in the rest of the world. Realization of an export-driven American economy requires an increase in the rest of the world's absorption levels. This obviously will affect the prospects for export-oriented growth strategies in large emerging economies like India.

In the past, especially during the Cold War era, the United States was often driven by political and strategic considerations to provide relatively open access to imports from countries such as Japan, West Germany, and the NIEs. A key factor that underlay the American policy of openness to foreign-made products was the strategic imperative to keep many of the above noted export dependent countries within its the orbit of influence, and to restrict the expansion of the Soviet/Communist power. Such policy considerations are obviously of little relevance in the current (and likely future) global environment. In fact, China (and to a lesser extent India) is perceived as a potential competitor to America's dominant position in global affairs.

Also, aversion towards globalization is increasingly widespread among the public in advanced economies. In a September 2007 NBC/*Wall Street Journal* poll, even the traditionally pro-trade Republicans were found wanting in their support for globalization. Almost 60% of the respondents in the survey agreed with the following statement: 'Foreign trade has been bad for the US economy, because imports from abroad have reduced demand for American-made goods, cost jobs here at home, and produced potentially unsafe products'.[2] It goes without saying that Democrats are even more strongly opposed to international trade and globalization. It is worth noting that this particular poll was conducted before the current US recession began in December 2007 (it is likely that public support for free trade is currently even lower). A less than favourable stance towards free trade is not limited to the layperson anymore. Recently, even some mainstream economists have expressed concerns over certain aspects of international trade, such as off-shoring. Prominent Princeton economist, Alan Blinder (2007), recently observed that off-shoring posed a serious risk to millions of American jobs in the future. According to Blinder (2007), the off-shoring 'of service jobs from rich countries such as the United States to poor countries such as India may pose major problems for tens of millions of American workers over the coming decades'.

Additionally, America's new found enthusiasm for regulating carbon emissions may lead to fresh trade protection measures via the imposition of a carbon tax (or green tariffs) on imports from large CO_2 emitters such as China and India (which is ironic, as the level of per-capita energy consumption and CO_2 emission in the US far exceeds that of China or India). The passage of any legislation aimed at limiting greenhouse gas emissions through the US Congress will likely require a tough stance on emerging market emitters that fail to accept binding targets.

The changing tide of opinion in the US is going to put pressure on policymakers to reduce the American trade deficit in the near future. Given the above noted factors, it is difficult to forecast a revival (or the future sustainability) of a Bretton Woods type arrangement. It is difficult to imagine a future where much of the emerging world (along with Germany and Japan) pursues an export-driven growth strategy, and where the US obligingly runs massive trade deficits.

3.2. Global saving glut hypothesis

In a couple of influential speeches, Ben Bernanke (2005, 2007), noted that the primary driver of the large US current account deficits was in fact the saving and spending decisions of emerging economies in Asia (and also similar decisions of Japan/Germany and a few oil-exporting countries). Bernanke's so-called 'global saving glut' hypothesis is controversial because of its emphasis on factors outside the US for the rise of global imbalances. The 'global saving glut' hypothesis gives the impression that domestic factors in the US were not the primary driver of the imbalances, and that in fact, the US was probably doing the world a favour by absorbing all the excess saving from emerging Asia and the Middle East.

According to Bernanke (2007), in the aftermath of the Asian financial crisis, many emerging market nations decided to pursue a pre-cautionary reserve accumulation strategy along with an emphasis on increasing domestic saving. Bernanke suggests that this shift in emerging economies from being primarily current account deficit regions to significant current account surplus regions was a key reason for the worsening of the US current account deficit in recent years.

Bernanke (2007) also points to the growth of current account surpluses in oil and gas exporting countries in recent years as a factor contributing to global imbalances. As money flowed in faster than governments and citizens could spend it, many oil and gas exporters' built-up large amounts of excess savings that needed to be invested abroad. Japan and Germany, due to their instinctive proclivity to be export-driven economies (and due to their rapidly aging populations) pursued current account surpluses as well.

Some economists (Cooper 2007; Caballero, Farhi and Gourinchas 2006) observe that due to the extraordinarily large and liquid US capital markets, it is natural for the US to absorb a significant portion of excess global saving. While the above noted economists are generally sanguine about the effects of the global imbalance in the near to medium term, there are several prominent economists who subscribe to more alarmist viewpoints regarding global imbalances. Obstfeld and Rogoff (2004) have warned of potential risks if foreign countries were to suddenly stop financing the US deficits. They specifically highlight the danger of a major dollar crisis with potentially serious consequences for the US and the rest of the world. Lawrence Summers (2006) has famously referred to the global imbalances as a 'financial balance of terror', with lenders (current account surplus countries) and borrowers (primarily the US) assured of mutual economic and financial destruction in the event of a sudden drying up of foreign funding of the large American deficits.

3.3. Dollar standard/pre-cautionary reserve accumulation

The American dollar's role as the pre-eminent global reserve currency may also be contributing to the rise of global imbalances. The ability of the US to simultaneously pursue large current account deficits and significant budget deficits is largely dependent on the centrality of the American dollar to the international financial system. With the dollar at the centre of global monetary system, the US can essentially borrow abroad for extended periods in its own currency to offset its low level of domestic saving (McKinnon 2009).

The dramatic surge in the reserve holdings of key emerging economies in Asia is driven by a desire to avoid the risks associated with a sudden stop in capital inflows (Calvo 2006). Faced with pro-cyclical and leverage driven capital flows (Goyal 2009), many emerging economies have hoarded an unprecedented amount of foreign exchange reserves to insulate themselves from a potential shock arising from the sudden curtailment of overseas capital flows. The US, by virtue of its position as the sole issuer of the pre-eminent global reserve currency, is able to enjoy easy financing of its massive deficits as emerging economies undertake pre-cautionary reserve accumulation.

However, the appetite for dollar reserves (and US securities) may be on the wane as countries around the world increasingly worry about the enormous current and projected US budget deficits. For fiscal year 2009, the US budget deficit reached an astounding $1.417 trillion, and, according to the non-partisan Congressional Budget Office (CBO), the cumulative US budget deficits between 2010 and 2019 will exceed $7 trillion.[3] Amongst many emerging economies, there is genuine fear about the possibility of significant capital loss due to a sharp decline in the value of the dollar. Foreigners are rightly concerned that the US may try to inflate away some of its debt burden by letting the dollar weaken. While an *en masse* rush by emerging economies to sell their dollar reserves is unlikely (Goyal 2005), there is a growing push to reduce the dollar's global clout.

Prior to the G20 London Summit, Zhou Xiaochuan, the governor of the People's Bank of China (PBOC), issued a statement in March 2009 calling for a radical overhaul of the international monetary system.[4] Mr Xiaochuan specifically noted that the current US dollar based international financial system was in need of reform and suggested that a super-sovereign reserve currency be created to replace the dollar as the global reserve standard. Given China's growing stature on the global stage and its current status as America's primary creditor, the views expressed by the Chinese central banker did not go unnoticed, especially in the US.

Several prominent economists have also highlighted the need to consider a broad based reform of the global monetary system. Bergsten (2009) and Stiglitz (2009) have called for a radical reworking of the international financial architecture. They suggest a reduction in dollar's role in global affairs and recommend greater prominence for the International Monetary Fund's (IMF) synthetic reserve-currency, the Special Drawing Rights (SDRs). While no imminent challenge to the current global monetary order is expected, declining confidence in the US dollar will encourage the search for alternatives.

Increased availability of official financing during periods of capital flow disruption through mechanisms such as IMF's newly created Flexible Credit Line programme, and the G-20 decision in April 2009 to triple IMF's lending facility (from $250 billion to $750 billion) will reduce the need for excessive accumulation of dollar reserves. Recent expansion of SDR allocations is also a step in the right direction. Such changes are likely to gradually diminish the dollar's international role and hence affect America's ability to sustain large deficits in the future.

3.4. Profligate American consumption

Due to the magnitude of its current account deficits (and its voracious appetite for imports), the US is the central player in any debate involving global imbalances. The gap between US gross saving and investment has grown dramatically in recent years mainly due to a decline in gross saving. To fathom some of the recent changes experienced by the US economy, it is helpful to reconsider Equation (2). If we were to breakdown national saving into private saving (S_i^{pvt}) and government saving (S_i^{gov}), we can rewrite Equation (2) as:

$$S_i^{pvt} + S_i^{gov} = I_i + CA_i \tag{5}$$

Furthermore, private saving can be separated into personal (or household) saving and corporate (or business) saving. For the US, both government saving and personal saving have been abysmally low in recent years (see Figure 4). Government saving has been consistently negative (except for a brief period during the late 1990s) in recent decades. More importantly, the US personal saving rate declined precipitously in recent years (in fact, personal saving rate hovered near zero during much of the 2005–2007 period).

There has been considerable debate regarding the causes of the low US personal saving rate. Lansing (2005) and Glick and Lansing (2009), amongst others, have suggested that the primary factors behind the decline in US personal saving rate were the asset bubbles (equity market as well as real estate market bubbles) experienced by the American economy between 1996 and 2006. Additionally, the excessive borrowing by households was a critical factor driving the increase in consumption

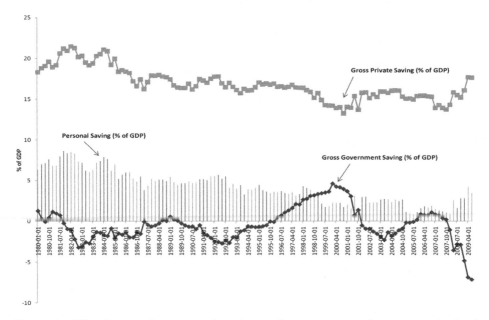

Figure 4.   US private saving, personal saving, and government saving – quarterly data/ seasonally adjusted annual rate.
Source: *FRED II Database* – Federal Reserve Bank of St. Louis (http://research. stlouisfed.org/fred2/categories/112).

and decrease in saving. Here we briefly examine the links between asset market bubbles, excessive household debt, low personal saving (and the correspondingly high consumption), and large trade deficits in the US.

Between 1997 and 2006, back to back asset bubbles (first in equity markets and then in real estate markets) impacted the US economy. Domestic factors (such as, the dot-com bubble, generally accommodative Federal Reserve interest rate policy, easy credit, financial engineering, lax regulatory supervision, government emphasis on expanding US homeownership levels) helped fuel the asset bubbles. The argument that inflated asset valuations along with debt-fuelled household consumption led to lower personal saving and rising trade deficits in the US is critical for understanding the global imbalance picture.

The American consumer, during the late 1990s and for much of the past decade, was the world's most dependable customer. The US personal consumption expenditure rose in recent years to over 70% of GDP (up from around 62% of GDP in 1981). But much of this consumption drive was based on the rise in household wealth (associated with rising equity and real estate values). In addition the lax regulatory environment, combined with financial innovation, allowed American consumers to dramatically expand their household debt levels (total outstanding household debt to personal disposable income ratio rose sharply during the past decade, exceeding 130% in 2006 and 2007).

Empirically, we investigate the link between personal saving rate and measures of asset values, wealth level, and borrowing levels in the US. The natural log of the US personal saving rate ($LN\_PSAVERATE$) is the used in our analysis. The two specific measures of household wealth considered here are: the natural log of the ratio of the sum of the market value of owner's equity in household real estate and equity shares held by households to personal disposable income ($LN\_RE\_EQ\_RATIO$); and, the natural log of the ratio of overall household net worth to personal disposable income ($LN\_NWRATIO$). To capture the effect of borrowing, we use the natural log of the ratio of annual borrowing to personal disposable income (LN_BORROW_RATIO). We also consider the natural log of the yield on the 10-year Treasury note ($LN\_TNYIELD$) in our empirical analysis. The Treasury note yield may act as a gauge of the 'perceived return to saving' (Lansing 2005).

Data on personal saving rate and 10-year Treasury note yield were obtained from website of the Federal Reserve Bank of St, Louis (annual rates were calculated as an average of the monthly rates). Personal disposable income, owner's equity in household real estate, equity shares at market value held by households, and household net worth ratio data were obtained from the *Flow of Funds Accounts* (various issues) published by the Federal Reserve Board. Our regression analysis covers the period from 1959 to 2008.

Graphically (see Figure 5), the sharp drop in personal saving rates during the past decade closely corresponds to rapid growth (relative to personal disposable income) in the value of real estate and equity assets held by households. Overall increase in the household net worth (relative to personal disposable income) also appears to reduce personal saving rate. Additionally, a dramatic rise in borrowing (relative to personal disposable income) in recent years appears to be related to the low personal saving rate.

Estimating a regression of the form shown in Equation (6), where LN_X_t is $LN\_RE\_EQ\_RATIO$ or $LN\_NWRATIO$ or LN_BORROW_RATIO, is complicated by the fact that many macroeconomic time series variables are non-stationary.

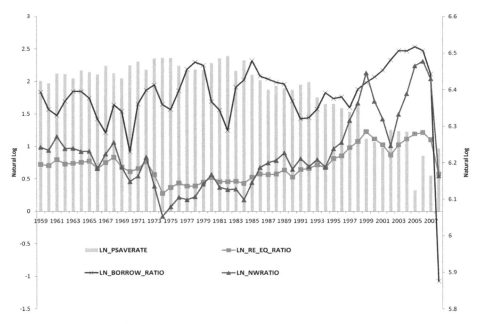

Figure 5. US personal saving rate, household real estate and equity value ratio, household net worth ratio, and annual borrowing ratio.
Source: Author's calculations using data from Federal Reserve Board – *Flow of Funds Account* (http://www.federalreserve.gov/releases/z1/), Various Issues; *FRED II Database* – Federal Reserve Bank of St. Louis (http://research.stlouisfed.org/fred2/categories/112).

Hence, we first check for the presence of unit roots using the Augmented Dickey-Fuller test and the Phillips-Perron test. The presence of unit roots is indicated for all the variables considered in our empirical model (Table A1 in the Appendix). To overcome non-stationarity related concerns, our regression analysis is based on the first difference of the natural log of personal saving rate, and the first or second difference of the independent variables. We use unit root tests to verify the appropriate transformation of the variables of interest to achieve stationarity. First differencing was enough to overcome non-stationarity for LN_PSAVERATE, LN_RE_EQ_RATIO and LN_TNYIELD, but twice differencing was more appropriate for LN_NWRATIO and LN_BORROW_RATIO.

$$LN\_PSAVERATE_t = \alpha_1 + \alpha_2 LN\_X_t + \alpha_3 LN\_TNYIELD_t + \varepsilon_t \qquad (6)$$

Our regression results (see Table 1 columns (*a*) and (*b*)) suggest that the US personal saving rate is significantly (at the 5% level) and *negatively* affected by increases in household asset values. Specifically, an increase in the market value of household real estate and equity holdings (relative to personal disposable income) causes the personal saving rate to decline. Additionally (see Table 1 columns (*c*) and (*d*)), increase in household net worth (relative to personal disposable income) affects the personal saving rate negatively and significantly (at the 10% level). Household net worth captures the difference between the total assets and the total liabilities of households, and hence the impact of net worth may be somewhat muted due to the fact that household borrowing (liabilities) was rising along with increases in real estate and equity values (assets). We find that the borrowing ratio (ratio of annual

Table 1. Results from OLS regressions – dependent variable D(LN_PSAVERATE).

Independent variables	(a)	(b)	(c)	(d)	(e)	(f)
CONSTANT	-0.022762	-0.022915	-0.025289	-0.025224	-0.027210	-0.027388
	(0.029415)	(0.029097)	(0.030940)	(0.030582)	(0.030783)	(0.030470)
D(LN_TNYIELD)	0.042838		-0.014865		0.075228	
	(0.247837)		(0.262543)		(0.255339)	
D(LN_RE_EQ_RATIO)	-0.566494	-0.568725				
	(0.241417)**	(0.238571)**				
D(LN_NW_RATIO, 2)			-0.797929	-0.792563		
			(0.474584)*	(0.459962)*		
D(LN_BORROW_RATIO, 2)					-0.105450	-0.105383
					(0.055977)*	(0.055418)*
R-Squared	0.108449	0.107870	0.060699	0.060632	0.074665	0.072881
F-statistic	2.797737	5.682898	1.453978	2.969089	1.815529	3.616043
Prob.(F-Statistic)	0.071345	0.021221	0.244405	0.091587	0.174471	0.063499

Notes: LN_VARIABLE refers to the natural log of the variable; D(LN_VARIABLE) refers to the first difference; and, D(LN_VARIABLE, 2) refers to the second difference. Also, *denotes significance at the 10% level and **denotes significance at the 5% level. All regressions were performed using EVIEWS 6.

household borrowing to personal disposable income) impacts personal saving rate negatively and significantly (at the 10% level) as well (see Table 1 columns (e) and (f)).

Figure 6 shows the market value of the sum of household real estate asset holdings and equity share holdings along with the US trade balance for the period 1960–2008. The figure also shows annual household borrowing levels. It is apparent that the dramatic increase in asset values, especially during the past decade or so, is tied to the widening of the trade deficit (reflective of high consumption levels and low personal savings levels). Another key driver of high levels of American consumption (and low personal saving) was the explosion in household borrowing levels.

US stock markets fell sharply in 2008 and early 2009 (despite a solid performance during the second half of 2009, major stock indexes in the US are still near their 1999 levels), and the severe downturn in the housing sector has led to historic reversals in residential property values as well. The sharp reduction in household wealth levels and an increased desire to save amongst Americans will negatively impact consumption going forward, and lead to a gradual improvement in the US trade balance. Signs also point to consumer deleveraging going forward (new household borrowing collapsed in 2008), which will impact consumption and US trade deficit levels (Juvenal 2009). A positive aspect is the uptick in personal saving rate seen in recent months.

It is worth noting that some of the factors highlighted in this section are applicable to Britain and Spain as well. Recently, Britain and Spain experienced significant current account deficits, and, just like the US, asset bubbles and debt-fuelled consumption were the key contributors. Consumer debt is a big concern in Britain and Spain (British household debt exposure is even greater than that of their

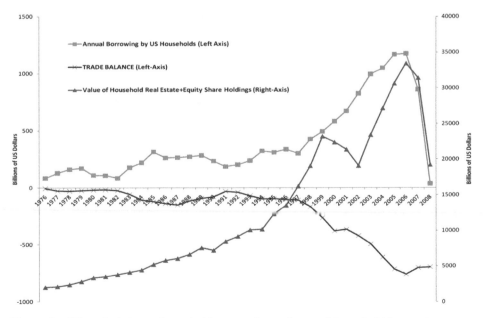

Figure 6. US trade balance, household asset value and annual household borrowing.
Source: US Department of Commerce: Bureau of Economic Analysis and Federal Reserve Board – *Flow of Funds Account*, various issues (http://www.bea.gov/international/index.htm#trade).

American counterparts). With the bursting of asset bubbles and with constraints on credit, Britain and Spain will see consumer retrenchment, and this will also contribute to a potential reduction in global imbalances.

4. Comparing India and China's recent growth patterns

While the Asian giants – India and China – are often jointly referenced in the press and in policy circles, there are important economic distinctions between the two countries. Here we discuss the specific economic approaches undertaken by China and India in recent decades, and attempt to highlight the relevance of the two countries to the broader global imbalance story.

According to the Nobel Prize winning economist Mike Spence (2007a, 2007b), several common features exist amongst the dozen or so countries (most located in East Asia) that achieved sustained high economic growth rates (defined as average economic growth of over 7% for 25 years or more) in the post-World War II era. Countries with exceptional growth performance displayed the following character-istics: high levels of domestic saving and investment, significant resource mobility (shift of population from low productivity sectors such as agriculture to high productivity sectors such as manufacturing industries), openness to foreign direct investment and technology transfer, functioning market system with respect for property rights, and trade openness (access to global demand, enabling exports to consumers in the global/developed country market).

The recipe for sustained high growth rates has apparently been discovered by China during the past three decades. An impressive achievement by China in recent years has been its ability to maintain saving and investment at unprecedented levels. China's investment has exceeded 42% of GDP of late, and its trade surplus (net exports) currently hovers around 8% of GDP (see Figure 7). Gross saving in China

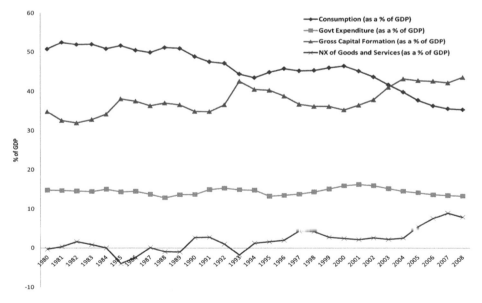

Figure 7.   China's GDP expenditure by components.
Source: China Premier Database, CEIC Data Company, Ltd. (http://www.ceicdata.com/China.html).

has reached an astounding 50% of GDP. While American household consumption exceeds 70% of GDP, China's household consumption has been closer to 35% of GDP recently. China, which just celebrated the 30-year anniversary of Deng Xiaoping's historical economic reform programme, has rightly captured the world's imagination with its extraordinary achievements. Over the past three decades, the country has averaged growth rates of over 9%, and it has gone from being a nearly closed economy with a negligible share of world trade in 1979 to becoming the world's biggest exporter (ahead of Germany) in 2009.

An examination of India's macroeconomic conditions reveals the stark differences with China (see Figure 8). While India's private consumption share of GDP has declined over time, it still exceeds 55% of GDP. India has experienced strong growth in investment (gross capital formation) in recent years though it still has some distance to go to attain Chinese levels. Since opening up to the rest of the world economy (following economic liberalization in 1991), India's exports and imports have grown steadily. However, unlike China, India's trade is relatively balanced (though trade deficits have increased in size of late).

According to IMF's *World Economic Outlook Database* (2009), India's current account saw a deficit of $26.6 billion in 2008, whereas China experienced a current account surplus of $426.1 billion in 2008. It is clear that India (which experienced current deficits of around $10 billion between 2005 and 2007, and smaller deficits prior to that), has not been a major factor in the rise in global imbalances. China, meanwhile, appears to be the mirror image of the US. China's current account surplus has exceeded $250 billion since 2006.

While China's achievements as a manufacturing and export powerhouse are well documented, India's distinct economic approach is less well-known (especially outside India). India has followed a somewhat idiosyncratic development strategy. India has certainly taken advantage of a shift away from autarkic policies and

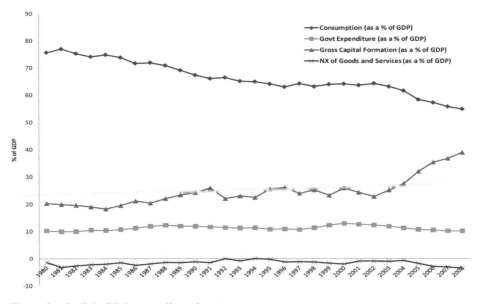

Figure 8. India's GDP expenditure by components.
Source: India Premier Database, CEIC Data Company, Ltd. (http://www.ceicdata.com/India.html).

towards policies aimed at achieving greater global integration; however, its approach is not primarily export-oriented.

The Indian growth story starkly differs from that of China and other East Asian success stories in four critical aspects. First, during much of its recent rapid growth phase, India has been running current account deficits. So, unlike the mercantilist leanings of East Asian economies, India has not pursued an export dominated growth strategy (with an emphasis on running trade surpluses). Second, India decided to adopt a managed floating exchange rate regime relatively early in its economic liberalization programme. Most East Asian countries, unlike India, maintained solid pegs to the US dollar during their initial liberalization and rapid growth phases. Third, India's exports have to a significant extent been service sector driven rather than manufacturing driven. The standard formula of specializing in low cost export-oriented manufacturing has been largely absent in India's development strategy so far. In fact, manufacturing success stories in India are more likely to be found in the relatively high skill and capital-intensive sectors. As shown in Figure 9, India's economy is already dominated by the service sector, and unlike China, industry's share of GDP has stayed well below 30% (even during the recent rapid growth phase). Finally, India started out as a democracy (following Independence in 1947) and the lack of an authoritarian regime contrasts sharply with the experiences of China and other East Asian countries. We expand on some of the issues noted here in the next section.

Overall, India's growth story, unlike China's, is not dominated by the explosive growth of exports or by large-scale manufacturing. Instead, the underlying economic structure of India is more balanced, with healthy domestic consumption levels and significant service sector contribution to output. India's trade balance is also far less skewed.

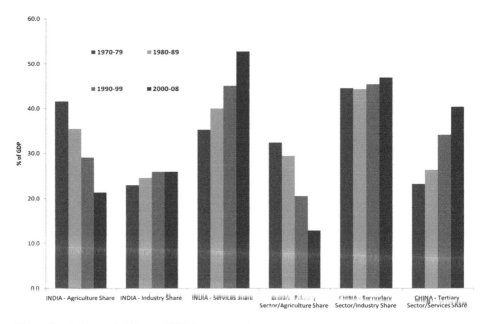

Figure 9.   India and China's GDP by sector share.
Source: India Premier Database (http://www.ceicdata.com/India.html) and China Premier Database (http://www.ceicdata.com/China.html), CEIC Data Company, Ltd.

5. Can India become the next China?

The economic achievements of China in recent years should rightly be lauded and its rise as an export powerhouse deserves acknowledgement. As global economic conditions shift, it is difficult to foresee India successfully replicating the China model. This section highlights the factors that are likely to hinder India from pursuing an export-oriented growth model anytime soon. Our arguments are organized under three categories – global conditions, domestic realities and policy environment.

5.1. Global conditions

Given the expected unwinding of large global imbalances, the prospects for the emergence of India as a major export driven powerhouse appear limited. While China has run up massive trade surpluses with the EU and the US, India's trade with the two major industrialized regions is far more modest and balanced (see Figure 10). As recent experience suggest, India has difficulty in achieving or sustaining trade surpluses even with the two largest consumer markets in the world.

The subdued recovery from the Global Credit Crisis of 2008–2009 in the US and key EU countries, such as the UK and Spain, and the high unemployment rates prevalent in those advanced economies (UK unemployment rate is around 8%, US unemployment rate is around 10%, and Spain's unemployment rate exceeds 19%) will impact their ability to import at pre-crisis levels. In addition, the expected consumer retrenchment (driven by reduced asset values and diminished credit access) in advanced economies, along with growing protectionism (including a backlash against outsourcing) in the EU and the US, will affect the level of imports from Asia. These factors imply that India will find it difficult to replicate China's export performance.

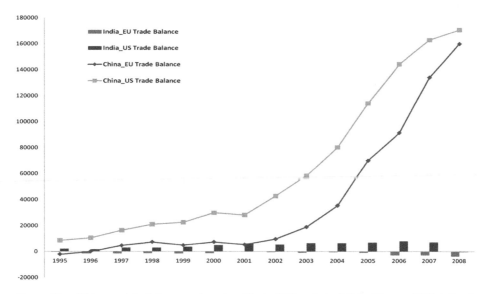

Figure 10. China and India's annual trade with the EU and the US (millions of US dollars). Source: India Premier Database (http://www.ceicdata.com/India.html) and China Premier Database (http://www.ceicdata.com/China.html), CEIC Data Company, Ltd.

If not the EU or the US, could India pursue a strategy focused on rapidly increasing exports to China and running large trade surpluses with its Asian neighbour? Again, this is not a feasible strategy given China's relative strength in manufacturing and the limited scope for Indian service exports to China. Imports from China have quickly outpaced Indian exports to its northern neighbour, and this is indicated by the widening of the bilateral trade deficit (see Figure 11).

5.2. Domestic realities

While India is endowed with cheap labour, it is certainly not a preferred destination for large scale assembly of cheap electronics or textiles. Inadequate transportation infrastructure (deficiencies in road networks, lack of modern ports, etc.) and unreliable and limited power supply (caused by insufficient power generation and widespread power theft) are two of the more glaring infrastructure defects that handicap India. Labour market rigidities caused by draconian regulations (such as the Industrial Disputes Act) also hinder the establishment of huge production facilities. For instance, firms with 100 or more employees require Labour Department permission in order to undertake layoffs, retrenchment or closure. Credit constraints resulting from financial sector weakness (such as the high share of public ownership in the banking sector and the low levels of financial intermediation by the banking sector) also affect the development of India's manufacturing capability (Gupta, Hasan and Kumar 2008).

Prominent international trade expert, Panagariya (2008), suggests that unskilled labour-intensive manufacturing has generally taken a backseat to capital intensive or skilled-labour intensive manufacturing in India's organized sectors. This, according to Panagariya (2008), has kept the transition of the labour force from agriculture to non-agricultural activities at a much lower level in India relative to China.

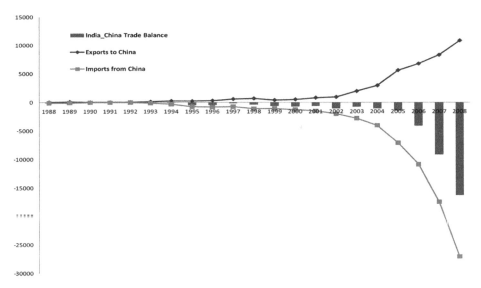

Figure 11.   India's trade with China (millions of US dollars).
Source: India Premier Database, CEIC Data Company, Ltd. (http://www.ceicdata.com/India.html).

Panagariya (2008) emphasizes that India still needs to develop its capacity to produce light manufactured goods in order to ease the transition from agriculture to the industrial sector for hundreds of millions of low skilled workers. He is also sceptical of the notion that India could skip the manufacturing stage of development and become a service oriented economy directly. The argument that 'India need not become South Korea on the way to becoming the United States' does not carry much weight with him. Panagariya (2008) rightly notes that current growth in jobs in formal service sectors such as software and communication services is a very small portion (employing around two million workers or so) of the overall labour market and that India is not positioned to generate sizeable future growth in formal service sectors like banking, insurance, finance and information technology due to a limited supply of highly skilled labour.

Though India needs to develop a competitive low cost manufacturing sector that employs millions of low-skilled workers, it is unlikely that India will challenge China's current status as the world's factory anytime soon.

5.3. *Policy environment*

India, unlike many East Asian economies, started out as a democracy despite being a very poor country and is pursuing an economic development strategy in the full glare of public and media scrutiny. East Asian countries, typically characterized by authoritarian rule during their rapid growth phase, were generally unencumbered by opposing views and able to push forth painful changes rapidly and sometimes forcibly. Being a large multi-cultural democracy with a parliamentary system and coalition politics, India is often seen as a lumbering giant that is slow to adapt.

The recent episode involving Tata Motors' attempt to set up a car plant in West Bengal crystallizes some of the challenges encountered by Indian manufacturers (Tata Motors ultimately was forced to shift the car plant to Gujarat). Poorly coordinated land acquisition deals by the West Bengal government led to protests and a political firestorm that eventually scuttled the proposed car plant. India may be at a disadvantage when juxtaposed against countries where it may be feasible to rapidly develop large scale manufacturing without much regard for environmental or labour standards, or where it may be possible to undertaking large scale infrastructure projects that may require overriding opposition from large numbers of private landowners and citizens.

India, however, does enjoy certain advantages arising out of its early adoption of democratic ideals. It has developed a solid domestic private sector and an entrepreneurial class that is globally competitive in many sectors. Much of the credit for this must go to India's open and democratic system of governance that despite its various defects still makes the country relatively unique (Huang 2008). While India may not be able to achieve China's speedy infrastructure development or its large scale export-oriented industrial zones in the near term, it should not despair.

In light of our discussion thus far, it is apparent that India's growth strategy needs to stay distinct from China's strategy. However, while India may not match China's export powerhouse status, it is still important to undertake policies that encourage exports as part of a broadly diversified growth strategy. Solid growth in export earnings provide India with the ability to pay for the importation of energy supplies (oil and natural gas consumption is expected to increase significantly) and other foreign products. Additionally, export sectors typically experience rapid productivity growth and generate higher paying jobs. Effective government action can help domestic producers compete in the global market place. Reducing or removing the various bottlenecks that prevent rapid interstate movement of goods would be quite beneficial to exporters. Improved turnaround times at India's major ports would also provide a boost. Widespread disparities in educational quality and insufficient supply of skilled workers are also critical challenges facing Indian exporters. India's ability to continue to generate tremendous growth rates in service sector exports is largely dependent upon the country's ability to radically upgrade its education system.

6. Conclusion

As we have discussed in this article, there is a high likelihood that global imbalances will unwind in the near to medium term. In fact, the unwinding may already be underway as consumers in key advanced economies face up to the prospect of an extended period of subdued economic growth and high unemployment rates. Households in advanced economies also realize the need to fix their balance sheets by reducing consumption, raising saving and lowering debt levels.

India, despite the challenges noted earlier, can continue its economic success story if it strives for a more balanced growth path. Given its size, India has the natural advantage of a large domestic market and businesses need not rely purely upon export sales to achieve economies of scale. The healthy consumer driven economy that already exists needs to be encouraged and enlarged through the inclusion of rural households in the growth story. Since India is still a land of many villages, ability to generate growth and decent standards of living in the rural sector is a must for the future development of the country. Reform of the agricultural sector (better access roads, improved refrigeration facilities, improved price discovery mechanisms) and greater formal financial system access in rural areas could jump start the process.

There is a clear need for a competitive manufacturing sector that targets both domestic and foreign markets. However, this requires significant labour market reform and fixes for infrastructure bottlenecks. Banking sector liberalization aimed at increasing lending to the corporate sector (especially to small and medium scale enterprises) will provide a boost to the manufacturing sector as well. Foreign direct investment (FDI) in the manufacturing sector should be encouraged as it often leads to the transfer of the latest technologies and management techniques. India should also continue to reduce trade barriers. The productivity gains in the manufacturing sector from exposure to international competition can be enormously beneficial in the long run.

For any emerging economy, getting the right balance in its policies towards exchange rates and capital flows is vital. The central bank of India, the Reserve Bank of India (RBI), has gradually allowed greater exchange rate flexibility in recent years. In light of growing capital flows and concerns about price stability, the RBI has reduced its emphasis on maintaining the stability of the rupee–dollar exchange rates. To achieve a degree of monetary policy independence, while still maintaining external competitiveness, the RBI should consider the following three steps. First, given the extraordinary fluctuations observed in the value of the US dollar (relative to other major currencies) recently, the RBI may be better off focusing on the gyrations of the nominal exchange rate relative to a basket of currencies (consisting of the dollar, euro, and yen, for instance). Wild swings in the rupee–dollar rates may overstate the degree of overall exchange rate volatility. Second, the RBI could limit the consequences of currency volatility by further encouraging the development of currency derivatives (allowing futures trading in currencies such as the euro, yen and pound, and removing the ban on options trading would help). Lastly, the RBI should emphasize stability of the real exchange rate, which is adjusted for price levels. Ultimately, from the perspective of maintaining external competitiveness, the real exchange rate matters more than the nominal exchange rate. Given that India is still a developing country, preventing excessive real exchange rate appreciation needs to be a priority for the central bank.

While India certainly needs to attract capital flows to meet its immense investment needs, the country should be cognizant of the risks associated with short-term flows. An intelligent approach in this regard might be to limit foreign currency borrowings by lending institutions and corporations while further encouraging foreign investor entry into domestic equity and bond investments. Foreign investment in equity markets can boost the size and liquidity of domestic markets. Foreign portfolio investors also bear some of the costs in the event of a sudden stop in capital flows. Growth of local currency denominated bond issues need to be emphasized as they provide domestic companies with an important avenue for raising capital. As in the case of equity investments, allowing foreign investors to partake in local currency denominated bonds (especially, long-maturity corporate bonds) will expand the size and the liquidity of the bond market. Foreign investments in rupee denominated bonds will spread the burden (in the event of a sudden stop) as overseas investors looking for a quick exit will be forced to sell their bond holdings in the secondary market at a significant loss.

Overall, India has pursued a relatively unique development strategy during the past two decades. With further reforms, India may yet fulfil its long held promise and achieve sharp increases in per-capita income levels. The ability to utilize its intrinsic advantages rather than a dependence on export-driven growth will prove ultimately to be India's best path to success.

Acknowledgements
I thank Dr Ashima Goyal for her extremely valuable comments and suggestions. I also want to acknowledge funding for databases from the Project Edge Grant (University of Tampa) and the Delo Grant (University of Tampa).

Notes
1. Note that in practice total global saving might not equal total global investment due to measurement errors.
2. NBC/*Wall Street Journal* GOP Primary Voters Survey, September 2007, available at http://online.wsj.com/public/resources/documents/WSJ-POLL-20071003.pdf
3. See the CBO's 'The long-term budget outlook', June 2009, available at http://www.cbo.gov/doc.cfm?index=10297&type=1
4. Zhou Xiaochuan, 'Reform the International Monetary System', 23 March 2009, http://www.pbc.gov.cn/english//detail.asp?col=6500&ID=178

References

Bergsten, C. Fred. 2009. The dollar and the deficits: how Washington can prevent the next crisis. *Foreign Affairs* 88, no. 6: 20–38.

Bernanke, Ben S. 2005. The global saving glut and the U.S. current account deficit. Homer Jones Lecture, St. Louis, Missouri, April 14.

Bernanke, Ben S. 2007. Global imbalances: recent developments and prospects. Bundesbank Lecture, Berlin, Germany, September 11.

Blinder, Alan S. 2007. Free trade's great, but offshoring rattles me. *The Washington Post*, May 6: B04.

Caballero, Richard J., Emmanuel Farhi, and Pierre-Olivier Gourinchas. 2006. An equilibrium model of 'global imbalances' and low interest rates. NBER Working Paper No. 11996.

Calvo, Guillermo A. 2006. Monetary policy challenges in emerging markets: sudden stop, liability dollarization, and lender of last resort. NBER Working Paper No. 12788.

Cooper, Richard N. 2007. Living with global imbalances. *Brookings Papers on Economic Activity*, 2: 91–107.

Dooley, Michael P., David Folkerts-Landau, and Peter M. Garber. 2003. An essay on the revived Bretton Woods system. NBER Working Paper No.9971.

Dooley, Michael P., David Folkerts-Landau, and Peter M. Garber. 2004. The revived Bretton Woods system: the effects of periphery intervention and reserve management on interest rates and exchange rates in center countries. NBER Working Paper No.10332.

Dooley, Michael P., David Folkerts-Landau, and Peter M. Garber. 2005. *International Financial Stability: Asia, Interest Rates, and the Dollar*. New York: Deutsche Bank Global Research.

Eichengreen, Barry. 2007. *Global Imbalances and the Lessons of Bretton Woods*. Cambridge: MIT Press.

Glick, Reuven, and Kevin J. Lansing. 2009. U.S. household deleveraging and future consumption growth. *FRBSF Economic Letter* 2009–16 (May 15).

Goyal, Ashima. 2005. Asian reserves and the dollar: is gradual adjustment possible? *Global Economy Journal* 5, no. 3, Article 3.

Goyal, Ashima. 2009. Financial crises: reducing pro-cyclicality. *Macroeconomics and Finance in Emerging Market Economies* 2, no. 1: 213–23.

Gupta, Poonam, Rana Hasan, and Utsav Kumar. 2008. What constraints Indian manufacturing? ERD Working Paper No. 119, Asian Development Bank.

Huang, Yasheng. 2008. The next Asian miracle. *Foreign Policy*, July/August 167: 32–40.

IMF. 2009. *World Economic Outlook*, October. Washington, DC: International Monetary Fund.

Juvenal, Luciana. 2009. Asset prices and their effect on the U.S. trade balance. *FRBSL Economic Synopsis*, No. 31 (July 6).

Lansing, Kevin J. 2005. Spendthrift nation. *FRBSF Economic Letter* 2005–30 (November 10).

McKinnon, Ronald. 2009. U.S. Current account deficits and the dollar standard's sustainability: a monetary approach. In *The Future of the Dollar*, ed. Eric Helleiner and Jonathan Kirshner, 45–68. Ithaca: Cornell University Press.

Obstfeld, Maurice, and Kenneth S. Rogoff. 2004. The unsustainable US current account position revisited. NBER Working Paper No.10869.

Panagariya, Arvind. 2008. *India: The Emerging Giant*. New York: Oxford University Press.

Spence, Mike. 2007a. Wealth of nations: why China grows so fast. *The Wall Street Journal*, January 23: A19.

Spence, Mike. 2007b. Wealth of nations: what drives high growth rates? *The Wall Street Journal*, January 24: A13.

Stiglitz, Joseph E. 2009. Death cometh for the greenback. *The National Interest* 104 (November/December): 50–9.

Summers, Lawrence H. 2006. Reflections on Global Account Imbalances and Emerging Markets Reserve Accumulation. L.K. Jha Memorial Lectures: Reserve Bank of India, Mumbai, India, March 24.

Summers, Lawrence H. 2009. Rescuing and rebuilding the US economy: a progress report. Petersen Institute of International Economics, Washington DC, July 17.

Appendix

Table A1. Unit root tests – null hypothesis: variable has a unit root, exogenous: constant, linear trend.

Variable	Augmented Dickey-Fuller test statistic	Phillips-Perron test statistic	Prob. (one-sided p-values)	Test critical values	
LN_PSAVERATE	−0.325935		0.9874	1% level	−4.180911
				5% level	−3.515523
				10% level	−3.188259
LN_PSAVERATE		−2.565747	0.2971	1% level	−4.156734
				5% level	−3.504330
				10% level	−3.181826
D(LN_PSAVERATE)	−5.103125		**0.0009**	1% level	−4.211868
				5% level	−3.529758
				10% level	−3.196411
D(LN_PSAVERATE)		−22.44364	**0.0000**	1% level	−4.161144
				5% level	−3.506374
				10% level	−3.183002
LN_RE_EQ_RATIO	−1.863203		0.6582	1% level	−4.156734
				5% level	−3.504330
				10% level	−3.181826
LN_RE_EQ_RATIO		−1.889945	0.6446	1% level	−4.156734
				5% level	−3.504330
				10% level	−3.181826
D(LN_RE_EQ_RATIO)	−4.305575		**0.0068**	1% level	−4.161144
				5% level	−3.506374
				10% level	−3.183002
D(LN_RE_EQ_RATIO)		−3.702640	**0.0317**	1% level	−4.161144
				5% level	−3.506374
				10% level	−3.183002
LN_NWRATIO	−1.756155		0.7087	1% level	−4.180911
				5% level	−3.515523
				10% level	−3.188259
LN_NWRATIO		−2.055517	0.5569	1% level	−4.156734
				5% level	−3.504330
				10% level	−3.181826
D(LN_NWRATIO, 2)	−5.219943		**0.0006**	1% level	−4.198503
				5% level	−3.523623
				10% level	−3.192902
D(LN_NWRATIO, 2)		−8.433098	**0.0000**	1% level	−4.165756
				5% level	−3.508508
				10% level	−3.184230
LN_BORROW_RATIO	−2.220220		0.4679	1% level	−4.161144
				5% level	−3.506374
				10% level	−3.183002
LN_BORROW_RATIO		−1.757063	0.7101	1% level	−4.156734
				5% level	−3.504330
				10% level	−3.181826
D(LN_BORROW_RATIO,2)	−6.082826		**0.0000**	1% level	−4.165756
				5% level	−3.508508
				10% level	−3.184230

(*continued*)

Table A1. (*Continued*).

Variable	Augmented Dickey-Fuller test statistic	Phillips-Perron test statistic	Prob. (one-sided p-values)	Test critical values	
D(LN_BORROW_ RATIO,2)		− 5.759050	**0.0001**	1% level 5% level 10% level	− 4.165756 − 3.508508 − 3.184230
LN_TNYIELD	− 0.821846		0.9564	1% level 5% level 10% level	− 4.156734 − 3.504330 − 3.181826
LN_TNYIELD		− 0.766718	0.9617	1% level 5% level 10% level	− 4.156734 − 3.504330 − 3.181826
D(LN_TNYIELD)	− 6.129814		**0.0000**	1% level 5% level 10% level	− 4.161144 − 3.506374 − 3.183002
D(LN_TNYIELD)		− 6.120313	**0.0000**	1% level 5% level 10% level	− 4.161144 − 3.506374 − 3.183002

Note: LN_VARIABLE refers to the natural log of the variable; D(LN_VARIABLE) refers to the first difference; and, D(LN_VARIABLE, 2) refers to the second difference. All unit root tests were conducted using EVIEWS 6.

Volatility in interest rates: its impact and management

V. Shunmugam[a] and Danish A. Hashim[b]

[a]Multi Commodity Exchange of India Ltd, Mumbai, India; [b]Financial Technologies India Ltd, Mumbai, India

Volatility in interest rates has direct and indirect effects on the economy, particularly on businesses. Studies indicate that due to deregulation, following liberalization of economies, the interest rate volatility has surged worldwide, with India among the highest-volatility counties. Hedging in interest rate futures helps stabilize interest costs enabling businesses to remain competitive. Transparency of futures leads to increased lending at market determined rates, moderation of external shocks, better operating decisions, etc. India's maiden effort to start interest rate futures in 2003 failed due to certain inadequacies in product design. Here is an attempt to look at the need for and development of interest rate futures market in India.

1. Introduction

There has never been a monetary system without interest rate fluctuations. Interest rates have fluctuated under all monetary regimes – a gold standard, a currency board, a normal fixed exchange rate, a monetary target, an inflation target, or a regime of pure discretion by central banks (Macfarlane 2001). In fact, fixed interest rates lead to an inflationary or a deflationary spiral.

If a central bank keeps interest rates fixed at low levels, demand tends to outstrip supply in the long run, resulting in inflation and lowering of real interest rate. And a reduction in the real interest rate further stimulates demand and, thus, increases inflation thereby causing a further lowering of the real interest rate. This cycle continues through rounds to end up in an inflationary spiral. Two centuries ago, Henry Thornton (1802) concluded that the low fixed interest rate policy of the Bank of England had caused inflation. On the other hand, if a central bank keeps interest rates at high levels, the cyclical movement will be a reverse one to eventually culminate in a deflationary spiral. These two extreme situations can be avoided only if rates are set at equilibrium through a flexible monetary policy. Friedman and Schwartz (1963) argued that if the US had an accommodative monetary policy, the severity of the Great Depression would have been much less.

Since with the opening of economies across globe and continuous financial sector reforms, most economies have moved from the fixed interest rates regime into the zone of market determined volatility in interest rates, only 'excessive' volatility is considered a cause for worry now. The term 'excessive' is not absolute or fixed and depends on a number of factors in a given country. First and foremost is the economic condition. If a given economy is not undergoing any abnormal business cycle, even high volatility in interest rates may not be considered excessive. Second, how responsive the economy is to a given change in interest rates. In a normal situation, the less elastic the economic activities (with respect to the interest rate), the less is the cause for concern. Third, very importantly, availability and efficiency of a risk management tool in the form of derivative markets. An economy armed with an efficient risk management tool to hedge against the volatility in interest rates can withstand even high volatility and minimize the need for corrective actions on the part of the central bank.

The rapid move towards financial sector liberalization has induced countries to develop the derivative market to tackle the issue of volatility associated with interest rates. Derivatives not only provide market participants with a tool to hedge the risk of volatility in interest rates but also help reduce the volatility itself. The risk of interest rate volatility is so high that, today, interest rate derivatives alone constitute around 65% of all derivatives transactions across the globe. In India, efforts are on to strengthen the derivative market to face high interest rate volatility caused by financial reforms. The Reserve Bank of India (RBI) in 1999 introduced over-the-counter (OTC) interest rate derivatives. Subsequently, on the recommendations of the Bindra group (2003), the central bank also introduced exchange operated futures in interest rates in June 2003.[1] Exchange traded interest rate derivatives were recommended on the ground that, in comparison to the OTC market, they provided a more efficient trading system, entailing lower transaction cost, full transparency and a better risk management tool.[2] Besides, they were also expected to meet hedging requirements of entities engaged in providing OTC products. However, due to inappropriate specifications of products, futures trading in interest rate derivatives could not take off (Sharma Group Report 2008). Initiatives have been taken yet again to give a headstart to this trade, after taking some corrective measures, from early 2009. This raises two basic questions: do interest rate futures deserve a second chance? Have enough safeguards been taken to ensure success this time around?

This article attempts to answer these two broad questions. Attention is paid to understand how volatility in interest rates has behaved in India during the pre- and post-administered regime. The article also analyzes the impact of interest rate volatility on various economic parameters, with supportive case studies. A look at available literatures is made to find if strengthening of the derivative market is a way forward to tackle high volatility in interest rates, citing experiences of other countries. An attempt is also made to understand the general products traded worldwide, and India's brief experience in interest rate futures. Mistakes of the earlier attempt to launch interest rate futures and the way forward are discussed in the light of various 'group' reports.

2. Interest rate and its volatility in India

Between 1960 and 1985 virtually all interest rates were directly or indirectly administered through levels such as fixed, ceiling, and differential, by the government, the RBI or other authorities like the Indian Banks Association (Sahu and Virmani 2005). Many economists disapproved of such administration of interest rates. Bhattacharya (1985), for instance, contended that pegging of interest rates causes demand for institutional credit to exceed supply, thereby warranting measures such as credit rationing and other non-price controls on institutional credit. Bhole (1985) found that the nailing down of interest rates caused savings and investments to behave inappropriately, misdistribution of financial resources and weakening of the effectiveness of monetary policy. Administration of interest rates also tends to create a huge difference between nominal and real interest rates due to varying inflation figures. As part of financial sector reforms, determination of interest rates in India started being linked to market forces in the mid-1980s. Most debt market rates including call rates, 182-day T-Bill rates, commercial papers and certificates of deposits rates were deregulated. Even larger administrative deregulation of interest rates began in 1993, as part of further reforms (Patnaik and Shah 2004). At present, most interest rates are supposed to be market determined, while the government controls them indirectly through fiscal and monetary measures.

As a result of deregulation, volatility in interest rates has increased significantly with a rise in volatility of factors that influence it. Economic growth, inflation, monetary and fiscal policy, and foreign reserves all have become very volatile in today's context, thereby making interest rates vulnerable. Reflecting the increased volatility in the post-liberalized regime, standard deviation (SD) of yearly interest rates on 1–3 years' deposits increased from 1.7 during 1970–92 to 2.3 during 1993–2008. The case was similar with interest rates on longer-term deposits (see Figure 1). Volatility in interest rates continues to remain high even now (see Figure 2). In one year, from 1 January 2008 to 1 January 2009, the yield on 3-month T-Bills moved in the range of 9.3% to 4.5%. Similarly, volatility in the yield of 10-year government securities (G-Sec) moved between 9.5% and 5.2%. While the rise in volatility is

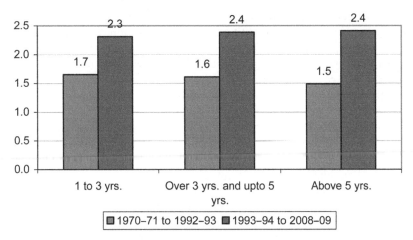

Figure 1.   Deregulation of interest rates and volatility in deposit rates.
Note: Volatility is measured in standard deviation (SD). Deposit rates pertain to the rates at five major public sector banks as at end-March. The data for FY 2008 is up to 12 September 2008.
Source: *Handbook of Statistics on Indian Economy 2008–2009*, Reserve Bank of India.

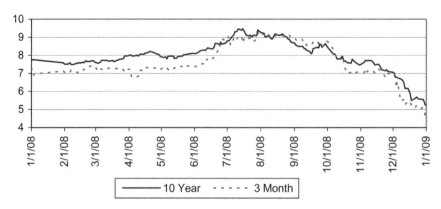

Figure 2. Daily movement of yield on 3-month T-Bill and 10-year G-Sec (%).
Source: Bloomberg.

expected in the post-deregulation regime, its extent appears quite higher compared with that in other countries. In a cross-country analysis of differences in volatility of short-term interest rates for 2000, Baig (2001) observed India to be among the counties with the highest volatility. For India, SD measured 1.74 *vis-à-vis* 0.91 for the UK, 0.16 for Canada, 0.11 for Germany, and 0.06 for Malaysia.

3. Impact of interest rate volatility

Volatility in interest rates can have direct and indirect effects on the whole economy. Financial institutions are among those that are directly exposed to the risk of interest rate volatility. They face risk on their Statutory Liquidity Ratio (SLR) portfolios, consisting of dated government bonds and T-Bills. They also hold corporate bonds in banks' portfolios, which, likewise, are subject to interest rate risk. Volatility in interest rates may also affect others, such as institutional investors, mutual funds and the corporate sector. Institutional investors and mutual funds are holders of corporate bonds and, therefore, with any movement in interest rates, they stand to confront risk. Corporates face the risk of interest rate escalation for their short-term working capital funding and long-term funding through bond market issuance. Due to the high degree of forward and backward linkages of the financial and corporate sectors with the rest of the economy, the impact may easily spread and engulf the whole economy.

There are numerous literatures that analyze the impact of interest rate volatility on various economic parameters. Most of these are on the impact of the US Federal Reserve putting a stop to its interest rate stabilization policy since October 1979, which resulted in high volatility in interest rates and a deterioration of the US economy. Evans (1984) observed that post-1979, US output shrank. An unanticipated rise in interest rate volatility had cut output by about 1% in 1980 and 2.5% in 1981 and 1982. Tatom (1984) noted that high volatility in interest rates had resulted in lower output by impacting supply, investment, and productivity growth. Friedman (1982) contended that increased interest rate volatility had affected output by way of disrupting the financial markets, thereby increasing the risk elements for various economic participants and raising the risk premiums in interest. Employment too was found to be adversely affected by interest rate volatility.

Dutkowsky (1987) found a significant rise in unemployment post-1979, when volatility in interest rates heightened.

As for non-US countries, Naudé (1995) noted that financial liberalization and subsequent interest rate volatility had adversely impacted the banking system in African countries. It was believed that the risk arising from interest rate volatility motivated banks' activities towards brokerage rather than maturity-transformation functions there. Aydogan (1991) observed that financial liberalization in Turkey, during the 1980s, exposed the country's commercial banks to both interest rate and foreign exchange risks. The study concluded that while some banks converted high volatility in interest rates into opportunity through a proper risk management policy, many others that failed to do so because of one or the other reason suffered. Patnaik and Shah (2004) found that banks in India are highly exposed to the interest rate risk. According to them, 34 of the 42 sample banks stood to lose over 25% of their equity capital in the event of a 320 basis points (bps) shock in the interest rate in March 2002. Further, 15 banks were exposed to the risk of losing more than half their equity capital owing to an interest rate shock of the same magnitude.

4. Managing the interest rate risks

The interest rate volatility risk can be managed by participating in the derivatives market – by trading in interest rate futures to guard against a fall/rise in rates. By selling futures contract, also known as short hedging, a participant can protect themselves from an increase in interest rates, and by buying futures contract (long hedging) an investor can protect themselves from a decline in rates.

Studies have found a number of benefits associated with hedging of interest rate risk. First, many studies link participating in interest rate derivatives to higher growth in commercial and industrial lending of the banking sector. Brewer III et al. (2000) observed that banks using interest rate derivatives experienced greater growth in their commercial and industrial loan portfolios vis-à-vis other banks in the US during 1985–92. Use of derivatives clearly expedited lending activity, faster than it would have been done otherwise. So, the researchers concluded that excessive regulatory constraints on commercial banks' participation in derivative contracts may result in lower lending growth. Zhao and Moser (2006a) pointed out that the use of interest rate derivatives by US commercial banks directly impacted their growth of commercial and industrial loan portfolios between 1996 and 2004. This was in conformance with Diamond's (1984) model that a bank's use of derivatives allows better management of systematic risk exposure.[3] Zhao and Moser (2006b), in another study for a period 1998–2003 for US bank-holding companies, showed how useful derivatives were in reducing the interest rate volatility risk. They noted that interest rate derivatives allowed banks to lessen their systematic exposure to changes in interest rates.

Second, studies also relate greater hedging activity to less sensitivity to macroeconomic shocks, better operating decisions and higher liquidity. According to Kashyap and Stein (1995, 2000), lending activities of large banks are less sensitive to monetary policies than those of small banks because they have greater exposure to derivative markets. Similarly, Purnanandam (2007) noted that derivatives-user banks made fewer (or no) adjustments in lending, borrowing and investment policies in response to a change in Federal policy than non-users. Derivatives trading not only helped in generating cash flows in adverse market conditions but also facilitated smooth cash flows through better operating decisions – in line with a study by Froot et al. (1993) which suggested that hedging allows firms to adopt optimal investment policies. Esty et al. (1994) showed how hedging can help a bank garner higher liquidity. They contended that hedging allows a bank to enter the swap market on a short-term basis instead of going in for a long-term fixed rate investment. In times of liquidity shortage, for meeting large loan demand, such a bank can withdraw more easily, i.e. withdrawing from the swap market is easier than from a long-term fixed investment.

Non-financial firms are also exposed to interest rate risk like banks as discussed above. Bartram (2001), studying the interest rate risk of 490 non-financial corporations during 1987–95, found a negative relationship between the interest rate exposure and liquidity. Interest rate risk, theoretically, affects the value of non-financial corporations as well, due to changes in cash flows and valuations of their financial assets and liabilities. Moreover, interest rate movements are closely related to changes in the business cycle of the economy, and they influence – through the cost of capital – firms' investment behaviour. Besides, interest rate risk may have indirect effects on corporations' competitiveness, impacting the size of future cash flows and, thus, firm value.

5. Interest rate futures

Trading in interest rate futures involves buying or selling of a contract with an underlying package of debt instruments which is supposed to mature at a specified future date and price. By buying or selling the contract, a market participant can hedge his risk arising from the unfavourable movement of interest rates. He should 'buy' to mitigate the risk of a fall and 'sell' to reduce the risk of a rise in interest rates.

Debt instruments such as T-Notes, T-Bills, T-Bonds, and Deposits constitute the underlying. Contracts traded are either on short-term (less than a year) or medium/long-term (more than a year) underlying. Globally, short-term underlying includes T-Bills and reference rate futures (like London Inter-Bank Offer Rates (LIBOR)) whereas long-term underlying is a notional coupon bearing bond. In India, when interest rate futures were introduced in 2003, contracts were designed to include 91-day T-Bill, 10-year notional GoI security and 10-year notional zero-coupon GoI security underlying. These contracts, however, failed to elicit market participants' interest due to lack of a pricing benchmark and lacunae in contract design. According to the Sharma Group Report (2008), as was argued by others as well, interest rate futures could not take off mainly for two reasons: one, the approach of zero coupon yield curve (ZCYC) for determining the settlement and daily mark-to-market (MTM) rate caused large gaps between zero coupon yields and underlying bond yields. The gaps arose mainly because ZCYC was calculated, theoretically, in absence of observable values. And, two, the prohibition for banks to take trading (speculative) positions in futures contracts, depriving the market of some active participants that would bring in sufficient threshold liquidity for market efficiency. Banks were allowed to hedge only their interest rate risks in the futures market.

From time to time, various study groups suggested ways to overcome the challenges of developing a vibrant interest rates futures market in India. SEBI (2003) in its report on 'Exchange Traded Interest Rate Derivatives in India' offered some critical suggestions. While favouring the continuation of cash settlement of contracts, SEBI suggested that the contract on a 10-year coupon bearing notional bond be priced on the basis of the average 'yield to maturity' (YTM) of a basket comprising at least three most liquid bonds with maturity between nine and 11 years. SEBI was in favour of quotation of the contact price on the scale of 100 minus the YTM of the basket. The Padmanabhan working group (2003), studying the rupee interest rate derivatives in India, suggested banks to act as market-makers by taking trading positions in interest rate futures.

The Sharma group (2008), in its latest report, has endorsed most of the above suggestions but differed on cash settlement of futures contracts. It felt that while money market futures may continue to be cash-settled with the 91-day T-Bills/ MIBOR (Mumbai Inter-Bank Offered Rate)/actual call rates serving as benchmarks, bond futures contract(s) should be settled physically, following the norms in matured financial markets around the world. The report has also favoured Foreign Institutional Investors (FIIs) taking long position in the interest rate futures market, subject to the condition that total gross exposure in the cash and interest rate futures markets does not exceed the extant maximum permissible cash market exposure limit. FIIs could take short position only to hedge exposure in the cash market.

6. Summing up

Reforms in the financial sector tend to increase volatility in interest rates – something which, as found by numerous studies, has several detrimental effects on an economy. This is precisely what drove most advanced economies to develop futures markets for interest rates, the most efficient form of the derivative market and an integral part of overall reforms in the financial sector. India, too, has taken some initiatives in this direction, allowing trading in interest rate futures in 2003 to begin with. But due to certain inadequacies in the designing of products, the trade could not really take off then. However, the whole exercise did, of course, throw some lessons at our policymakers for their future initiatives in this regard.

Currently, there is a proposal to jump-start the futures market in interest rates early in 2009. This is clearly a good sign not only from the point of view of providing various stakeholders with a risk management tool to hedge against high volatility of interest rates in the country but also to facilitate mitigation of such volatility. If the Sharma group (2008) suggestions are incorporated in the policy measures, interest rate futures seem to be all set for a successful launch this time. And no doubt, this would mean India taking a big leap forward in its next-level reforms in the financial sector.

Notes

1. The first exchange traded interest rates futures in the world were launched at the Chicago Board of Trade on 20 October 1975.
2. The basic difference between OTC and exchange traded derivatives (also called as futures) is the way buyers and sellers interact with each other. While in OTC, the contracts are traded on one-to-one basis, in case of futures, contracts are trade through an exchange.
3. According to Diamond's (1984) model, banks can reduce the cost of delegated monitoring by holding a diversified portfolio. Diamond showed that diversification within a bank lowers the cost of delegated monitoring. On this basis he argued that banks should hedge all market risks in which they do not have any special monitoring advantages. By hedging

in derivative activities, banks stand to reduce the cost of monitoring contracts issued to their loan customers, which enable them to increase their lending activities without escalating the total risk level.

References

Aydogan, K. 1991. Interest Rate Risk and Bank Profitability: The Case of Turkey. Discussion Paper: 9105, Central Bank of the Republic of Turkey.

Baig, T. 2001. Characterizing Exchange Rate Regimes in Post-Crisis East Asia. IMF Working Paper 01/152.

Bartram, S.M. 2001. The Interest Rate Exposure of Non-financial Corporations. PhD. dissertation, Limburg Institute of Financial Economics, Maastricht University.

Bhattacharya, B.B. 1985. Role of interest rates as an incentive for household saving in India, 1960–61 to 1980–81. Delhi: Mimeo, Institute of Economic Growth.

Bhole, L.M. 1985. Administered interest rates in India. *Economic and Political Weekly* June 22–29, no. 25–26: 1089–1104.

Bindra, Jaspal Working Group Report. 2003. Over-the-Counter Rupee Derivatives. Mumbai: Reserve Bank of India. January.

Brewer, III, E., B.A. Minton, and J.T. Moser. 2000. Interest-rate derivatives and bank lending. *Journal of Banking & Finance* 24: 353–79.

Diamond, D.W. 1984. Financial intermediation and delegated monitoring. *Review of Economic Studies* 51: 393–414.

Dutkowsky, D.H. 1987. Unanticipated Money Growth, Interest Rate Volatility, and Unemployment in the U.S. *Review of Economics and Statistics*, 144–8.

Esty, B., P. Tufano, and J. Headley. 1994. Banc One Corporation: asset and liability management. *Journal of Applied Corporate Finance* 7: 33–51.

Evans, P. 1984. The effects on output of money growth and interest rate volatility in the U.S. *Journal of Political Economy* April: 204–22.

Friedman, B. 1982. Federal reserve policy, interest rate volatility, and the U.S. capital rationing mechanism. *Journal of Money Credit and Banking* Part 2, November: 721–45.

Friedman, M., and A.J. Schwartz. 1963. *A Monetary History of the United States, 1867–1960.* Princeton: Princeton University Press

Froot, K.A., D.S. Scharfstein, and J.C. Stein. 1993. Risk management: coordinating corporate investments and financing policies. *Journal of Finance* 5: 1629–58.

Kashyap, A.K., and J.C. Stein. 1995. The Impact of Monetary Policy on Bank Balance Sheet. *Carnegie-Rochester Series on Public Policy* 42.

Kashyap, A.K., and J.C. Stein. 2000. What do a million observations of banks say about the transmission of monetary policy? *American Economic Review* 90: 407–28.

Macfarlane, I.J. 2001. The Movement of Interest Rates. Australia: University of Tasmania. Occasional Paper No.5.

Naudé, W. 1995. Financial Liberalisation and Interest Rate Risk Management in Sub-Saharan Africa. University of Oxford. WPS/ 96-12, Centre for the Study of African Economies.

Patnaik, I., and A. Shah. 2004. Interest Rate Volatility and Risk in Indian Banking. IMF Working Paper, 04/17.

Padmanabhan, G. 2003. Group on Rupee Interest Rate Derivatives. Reserve Bank of India. December.

Purnanandam, A. 2007. Interest rate derivatives at commercial banks: an empirical investigation. *Journal of Monetary Economics* 54, no. 6: 1769–1808.

Sahu, S., and A. Virmani 2005 Structure of the household sector asset portfolio in India. Working paper 157, Indian Council for Research on International Economic Relations, New Delhi.

SEBI 2003 Exchange Traded Interest Rate Derivatives in India. Consultative Document, Group on Secondary Market Risk Management, Securities and Exchange Board of India, March.

Sharma group report. 2008. Report of the Working Group on Interest rate Futures. Reserve Bank of India, February.

Tatom, J.A. 1984. *Interest rate variability: its link to the variability of monetary growth and economic performance.* Review, Federal Reserve Bank of St. Louis, November.

Thornton, H. 1802[1939]. An Enquiry into the Nature and Effects of the Paper Credit of Great Britain. ed. F.A. von Hayek. London: George Allen and Unwin.

Zhao, F., and J. Moser. 2006a. Bank lending and Interest Rate Derivatives. Working Paper, Siena College, USA.

Zhao, F., and J. Moser. 2006b. Use of Derivatives and Bank Holding Company Interest Rate Risk. Working Paper, Siena College, USA.

Exchange traded currency derivatives markets in India: the road ahead

Ranjan R. Chakravarty and D.G. Praveen

Research & Product Development, MCX-SX, Mumbai, India

Indian exchanges have recently been permitted to offer currency futures on their platforms to the market participants. The paper outlines the contract, and charts the development and growth of currency futures in India since their inception in 2008. It emphasizes the existing close connectivity between commodity and currency markets. It highlights the increased exchange rate volatility of Indian exchange rate against US dollar (INRUSD) during conventional and non conventional trading hours and argues for the ability of the market to quickly adapt to extended trading hours. The paper recommends some new products and an alternative mechanism to settle the contracts.

1. Futures market to cohabit with OTC market

The government has played an important role in initiating the launch of exchange traded currency futures in India. The introduction of the currency futures market has filled the need which was greatly felt by the market in the wake of deregulation in the 1990s and the resultant increased foreign exchange transactions and uncertainty in currency exchange rates. The average daily turnover in the foreign exchange (forex) market has increased from US$23.7 billion in March 2006 to US$33 billion in March 2007. It currently stands at around $48 billion in consonance with the increase in foreign exchange transactions (Reserve Bank of India).

The futures market will seamlessly cohabit with and complement the existing OTC market. The forex futures are permitted to provide greater depth and breadth to the forex market. The development of the futures market has brought in greater flexibility in hedging underlying currency exposure to market participants.

Exchange traded futures as compared to OTC forwards serve the same economic purpose, yet differ in fundamental ways. Forward contracts are entered into by individuals agreeing to transact at a forward price on a future date. No money changes hands except on maturity date. There is no mark to market (MTM) settlements in the OTC markets, while margins are collected up front from both parties (buyers and sellers) and the mark to market profits/losses are settled daily in the exchange traded currency derivatives market. This limits the scope of building up of mark to market losses in the books of participants and thereby default risk on an exchange traded platform.

The OTC market is bilateral and lacks transparency unlike the transparent exchange traded market which is multilateral and also anonymous. Exchange trading brings in greater transparency, efficiency and accessibility to this market. It also provides for the elimination of counterparty risk, as clearing corporation assumes counterparty guarantee and eliminates credit risk. In an exchange traded scenario where the market lot is fixed at a much smaller size than the OTC market, equitable opportunity is provided to all classes of investors whether large or small to participate in the futures market.

2. Introduction and growth of currency futures

Subsequent to recommendations made by a panel for trading in currency futures on dedicated exchanges and the report from the standing technical committee comprising of members from Reserve Bank of India (RBI) and the Securities Exchange Board of India (SEBI), the two regulatory bodies laid down the guidelines for setting up of currency futures market.

Currently, the USDINR futures contract with a contract size of US$1000 is allowed to be listed on exchanges. Market participants have received the product enthusiastically and the market has witnessed stupendous growth since its inception in August 2008. The Indian currency futures market, with three national exchanges offering the product, has an average daily turnover of over Rs. 17,000 core (US$4 billion).

The MCX Stock Exchange (MCX-SX) had an average daily turnover of Rs.57.72 Billion in the month of September 2009 with a record turnover of Rs.107.98 Billion on 7 October 2009. The MCX-SX has a market share of over 50%. As of 30 September 2009, the exchange had 621 members registered with SEBI, spread across over 475 centres (MCX-SX Currency Update).

Such growth witnessed in exchange traded forex derivatives volume within a short span of time should be credited to exchanges, regulators, market participants and supporting agencies. Before proceeding further to analyze ways to deepen the currency markets in India, we need to understand the strong fundamental relationship between commodities and currencies, and the volatility behaviour of our currency. The next section of this paper discusses the linkage between the two markets.

3. Linkage between securities, commodities and currency markets

There exists an intricate linkage between commodity prices and the movement of global currency prices. This linkage assumes importance especially for corporate firms dealing in commodities like gold, copper, zinc, edible oil, crude oil and petroleum products, which India has a large exposure to global markets as India is one of the major importers, consumers and exporters of some of these commodities and their derivatives. This risk exposure has a bearing on the profitability of the firm and, thereby, on their stock prices.

An Indian exporter, for instance, would face severe currency risk if the Indian rupee posts a steep appreciation against US dollar post the sale of goods abroad. The steep appreciation would have a startling impact on his revenues in Indian rupee as the US dollar fetches him fewer Indian rupees when the payment is received. Contrarily, an importer is apprehensive about Indian rupee depreciation, while a re-exporter, like a jewellery exporter who imports gold and export jewellery, is exposed to both appreciation and depreciation of the Indian rupee. All these lead to a recommendation for locking the US dollar rate against the Indian rupee to protect profit margins and stabilize revenues.

As an illustration, it is notable that the steep correction in global oil prices, which came down to around $50 a barrel in 2009 from a peak of $140 a barrel in 2008, were not fully reflected in import prices of crude oil for Indian oil firms on account of a simultaneous depreciation in the Indian rupee during this period.

Typically, almost all exporters, importers and other intermediaries in foreign trade are exposed to both commodity price risk and exchange rate risk. Such scenarios call for comprehensive price risk management. Lock-in of trade margins through hedging help the business community to manage better and improve overall profitability of their companies.

Commodity traders always look for avenues for the effective and efficient hedging of their commodity and currency risks. Although commodities were traded on exchanges for some time, until August 2008 currencies were not traded on Indian exchanges. This absence constrained commodity/currency traders to be confined to an OTC forward currency platform.

4. Volatility in exchange rates

Since the 1990s, the value of the Indian rupee has become more market driven. The increasing primacy of demand–supply dynamics have brought together domestic and global market factors in determining this value. This co-integration is in line with the fact that a significant portion of Indian exports are destined for the United States and Europe or to other countries in dollar denominated trade and it is likewise for imports.

Coming to actual market dynamics, there is an active OTC forex market for the Indian rupee during evening hours when US and European markets are active. Most of the key macroeconomic data releases and other policy announcements for these countries occur during these hours and these have a significant impact on the value of the US dollar and other currencies, which in turn has a spill over impact on the value of the Indian rupee. The Indian rupee movements against foreign currency in the evening hours, therefore, cause the exposure of Indian foreign trade participants to fluctuate, not only during traditional Indian trading hours but also during active times of western markets. Table 1 shows how traded USDINR futures' prices have

Table 1. Volatility in near-month USDINR futures contracts (2009) (in %).

Month	Day's open/ previous day's close (i.e. during closed hours)	Day's close/ day's open (i.e. during trading hours)	Day's close/ previous day's close (i.e. for full day)	Day's high/ day's low (intraday trading volatility)
March	0.341%	0.66%	0.82%	0.41%
April	0.432%	0.66%	0.50%	0.32%
May	0.497%	0.75%	0.91%	0.47%
June	0.291%	0.41%	0.45%	0.29%
July	0.260%	0.39%	0.49%	0.28%
August	0.289%	0.36%	0.48%	0.23%

Source: MCX-SX Research.

changed during these conventional trading and non-trading hours on the MCX-SX. It is evident from the data that there exists significant volatility both during trading and non-trading hours. The price change during closed hours (i.e. day's open over previous day's close) and during trading hours (i.e. day's close over day's open) are both significant, and are imbibed in full over the day's price change (observed in day's close over previous day's close).

Given the above, we now turn our focus to measures that can be considered for deepening the currency futures market.

5. Extension of trading timings

Indian export and import (EXIM) businesses are active in the late evening hours. Markets for global commodities like gold, crude oil, copper and edible oil are very vibrant during the same hours; it could be surmised that their prices are substantially influenced by the value of the US dollar, which still acts as a universal medium of exchange in international trade. The availability of late evening trading hours on the Indian commodity markets enables traders to partially cover their commodity price risk, as they are otherwise required to keep the currency risk exposure until the market re-opens. Hence, if the currency derivatives segment, which is currently operational between 9 am to 5 pm, can also be kept open during late evening hours it would enable a larger number of stakeholders to cover their risk arising out of commodity prices and exchange rates in global markets on the domestic exchanges.

Certain specific measures could be taken in order to synchronize Indian trading hours across geographies and markets. For instance, trading hours could be extended till 11:30 pm in order to have a significant overlap of trading hours of Indian markets with that of Far Eastern, European and US markets. Late evening trading hours are not new to the Indian markets as almost all trading members in equity markets operate in commodity markets and they keep their commodity market segment operational from 10 am to 11:30 pm.

To take a hint from global markets, the electronic platform of the world's leading currency derivatives exchange, the Chicago Mercantile Exchange (CME) of the United States, operates nearly 24 hours a day from 5 pm to 4 pm CST (next day).

It is also a known fact that a section of firms use the non delivery forwards (NDF) market to hedge the currency risk as the onshore market is not available for hedging during the entire time zone from Tokyo to New York. It is also a known fact that major volatility is seen once the New York market opens which is after 5:50 pm IST and firms with genuine exposures have to keep their currency risk exposures open until the market reopens the next day. Extension of market timings enables the market participants to hedge their exposures and to manage volatility.

Whilst the other asset classes, viz. equity cash and equity futures and options (F&O), are largely indigenous products with a domestic asset base, the currency and commodity derivatives segment are international asset classes, which have a direct correlation with movements in the global currency market. The availability of domestic currency exchanges operating across international timings will facilitate domestic market players including exporters, importers, firms, banks and institutions having currency exposures, to hedge in local exchanges. Hence, the need is to provide the enabling environment for these participants to effectively manage and hedge their exposures.

The extended hours would not put excessive strain on the infrastructural or manpower resources of traders. Clearing banks are ready to provide clearing activities, even if the trading time is extended beyond 5 pm. There could be occasions when the members or clients banks have electronic banking facilities where collection of funds intraday is not a challenge even during a highly volatile day. In fact, banks have started keeping their branches open until 11:30 pm to support exchanges for collection of funds and sharing of information until end of the trading day.

Recently, SEBI has allowed exchanges to extend trading hours in the equity cash and derivatives segment from 9:55 am to 3:30 pm, to between 9 am to 5 pm in order have greater overlap with Singapore and Indian markets. While this would align Indian markets more with Far Eastern markets, there is greater need to align Indian markets with European and US markets which would require markets to extend trading up to midnight. This would make the global securities market aligned with commodity markets in India and global markets so that there is no distortion or lag in price discovery. We are sure the regulators will gradually permit the industry to bridge this risk of time lag, especially for the global asset class such as currency. Globally it is seen that the underlying cash market operates for a shorter interval whereas the derivatives market operates for longer hours as these are risk management products and not principal cash products.

6. Options on currency to widen scope

Option contracts serve the participants in a way different from that of futures contracts. Options attract risk averse participants who are apprehensive about futures products because of the involvement of higher risk which needs to be met on a daily basis. The market would never be complete without exchange traded option products. The volatility in the Indian rupee against foreign currency has significantly increased over the recent times and this emphasizes the need for options contracts meant for those who are averse to huge risks.

Globally, option products are available in many markets that have forex products. Those exchanges offering forex futures products are also trading in options contracts. For instance, the leading forex exchanges like CME in United States, ICE Futures US, NYSE Euronext.Liffe in Europe, and Brazilian Mercantile Exchange (BM & F), all offer forex option products to their customers.

In an emerging country like Brazil, BM & F option volume accounts for 35% of futures volume (in 2008). The options are also active on CME. Interestingly, at NYSE Liffe volume in option products is significantly larger than forex futures products. When we consider all markets, forex options market is about 15% of futures market (World Federation of exchanges).

The introduction of option products in the Indian market would be a timely move, where the foreign currency futures products by now have become successful and completed a full one year cycle. The successful past of the derivatives market shows the path India can smoothly tread. Index options have been re-introduced soon after the successful introduction of index futures products in equity markets, while stock options are allowed ahead of stock futures.

To be precise, in the equity segment, derivative products have been introduced in a phased manner, starting with index futures contracts in June 2000. Index options and stock options were introduced in June 2001 and July 2001 respectively. All these put the Indian markets on the global map. To date, it is clear that the market needs a logical extension to the foreign currency product list.

7. Other currencies and crosses

There has been demand from the market participants for the introduction of the new currency pairs such as Euro-Indian Rupee (EURINR), Japanese Yen-Indian Rupee (JPYINR), British Pound-Indian Rupee (GBPINR), etc. The daily foreign exchange market turnover has increased to US$48 billion in 2007–08 against US$34 billion in 2007. About 40% of foreign exchange transactions are in cross currency deals other than direct foreign currency to rupee (FCY/ INR) deals (Reserve Bank of India).

Forex market participants often enter deals in USDINR contract and cross currencies like Euro-US Dollar (EURUSD) and British Pound-US Dollar (GBPUSD) to hedge against the other currency pairs EURINR, GBPINR and JPYINR. The availability of other currency pairs enables market participants to hedge on exchanges on direct currency pairs (i.e. EURINR, GBPINR and JPYINR).

While USDINR rates are determined locally and in global markets, the cross currency pairs are determined mainly in global markets during Indian and non-Indian conventional trading hours. Those who are exposed to other currency exchange rates are highly susceptible to cross currency pairs.

With increased volatility and depreciation, countries like China and India prefer gold, EUR and other currencies to US dollar reserves. The entire information technology (IT) export industry has been severely impacted because of development in the US and UK markets. And, now Indian Information Technology companies are focusing on European, West Asia and Asia Pacific to offset slowing growth in the US and the UK. Small and Medium Enterprises (SMEs) have huge business transactions with countries other than US. And invoicing happens often in other currencies.

Globally, exchanges often offer more than one currency pair. BM & F in Brazil offer contracts on US dollar and euro, JSE in South Africa on US dollar, euro and pound sterling, KRX in South Korea on US dollar, JP yen and euro, RTS in Russia offers EUR/USD and Euro-Russian Ruble (EUR/RUR) contracts.

The world's largest currency derivatives exchange, Chicago Mercantile Exchange offers contracts on currencies of developed as well as emerging countries. It also offers contracts on cross currencies apart from direct currency pair contracts like EURUSD. The average daily turnover of CME is in excess of $100 billion. Over half a million contracts are traded daily in the currency segment and about 65% of volume is from currency pairs and cross currency contracts other than EURUSD.

The RBI proposal in the Credit Policy of October 2009 to permit the expansion of currency pairs of currency futures contracts beyond US dollar–rupee contracts is a welcome step in light of the successful one year completion of currency futures. It would facilitate the development of the market and ensure greater financial inclusion through direct hedging of risk in other currencies on exchanges. It signals the beginning of the next phase of robust growth in the exchange traded currency derivatives market.

As India's international trade is in multiple currencies, other currencies could be permitted for trading on the Exchange to minimize the cross currency risk of actual users in hedging. These contracts could settle at the cross currency rates vis-à-vis the US dollar on expiry. The suggested currencies initially could be British pound, the euro and the Japanese yen.

8. Option of physical settlement in currency futures

A physically settled contract would align the Indian foreign currency futures market with international standards, eliminate basis risk and reduce the cost of hedging. In addition, this will create transactional efficiency as in one transaction the actual user will be hedged and also be sure of obtaining delivery that will be taken only by actual users themselves. This would be operationally executed through approved clearing banks, subject to necessary compliance.

Globally, the most successful contracts on the EUR, JPY, GBP, Swiss franc, Canadian dollar traded on CME are all physically settled contracts. Other exchanges in South Korea and Mexico also offer physical settlement of contracts.

The foreign exchange futures market, which has a history of over one year in India, has garnered lot of interest among participants and is fast gaining popularity. What can be discerned from market feedback is that participants are keen to have some option for the physical settlement of currency futures contracts.

The following are important factors that endorse the demand for physical delivery contracts in India.

- A physical delivery contract provides for both the types of hedgers – those who are interested in rolling their positions for long-term hedging and those who are looking for delivery of the foreign currency.
- The share of forward and cancellation constitutes 40% of the merchant market and forward cancellation around 37% of the total forward volume. A physical delivery contract is sure to provide a parallel platform also for those who wish to obtain or cancel deliveries.
- It reduces the burden for hedgers for approaching the OTC spot market during delivery days for physical delivery and ensures smoother convergence of spot, and futures markets.
- Contracts settled through physical delivery provide a standard, efficient and cost effective parallel trading platform for all types of market participants irrespective of their size and nature of hedging.
- Competition helps in reducing the costs in physical forex spot/forward trading.
- The physical and futures market arbitrage becomes easier, effective and efficient, and this helps for bridging differences.

A mechanism suitable to both parties may be made available to participants, where delivery can be left at the option of buyers and sellers. Otherwise, the introduction of exchange of physicals for futures (EFP) can be considered. An EFP transaction involves simultaneous transactions in a spot/cash market and a futures market.

EFP is very popular globally and the mechanism gives market participants who have physical market exposure a smooth exit route through dealings in physical market as well as futures markets. In the absence of full capital account convertibility, the physical delivery could be given and taken only by actual users with foreign currency exposure and delivery could be handled through banking system. Conversely, with the assumption of full convertibility, in the absence of physical delivery in the futures contract by anyone without forex exposure on account of the full convertibility of the rupee, EFP can aid in the convergence of physical and futures market. Thus, under both scenarios one can envisage a boost in the efficiency of markets through this measure.

9. Conclusion

The launch of USDINR futures in India during 2008 has given participants in the foreign exchange market a new means to cover their foreign exchange rate risk on exchange trading platforms. Since its introduction, the market has seen volume on exchanges burgeon. However, the market has a great potential to achieve more. The time is opportune for implementation of some of the suggestions made in this paper such as the introduction of late evening sessions, options, and products on other currencies and crosses. These should help the Indian market grow bigger and more popular, and also to become deeper and more efficient.

The continued commitment of the two Indian regulatory bodies towards the orderly and well thought out development of financial markets, while maintaining financial stability and integrity, is commendable and encouraging at the same time. It is clear that there is a policy commitment at the highest levels of government towards the development of an efficient and transparent exchange traded currency derivatives market in the country, albeit with appropriate safeguards.

Bibliography

Government of India and Reserve Bank of India. 2009. Report of the Committee on Financial Sector Assessment.

Mistry, P.S. (Chairman). 2007. Report of the High Powered Expert Committee on making Mumbai an international financial centre. Ministry of Finance, Government of India.

Rajan, R.G. (Chairman). 2007. A hundred small steps: Report of the Committee on Financial Sector Reforms. Planning Commission, Government of India.

Rao, M.R. (Chairman). 2008. SEBI Derivatives Market Review Committee: Report on the developments and review of derivative markets in India. Securities and Exchange Board of India.

Reserve Bank of India and Securities and Exchange Board of India. 2008. Report of the RBI–SEBI standing technical committee on exchange traded currency futures.

Securities and Exchange Board of India. 2009. Discussion paper on increase in market hours of trading in exchanges.

Spread, volatility and monetary policy: empirical evidence from the Indian overnight money market

Saurabh Ghosh[a] and Indranil Bhattacharyya[b]

[a]Financial Markets Department, Reserve Bank of India, Reserve Bank of India, Fort, Mumbai, 400001, India; [b]Monetary Policy Department, Reserve Bank of India, Fort, Mumbai, 400001, India

This study uses a GARCH model to estimate conditional volatility in the Indian overnight money market during the period 1999–2006. It finds that the bid-ask spread in the overnight market was positively related to conditional volatility during 1999–2002. This relationship, however, has undergone a structural break since 2002 and lagged spread, along with conditional variance of the call rate, played an important role in determining spread during 2002–2006, indicating the improvement in market microstructure in recent years. Regarding monetary policy measures and money market volatility, the empirical findings indicate that expansionary monetary policy reduces volatility of both the weighted average call rate and the bid-ask spread. Among individual policy instruments, announcement of cash reserve ratio changes have a negative impact on the volatility of both call rate and spread. The other policy variables like Bank Rate, repo and reverse repo rates have a mixed impact on volatility of call rate and spread.

1. Introduction

The money market is the fulcrum of the financial system on which monetary operations are conducted by the central bank in its pursuit of policy objectives. It is now well established that central banks operate mainly at the short end of the money market and policy impulses get transmitted at the longer end of the financial system through the term structure of interest rates. Globally, operating procedures of monetary policy have converged on an increasing role of interest rates in the transmission mechanism. The sharper focus on interest rates as the operating target has gone hand in hand with a tendency to move towards targeting short-term interest rates. As a corollary, the overnight rate has emerged as the most commonly pursued operating target in the conduct of monetary policy.[1] The targeting of short-term interest rates is fully consistent with a market oriented approach whereby information about the expectations of future movements in interest rates is extracted from the prevailing market rates

Central banks realise their monetary policy objectives by careful management of liquidity conditions and facilitate money market transactions while ensuring stable market conditions. As excessive money market volatility could provide confusing signals to economic agents about the stance and intent of monetary policy, it is critical to ensure orderly market behaviour from a financial stability perspective. A well-functioning money market is, therefore, essential for conducting indirect, market-based monetary policy operations and developing the term structure of interest rates by providing the necessary liquidity for a market in government and corporate bonds.

Development of liquidity in the inter-bank market – the market for short-term funds amongst banks – provides the basis for growth and increased liquidity in the broader money market, including the secondary market for Treasury Bills and private sector money market instruments. Successful management of market liquidity and effective regulation of money market conditions requires modulation of volatility in order to smoothen short-term interest rates. In reality, however, money markets, particularly those in emerging market economies, are prone to volatile behaviour of short-term rates which calls for greater introspection on issues relating to market microstructure.

Market microstructure analyses how specific trading mechanisms affect the price formation process. It studies the process by which investors' latent demands are ultimately translated into prices and volumes. In particular, as information is important in decision-making, market outcome is highly sensitive to the assumed information structure. Research in this field has mainly focussed on the intertwined relationships between price volatility, liquidity (popularly proxied by bid-ask spreads and trading volumes), price discovery and market design. Market microstructure models relate price changes to order flows and provide deep insights on the determinants of a deep and liquid market.

Research in money market microstructure is a relatively recent phenomenon and has mainly focussed on developed markets. In contrast, research on emerging market economies (EMEs) is rather limited – perhaps attributable to the narrow and underdeveloped nature of this market in such economies. This paper makes an attempt to address this anomaly by extending a recently proliferating body of research on EMEs (Sánchez-Fung 2008) to India, where the transmission mechanism and operating procedure of monetary policy exhibit dynamics that are significantly different from more mature markets.

In the wake of rapid and significant developments of the financial sector in general, and the money market, in particular over the last decade, this paper focuses on the evolving role of market microstructure in the Indian inter-bank money market. Specifically, the paper has two objectives. First, it attempts to model the relationship between spread and volatility in the overnight segment of the money market, which would shed some light on the efficiency gains and institutional development at the short end of the yield curve. Second, after evaluating the role of market microstructure, it tries to assess the impact of various monetary policy instruments used by the Reserve Bank of India (RBI) on market volatility and draw policy perspectives for the future. This is particularly important as analysis of money market microstructure, so far, has largely escaped research attention in the Indian context.

The structure of the paper is as follows. Section 2 presents a brief review of the literature on money market microstructure. Some stylized facts about the Indian money market are presented in section 3. The data and methodology of the study along with the empirical results and its implications are presented in section 4. Concluding observations are presented in section 5.

2. Brief review of literature

The initial theoretical literature on market microstructure tried to explain the bid-ask spread through the use of two approaches. The first *viz.*, the inventory-based explanations beginning with Garman (1976) highlighted the importance of transaction costs in determining the bid-ask spread. The second, beginning with Bagehot (1971), emerged to explain market prices through the role of asymmetric information. In this approach, which draws heavily from the theory of adverse selection, new information gets reflected into prices as a result of the trading behaviour of informed and uninformed traders such that even in competitive markets without explicit transaction costs, spreads would exist.

Initially, the empirical literature on money markets related the behaviour of the overnight inter-bank market rates of a representative bank to monetary policy operating procedures and money market accounting conventions (Ho and Saunders 1985; Campbell 1987). More recently, Bartolini et al. (1998) introduce a role for central bank liquidity provision while examining market dynamics. Perez-Quiros and Rodriguez (2000) analyse the behaviour of a representative bank during the minimum reserve maintenance period when there is a symmetric pair of standing facilities.[2]

The empirical literature on money market microstructure is more recent in origin and rather limited in contrast to bond, equity or foreign exchange markets. Most studies follow a traditional macroeconomic approach or look at the time series properties of short rates at a daily (or longer) frequency for the US Federal funds market (Spindt and Hoffmeister 1988; Griffiths and Winters 1995; Hamilton 1996) and the euro overnight market (Perez-Quiros and Rodriguez 2000; Bindseil and Seitz 2001).

In the context of the US Federal funds market, Furfine (1999) describes the size, concentration, intra-day timing and analyses bank relationship patterns, particularly with respect to size of institutions. Angelini (2000) discusses the implications of timing of overnight transactions in the Italian electronic deposit market during periods of uncertain liquidity. Cassola and Morana (2006a, 2006b) estimate the factors that explain the volatility and its persistence in the overnight segment of the euro money market, which shows repetitive intra-day, daily and monthly patterns that can be explained by market microstructure.

In the euro area, studies on the microstructure of the money market have shown that it is heavily influenced by the institutional environment of the European Central Bank (ECB) and its monetary policy operations (Hartmann et al. 2001). This study analyses the intra-week and intra-day behaviour of bid-ask spreads, volatility, quoting frequency and trading volume and finds that overnight market rate volatility and spreads are relatively high on days with ECB monetary policy announcements, particularly during mid-day when the ECB's interest rate decisions are released. Similarly, recent work by Bartolini et al. (2002), Bartolini and Prati (2003a), and Prati et al. (2003) document the close connection between the operational frameworks of monetary policy and the behaviour of overnight interest rates in the US, the euro area and other G-7 countries. Bartolini and Prati (2003b) demonstrate that short-term interest rate volatility also reflects differences in central banks commitment to interest rate smoothing. Ayuso et al. (1997) show the relevance of institutional details in influencing money market rates and their volatility.

One related strand in the literature has investigated how well the markets are able to anticipate the monetary policy actions of the Federal (Krueger and Kuttner 1996; Poole and Rasche 2000; Kuttner 2001; Demiralp and Jordà 2004) and the ECB (Gaspar et al. 2001; Perez-Quiros and Sicilia 2002; Ross 2002; Bernoth and von Hagen 2004), drawing on the methods of extracting market expectations from financial instruments (Söderlind and Svennson 1997). Bernhardsen and Kloster (2002) and Coppel and Connolly (2003) provide cross-country comparison of some Organisation for Economic Cooperation and Development (OECD) countries. Their main findings indicate that market participants in advanced economies, given the increased public availability of information about how monetary policy decisions are taken, are better able to anticipate policy decisions in recent years than in the 1980s or early 1990s.

3. Indian money market: some stylized facts

3.1. Money market operations

The instruments used by the Reserve Bank of India are daily repo/reverse repo transactions under the Liquidity Adjustment Facility (LAF), standing facilities and reserve requirements. Daily open market operations under the LAF are used to manage temporary liquidity and guide interest rates in the desired direction. Additional liquidity through the standing facility of export credit refinance is made available to banks, who can access this facility as and when required. Moreover, the RBI has the discretion to conduct longer term repo auctions at fixed rate or at variable rates depending on market conditions and other relevant factors. Furthermore, the RBI also conducts auctions under the Market Stabilization Scheme (MSS) to modulate liquidity conditions emanating from large capital flows. This is done on a weekly basis against the issue of Treasury Bills and dated securities.

Under the LAF which became operational in June 2000, two policy rates, namely the repo[3] and the reverse repo rates, are specified for lending and borrowing of funds by the RBI. By accepting repo bids from banks and primary dealers, liquidity is injected while it is absorbed from the banking system through the acceptance of reverse repo bids. These operations are conducted regularly by means of daily tenders at fixed rates for repo transactions with an overnight maturity under a uniform price auction. In this process, the RBI determines the overall quantity to be absorbed/injected with inputs from its own assessment of the liquidity requirements of the banking system. The RBI influences liquidity conditions either by rejecting bids or by changing the LAF rates, which is, however, done only at discrete intervals.

With a view to absorb liquidity of a more enduring nature, the Reserve Bank operationalized the MSS as an instrument of sterilization, by issue of Treasury Bills and dated securities under the MSS from April 2004. The proceeds of the MSS are held by the government in a separate identifiable cash account maintained and operated by the RBI. The amounts credited into the MSS account are appropriated only for the purpose of redemption and/or buy back of the Treasury Bills and/or dated securities issued under the MSS. The auctions are conducted by the RBI who decides the amount, tenor, modalities and the timing of issue.

3.2. *Money market structure*

The last two decades have witnessed substantial developments in the Indian money market in terms of introduction of newer instruments, building up of appropriate market infrastructure and strengthening of prudential practices. The broad policy objectives are to ensure stability, minimize default risk and achieve a balanced development of various segments through introduction of new instruments, broadening of participants' base and strengthening of institutional infrastructure. The policy thrust given to the growth of the collateralized segment has improved options for liquidity management while reducing risks. Developments in institutional and technological infrastructure such as the introduction of screen-based dealing system have also helped in improving transparency, facilitating the price discovery process and providing avenues for better liquidity and risk management.

In India money market instruments mainly include call or notice money, term money, certificates of deposit, commercial papers, usance bills and any other debt instruments of original or initial maturity up to one year as specified by the RBI from time to time. In this paper, we focus on the overnight inter-bank deposit market, which is of particular interest to the central bank for liquidity management. Earlier, unsecured overnight call money trading was dominant over any of the other segments by a large margin. However, with concerted efforts being made by the Reserve Bank over the last few years to develop the collateralized segment through the introduction of market repo and Collateralized Borrowing and Lending Obligations (CBLO) – a repo instrument developed by the Clearing Corporation of India Limited (CCIL) for its members – the volume in the collateralized segment has overtaken that of the uncollateralized one (see Table 1). Since 6 August 2005, the uncollatersalized segment of the money market has become purely an inter-bank market. Gradually, the CBLO market is becoming the preferred option both for the banks and non-bank participants.

4. Empirical analysis

Financial markets suffer from contagion – both foreign and domestic. While the former defines financial contagion as a shock to one country's asset market that causes changes in asset prices in another country's financial market, the latter refers to turbulence in one market spilling over into other market segments of the same country. In the Indian context, for example, for the period April 2000–March 2007 the inter-bank call money rate was found to be positively correlated to both the exchange rate (0.06) and the BSE Sensex (0.01) (Report on Currency and Finance, 2005–2006, Reserve Bank of India, 2007). While volatility across financial markets are often synchronous in nature, particularly in EMEs, the crux of this paper is in

Table 1. Shares in money market in %.

Year	Call	Market repo	CBLO
2003–2004	55.67	41.59	2.74
2004–2005	31.88	51.84	16.29
2005–2006	30.45	35.77	33.78
2006–2007	24.61	38.92	36.47

trying to explain money market microstructure (*viz.*, the bid-ask spread) from the perspective of money market volatility. Hence, the focus of this paper is to examine the linkages between the bid-ask spread and volatility in the money market rather than exploring the impact of cross-market contagion on market volatility.

Money market liquidity is typically based on three dimensions, *viz.*, tightness, depth and resilience. Tightness refers to how far transaction prices diverge from the average market price, i.e., the general costs incurred irrespective of the level of market prices. One of the most frequently used measure of tightness is the bid-ask spread,[4] i.e. the differential between the lowest bid quote (the price at which a market participant is willing to borrow in the inter-bank market) and the highest ask quote (at which the agent is willing to lend), representing an operational measure of the price of the agents' services in the absence of other transaction costs. Depth denotes either the volume of trades possible without affecting prevailing market prices, or the amount of orders on the order books of market makers at any time period. Depth is reflected by the maximum size of a trade for any given bid-ask spread. The turnover ratio, i.e. the turnover in the money market as a percentage of total outstanding money market transactions, also provides an additional measure of the depth of the market.[5] Resilience refers either to the speed with which price fluctuations resulting from the trade are dissipated, or the speed with which imbalances in order flows are adjusted. While there is no appropriate measure of resilience, one approach is to examine the speed of the restoration of normal market conditions (such as the bid-ask spread and order volume) after transactions are completed. Other measures such as the number and volume of trades, trading frequency, turnover ratio, price volatility and the number of market participants are often regarded as readily available proxies for market liquidity. Thus, a relatively more liquid money market, *ceteris paribus*, requires less time to execute a transaction, operates on a narrower bid-ask spread, supports higher volumes for a given spread and requires relatively less time for the restoration of the 'normal' bid-ask spread following a high value transaction.

4.1. Data

For the empirical exercise, we restrict our analysis to the overnight segment of the money market. In the overnight segment, we use the daily data on weighted average call money rate and spread of the Mumbai Inter-bank Bid Rate (MIBID) and Mumbai Inter-bank Offer Rate (MIBOR) for the overnight money market from 1 April 1999 to 31 December 2006.[6] While weighted average call money rates are calculated based on actual data of transaction volumes and rates, the MIBID-MIBOR spread is based on data obtained by conducting a poll to get reference rates on bid and offer prices from eight market participants. In effect, while the former is based on actual market transactions, the latter is representative of market expectations. As mentioned above, the depth of the market is sought to be gauged from transaction volumes. The data of daily turnover in the overnight market, however, is only available from 1 October 2002.

Major features of the data on bid-ask spread in the overnight market is presented in Table 2a and Table 2b (also see Figure 1). While the relationship between spread, volatility and turnover sheds light on the evolving market microstructure and the institutional development in the Indian money market, the second part of the empirical exercise assess the impact of different monetary policy instruments on call

Table 2a. Bid-ask spread in the inter-bank money market in %.

	1999–2000			2000–2001			2001–2002			2002–2003		
	MIBID	MIBOR	Spread	MIBID	MIBOR	Spread	MIBID	MIBOR	Spread	MIBID	MIBOR	Spread
Average	8.82	9.12	0.31	9.03	9.32	0.29	7.08	7.31	0.23	5.83	5.97	0.14
SD	1.68	2.23	0.67	2.13	2.34	0.34	1.29	1.57	0.39	0.48	0.51	0.06
CV	0.19	0.24	2.19	0.24	0.25	1.17	0.18	0.22	1.72	0.08	0.09	0.43
Max	19.76	27.03	7.68	21.55	25.94	4.39	13.47	16.54	3.65	7.70	7.95	0.44
Min	5.26	5.88	0.06	2.60	3.60	0.06	6.29	6.47	0.08	4.89	5.06	0.06

	2003–2004			2004–2005			2005–2006			2006–2007		
	MIBID	MIBOR	Spread	MIBID	MIBOR	Spread	MIBID	MIBOR	Spread	MIBID	MIBOR	Spread
Average	4.53	4.71	0.17	4.56	4.76	0.20	5.54	5.68	0.14	6.96	7.24	0.28
SD	0.26	0.27	0.05	0.46	0.44	0.06	0.80	0.84	0.06	4.08	5.05	1.04
CV	0.06	0.06	0.30	0.10	0.09	0.30	0.14	0.15	0.42	0.59	0.70	3.76
Max	6.19	6.48	0.41	6.03	6.30	0.42	7.72	8.00	0.36	58.15	68.27	11.81
Min	4.19	4.41	0.07	4.11	4.41	0.08	4.67	4.78	0.06	4.80	5.21	0.07

Notes: MIBOR: Mumbai Inter-Bank Offered Rate; MIBID: Mumbai Inter-Bank Bid Rate; Spread: MIBOR–MIBID.
Source: Fixed Income Money Market and Derivatives Association of India (FIMMDA), National Stock Exchange (NSE).

Table 2b. Turnover and weighted average call rate.

| | 1999–2000 | | 2000–2001 | | 2001–2002 | | 2002–2003 | |
	Wt. Avg. Call (%)	Turnover (Rs. Crore)	Wt. Avg. Call (%)	Turnover (Rs. Crore)	Wt. Avg. Call (%)	Turnover (Rs. Crore)	Wt. Avg. Call (%)	Turnover (Rs. Crore)
Average	8.87	–	9.15	–	7.17	–	5.91	–
SD	1.73	–	2.23	–	0.81	–	0.52	–
CV	0.19	–	0.24	–	0.11	–	0.09	–
Max	18.79	–	20.34	–	13.13	–	10.35	–
Min	3.99	–	3.15	–	6.34	–	5.01	–

| | 2003–2004 | | 2004–2005 | | 2005–2006 | | 2006–2007 | |
	Wt. Avg. Call (%)	Turnover (Rs. Crore)	Wt. Avg. Call (%)	Turnover (Rs. Crore)	Wt. Avg. Call (%)	Turnover (Rs. Crore)	Wt. Avg. Call (%)	Turnover (Rs. Crore)
Average	4.64	17255	4.67	14160	5.59	17950	7.25	21767
SD	0.28	8543	0.47	7892	0.83	9961	4.79	13200
CV	0.06	0.50	0.10	0.56	0.15	0.55	0.66	0.61
Max	6.20	37909	6.30	36346	7.88	35086	54.32	51201
Min	4.16	76	3.50	20	3.19	1068	5.27	350

Note: Data on turnover is only available from 2003–2004 on a full financial year basis.
Source: Reserve Bank of India, *Handbook of Statistics on the Indian Economy, 2007–2008.*

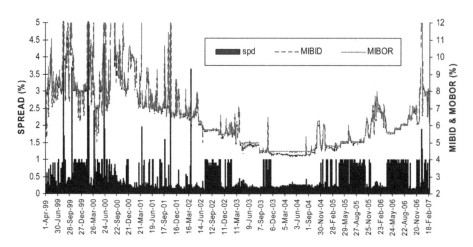

Figure 1.   MIBID, MIBOR and spread.

rate and spread volatility. In this regard, we take into account the changes in major monetary policy instruments of the Reserve Bank *viz.*, repo rate, reverse repo rate, Bank Rate and cash reserve ratio (CRR) changes used during this period.

From the data, it is pertinent to make few observations. First, the mean spread has been declining until 2005–2006 but has increased significantly in 2006–2007. Second, volatility, as measured by coefficient of variation (CV) of the bid-ask spread, has gone up alarmingly during 2006–2007 (Table 2a). Similar inferences can be drawn from the movements in the weighted average call rate and the turnover in the inter-bank overnight market (Table 2b). First, the mean weighted average rate has been declining steadily from 1999–2000 till 2004–2005 but has increased thereafter in 2005–2006 and more significantly in 2006–2007. Second, volatility of the weighted average call rate has gone up alarmingly during 2006–2007. Third, since the introduction of LAF, the weighted average call rate has been moving within a narrow range until 2005–2006 but widened significantly thereafter during 2006–2007. These patterns also get broadly reflected in the data on turnover which also is a pointer to the swings in liquidity conditions during 2006–2007.[7] It is interesting to note that there have been several monetary policy tightening announcements in response to large capital inflows during 2006–2007, and *prima facie* it appears that the overnight market has reacted significantly to these developments. Therefore, it would be interesting to look at the response of volatility of call rate and bid-ask spreads to various monetary policy measures of the RBI.

4.2. *Methodology*

In order to evaluate the underlying volatility of the overnight rate in the money market, we first try to explain it by using its own lagged values through the method of ordinary least squares (OLS). The residual from the OLS model, however, does not bear testimony to the assumption of constant volatility since overnight money market rates reflect phases of volatility clustering.[8] Therefore, in order to estimate the time varying volatility, we use the generalized autoregressive conditional heteroskedasticity (GARCH) model (Bollerslev 1986) – the standard methodology in estimating volatility of financial time series. We formally test the autoregressive conditional heteroskedasticity (ARCH)/ GARCH effect in the residual using Engel's LM test (up to five lags) and find that the null of no ARCH effect is strongly rejected by the data.

The GARCH model aims to describe more accurately the phenomenon of volatility clustering and related effects such as kurtosis. The main idea behind this model is that volatility is dependent upon past realizations of the data generating and related volatility process. This is a more precise formulation of the intuition that asset volatility tends to revert to some mean rather than remaining constant or moving in monotonic fashion over time.

If an autoregressive moving average model (ARMA model) is assumed for the error variance, the model is a GARCH model. The GARCH specification asserts that the best predictor of the variance in the next period is a weighted average of the long-run average variance, the variance predicted for this period, and the new information in this period that is captured by the most recent squared residual. Such an updating rule is a simple description of adaptive or learning behaviour and can be thought of as Bayesian updating.

In general, the GARCH (p,q) process models the residual of a time series regression with p referring to the number of autoregressive lags (ARCH) terms that appear in the equation, while q being the number of moving average lags. Specifically, the GARCH (1,1) model specified with a mean equation and the conditional variance equation with first lag of squared residuals and the conditional variance itself offers the most popular methodology for studying the volatility patterns of high frequency financial time series. Besides, the choice of the GARCH (1,1) model is also based on its attribute of parsimony and its capacity to outperform most other models (White 2000; Hansen 2001).

Accordingly, for studying the volatility patterns of overnight rates in the call money market, the GARCH (1,1) model is specified with a mean equation (Y_t) and the conditional variance equation (h_t) with first lag of squared residuals and the conditional variance itself. The GARCH model characterizes the distribution of the stochastic error ε_t conditional on the realized values of the set of variables $\Phi_{t-1} = \{Y_{t-1}, Y_{t-2}, \ldots\}$. The GARCH (1,1) model is specified as below:

$$\text{mean equation}: Y_t = \alpha Y_{t-1} + \varepsilon_t; \quad \text{where } \varepsilon_t/\phi_{t-1} \sim N(0, \ h_t) \tag{1}$$

$$\text{conditional variance equation}: h_t = \beta_o + \beta i \varepsilon_{t-1}^2 + \beta j \, h_{t-1} \tag{2}$$

In addition, the following constraints are placed on the coefficients to preserve stationarity of the variance process:

(1) $\beta_o > 0;\ \beta i \geq 0,\ \beta j \geq 0$
(2) $\beta i + \beta j < 1$ for all i and j.

4.3. Results

The coefficient of the mean equation and volatility equation of overnight rates derived from the above system of equations are summarized in Table 3. The significance of the coefficients of volatility equation below the 1% level indicates the presence of strong GARCH effect in the overnight rate volatility. Therefore, the rest

Table 3. Mean and volatility from GARCH (1,1).

	Co-efficient	P-value
	Mean equation	
C	0.19	0.005
WT_AVG(− 1)	0.96	0.001
	Variance equation	
C	0.0076	0.00
RESID(− 1)^2	0.46	0.00
GARCH(− 1)	0.51	0.00
R-squared	0.92	
D-W Stat	2.10	

Notes: Dependent variable: weighted average call money rate. RESID(− 1)^2: coefficient of square of past of residual. GARCH(− 1): coefficient of past residual in variance.

of this study uses the daily volatility estimated by the above mentioned GARCH equation in modelling spread.

4.3.1. Modelling spread and volatility relationship

After estimating the volatility of overnight rates, this section attempts to explain the relationship between volatility and money market spread (MIBOR-MIBID). Conventional wisdom from the existing literature suggests a positive relationship between volatility and bid-ask spread, as market makers are likely to respond to the additional risks (rise in volatility) by increasing the spread. The trading volume, on the other hand, is likely to have an inverse relationship as volume increases liquidity and thereby reduces the underlying risk to some extent.

Before modelling the spread-volatility relationship, we examine the monthly and daily patterns of MIBOR-MIBID spread by using monthly and day of the week dummies. The regression result using spread as dependent variables are summarized in the appendix (see Table A1 and A2). In terms of the day-of-the-week effect, the regression coefficients and their P-values indicate that spreads were significantly higher on Fridays during the week and in the month of March during the financial year.[9]

Data from March 1999 to December 2006 was considered for modelling the spread-volatility relationship. The regression results using spread as dependent variable and GARCH volatility as explanatory variable are presented in Table 4 (columns 2 and 3). The dummy variables for March and for Fridays were also included to control for the month and day of the week effect, respectively.

Though the coefficient of volatility (GARCH01) is found to be positive and significant in Table 4, the low value of R^2 clearly indicates poor explanatory power of the underlying model and suggested the possibility of structural changes/omitted variables over the period under consideration. To evaluate the possibility of a regime shift, we use a Markov regime switching model which computes the maximum likelihood step switch date for a deterministic change in regime based on time (Goldfeld and Quandt 1973) – drawing from the work of Sun (2005), who found evidence of such shifts in rate volatility in both the US and UK. The log-likelihood ratio (LR) and posterior odds ratio for step switching of the estimated Markov

Table 4. Spread-volatility relationship.

Period	Apr 1999–Dec 2006		Apr 1999–Dec 2002		Apr 2002–Dec 2006		Apr 2002–Dec 2006		Apr 2002–Dec 2006	
	Co-efficient	P-value	Co-efficient	P-value	Co-efficient	P-value	Co-efficient	P-value	Co-efficient	P-value
1	2	3	4	5	6	7	8	9	10	11
C	0.15	0	0.16	0	0.15	0	0.02	0	0.073	0
MAR	0.06	0	0.2	0	0	0.6	0.01	0.04	0.009	0.02
FRI	0.08	0	0.09	0.08	0.04	0	0.01	0.12	0.008	0.13
GARCH01	0.06	0	0.06	0	0.08	0	0.01	0	0.022	0
SPD(−1)							0.9	0	0.862	0
LTURNOVER									−0.005	0.01
R-squared	0.17		0.17		0.16		0.73		0.737	
Durbin-Watson stat	1.9		1.99		0.47		2.45		2.93	

Notes: Dependent variable: MIBOR-MIBID spread. Mar: dummy variable for month of March. Fri: dummy variable for Fridays. GARCH01: call money rate volatility estimated by GARCH(1,1) model (Table 3). LTURNOVER: log of turnover in the call money market. SPD(−1): lagged value of the dependent variable (Spread).

switching model identified the structural break for the Indian overnight market as that in April 2002 (see Figure 2). For checking the robustness of the above structural break, we also did a Chow's (1960) break point test, which confirms the existence of a regime shift as indicated by the statistically significant F-Statistics and the LR (see Table 5). In this context, it is worthwhile to note that the process of gradually phasing out non-bank participants from the inter-bank money market gathered momentum since 2002 and was completed by 2005. Furthermore, the CBLO was permitted as a money market instrument since 2002 which facilitated the emergence of the collateralized instruments as the dominant segment in the money market.

Based on evidence of structural break, the entire period was truncated into sub-periods (Apr 1999–Mar 2002 and Apr 2002–Dec 2006) and the regression results using same set of independent variables are presented in Table 4 (columns 4 and 5) and (columns 6 and 7).

The results indicate that for both the periods, the volatility term (GARCH01) has significant positive coefficient indicating that volatility had an incremental effect on MIBOR-MIBID spread. The dummy for March was significant for both the periods, while the Friday dummy was only significant for the first period. In the second period, however, the Durbin-Watson (DW) statistic was very low indicating the presence of autocorrelation. Therefore, lagged spread was introduced as an explanatory variable in the model for the period Apr 2002–Dec 2006, which significantly improved the DW statistic along with R^2 in the augmented model. The regression results found that the lagged spread had a significant positive coefficient which indicates evidence of adaptive learning from past experience (Table 4 columns 8 and 9).

Finally, the turnover series – constrained by the availability of data – was included in the model since October 2002 and the regression results indicate a negative coefficient for turnover (indicating negative impact of liquidity on spread)

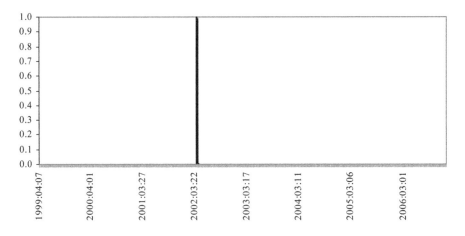

Figure 2. Markov switching model posterior odds ratio.
Note: Total number of switching points considered is 2820.

Table 5. Chow breakpoint test.

| F-statistic | 14.90942 | Prob. F(4,2230) | 0.000000 |
| Log likelihood ratio | 59.06546 | Prob. Chi-Square(4) | 0.000000 |

(Table 4 columns 10 and 11). Both GARCH volatility and lagged spread recorded positive coefficients as found earlier. The movement of actual and fitted spreads is shown in Figure 3.

To sum up, money market microstructure improved significantly in India as evident from the evolving spread-volatility relationship in recent years. During the first part of the truncated period, while rate volatility had a marginal impact on money market spread in a contemporaneous sense, the relationship has undergone a change since April 2002. In the second period, lagged spread has become more significant in determining spread along with GARCH volatility. This would indicate that the spread evaluated from market expectations – reflected in conducted polls – has increasingly aligned with the underlying market movement over time and the progressive development of the market. Finally, the expected negative impact of turnover on spread is reflective of greater depth in liquidity and improvement in market microstructure consequent to the series of measures initiated by the RBI to develop the overnight money market since 2002 and the institutionalization of LAF and MSS in modulating liquidity conditions at the short end of the market.

4.3.2. Impact of policy announcements on money market volatility

Having explored the changing dynamics of the spread-volatility relationship and the improvement in market microstructure over the last five years, we now concentrate on the impact of monetary policy measures on market volatility during Apr 2002– Dec 2006. As noted earlier, the short term money market has emerged as the main arena for signalling monetary policy changes. Changes in policy instruments[10] tend to have two distinct type of impact on the market, *viz.*, the direct announcement impact and the indirect liquidity effect. While changes in Bank Rate, repo/reverse repo rates become immediately effective i.e., from the next day, CRR changes are typically implemented with a lag. Therefore, while the market reaction to Bank Rate and repo/reverse repo rates gets reflected on financial market behaviour on the very next day, the reaction to changes in CRR gets reflected in two phases. While the next

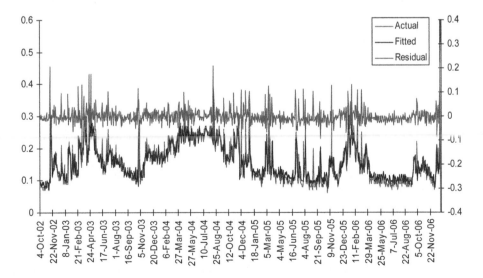

Figure 3.   Actual, fitted and residual spread.

day data would capture the announcement effect, the liquidity impact would be discernible once the CRR changes become effective. As a result, we consider both the announcement and effective dates for changes in CRR.

While the rate in the overnight market almost instantaneously reacts to policy measures, this section analyses the effect of monetary policy changes on the volatility of the same. In the Indian context, while the impact of alternative policy instruments on the weighted average call rate has been examined recently (Bhattacharyya & Sensarma 2008), it is more interesting to study the impact of these instruments on volatility of both weighted average call rate and spread from the perspective of market microstructure. For estimating the announcement impact of policy changes on the underlying volatility of these two variables, we have considered announcement dates of changes in Bank Rate, repo and reverse repo rate and the CRR (also effective dates) during the period of study. In addition, we also explore the impact of expansionary/contractionary monetary policy in terms of rate cuts/hikes (using any or a combination of the above instruments) on the volatility of rate and spread.

For empirically evaluating the nature, magnitude and the significance of the policy changes on the underlying volatility of overnight money market rate and spread, the GARCH volatility equation used earlier (Equation 2) was augmented to include a dummy variable. The augmented set of information used for estimating GARCH volatility is as follows:

$$R_t = \alpha_0 + \alpha_1 R_{t-1} + \varepsilon_1 \quad \text{where } \varepsilon_t/\Phi_{t-1} \sim N(0, h_t) \tag{3}$$

$$h_t = \beta_0 + \beta_1 \varepsilon_{t-1}^2 + \beta_2 h_{t-1} + \lambda * \mathbf{D_f} \tag{4}$$

Where R_t is the dependent variable signifying the weighted average call rate/ spread, h_t is the conditional volatility of the weighted average call rate/spread augmented by $\mathbf{D_f}$ — a dummy variable which takes the value 1 on the date of monetary policy changes but 0 otherwise. $\mathbf{D_f}$ is created to capture the effect of changes in Bank Rate, repo rate, reverse repo rate, both effective/announcement dates for CRR and expansionary/contractionary policy. The magnitude, direction and significance of the coefficient λ would indicate the impact of a particular policy change on the volatility of both weighted average call rate and spread. The estimated results using the augmented GARCH model are presented in Table 6a and the observations are summarized in Table 6b. Together from these two tables, it is pertinent to reflect and draw some inferences on the impact of monetary policy measures on the underlying volatility of both the weighted average call rate and MIBID-MIBOR spread.

4.3.2.1. Impact of measures on volatility of weighted average call rate. The announcement of Bank Rate, repo and reverse repo rate changes, although having a marginal positive impact, is not statistically significant. Changes in CRR (both announcement and effective dates) have a negative impact on rate volatility which is statistically significant. This would imply that CRR changes tend to have a sobering influence on market volatility by reducing the uncertainty about policy after its announcement. Moreover, while unpansionary monetary policy reduces volatility by easing market conditions, contractionary policy increases volatility. While both the results are statistically significant, the magnitude of impact of the contractionary measure is higher than that of expansionary policy, i.e. the short-end of the money market seems to react more to monetary tightening than to monetary easing which is

Table 6a. Interaction of market volatility and monetary policy instruments.

Monetary policy instrument	GARCH using weighted average call rate as dependent variable						GARCH using MIBID-MIBOR spread as dependent variable					
	Mean eqn.		Variance eqn.				Mean eqn.		Variance eqn.			
	$\alpha 0$	$\alpha 1$	$\beta 0$	$\beta 1$	$\beta 2$	λ	$\alpha 0$	$\alpha 1$	$\beta 0$	$\beta 1$	$\beta 2$	λ
DBRATE	0.11 (0.00)	0.98 (0.00)	0.01 (0.00)	0.37 (0.00)	0.47 (0.00)	0.004 (0.88)	0.04 (0.78)	0.77 (0.00)	0.14 (0.00)	0.16 (0.00)	0.55 (0.00)	−0.30 (0.00)
DREPO	0.11 (0.00)	0.98 (0.00)	0.01 (0.00)	0.37 (0.00)	0.47 (0.00)	0.07 (0.24)	0.01 (0.00)	0.96 (0.00)	0.0002 (0.00)	0.70 (0.00)	0.51 (0.00)	0.005 (0.00)
DRREPO	0.10 (0.001)	0.98 (0.00)	0.01 (0.00)	0.36 (0.00)	0.48 (0.00)	0.04 (0.16)	0.01 (0.00)	0.95 (0.00)	0.0001 (0.00)	0.73 (0.00)	0.50 (0.00)	0.0001 (0.61)
DCRR	0.11 (0.00)	0.98 (0.00)	0.01 (0.00)	0.37 (0.00)	0.48 (0.00)	−0.01 (0.03)	0.01 (0.00)	0.95 (0.00)	0.00017 (0.00)	0.61 (0.00)	0.53 (0.00)	0.02 (0.00)
DCRRA	−0.11 (0.08)	1.02 (0.00)	0.03 (0.00)	0.15 (0.00)	0.45 (0.00)	−0.06 (0.00)	0.04 (0.00)	0.76 (0.00)	0.14 (0.00)	0.16 (0.00)	0.55 (0.00)	−0.30 (0.00)
DEXPAN	0.27 (0.001)	0.95 (0.00)	0.04 (0.00)	0.12 (0.00)	0.52 (0.00)	−0.04 (0.005)	0.04 (0.81)	0.75 (0.00)	0.14 (0.00)	0.16 (0.00)	0.57 (0.00)	−0.17 (0.00)
DCONTRA	0.11 (0.00)	0.98 (0.00)	0.01 (0.00)	0.40 (0.00)	0.45 (0.00)	0.08 (0.00)	0.01 (0.00)	0.95 (0.00)	0.0002 (0.00)	0.66 (0.00)	0.53 (0.00)	−0.0003 (0.00)

Notes: λ: coefficient of dummy variables. DBRATE: dummy variable for Bank Rate change. DREPO: dummy variable for repo rate change. DRREPO: dummy variable for reverse repo rate change. DCRR: dummy variable for effective cash reserve ration change. DCRRA: dummy variable for announcement date of CRR change. DEXPAN: dummy variable for expansionary monetary policy (viz., reduction in policy rates and CRR). DCONTRA: dummy variable for contractionary monetary policy (viz., hikes in policy rates and CRR). Figures in parenthesis represent P-values of the coefficients.

Table 6b.   Interaction of market volatility and monetary policy instruments.

Monetary policy instrument	Weighted average call rate	MIBID-MIBOR spread
DBRATE	Positive but not significant (P = 0.88)	Negative and significant (P ~ 0)
DREPO	Positive but not significant (P = 0.24)	Positive and significant (P ~ 0)
DRREPO	Positive but not significant (P = 0.16)	Positive but not significant (P = 0.61)
DCRR	Negative and significant (P = 0.03)	Positive and significant (P ~ 0)
DCRRA	Negative and significant (P ~ 0)	Negative and significant (P ~ 0)
DEXPAN	Negative and significant (P ~ 0)	Negative and significant (P ~ 0)
DCONTRA	Positive and significant (P ~ 0)	Negative and significant (P ~ 0)

Notes: DBRATE: dummy variable for Bank Rate change. DREPO: dummy variable for repo (injection) rate change. DRREPO: dummy variable for reverse repo (absorption) rate change. DCRR: dummy variable for effective cash reserve ration change. DCRRA: dummy variable for CRR announcement date of CRR change. DEXPAN: dummy variable for expansionary monetary policy. DCONTRA: dummy variable for contractionary monetary policy.

indicative of asymmetric market response. In other words, while rate cuts enhance the comfort level of market participants, rate hikes tend to heighten uncertainty relating to inflationary expectations in the market. We postulate that this dichotomy in expectation of market participants is indicative of risk-averse behaviour resulting in the downward rigidity of nominal interest rates in India.

Finally, the estimated relationship between the underlying volatility of weighted average call rate and monetary policy measures are found to be stable as reflected in the fact that the coefficients in the conditional variance equation (apart from the constant term) add up to less than one.

4.3.2.2.   Impact of measures on volatility of MIBID-MIBOR spread. While the announcement impact of Bank Rate changes is found to be negative and statistically significant on the volatility of spread, announcement of reverse repo rate, although having a negligible positive impact, is not significant. Similarly, CRR announcements have a negative (significant) impact while CRR effective dates have a positive (significant) impact on spread volatility. Moreover, both expansionary and contractionary monetary policies are statistically significant in reducing spread volatility, although the magnitude of the expansionary impact is much higher than that of contractionary policy reflecting the stronger impact of monetary easing on market expectations. It is important to note, however, that the relationship between the underlying volatility of spread and announcement of repo and reverse repo changes, effective dates of CRR changes along with contractionary policy are not stable from the criterion of variance stationarity.

Summing up, the GARCH volatility equation for both rate and spread shows a negative and statistically significant impact of CRR announcement and expansionary monetary policy. While expansionary monetary policy reduced volatility of both market rates and spread, contractionary policy had a negative impact on spread volatility but a positive impact on rate volatility. Thus, the impact of expansionary monetary policy is a stronger result in that it influences the volatility of both rate and spread in the same direction in contrast to that of contractionary policy. The other policy changes (e.g. changes in LAF rates, Bank Rate) had mixed effect on rate and spread volatility.

5. Conclusion

This paper makes an attempt to understand the determinants of volatility and spread in the overnight segment of the Indian money market from 1999–2006 – a period that has witnessed both significant shifts in the operating procedures of monetary policy and the rapid strides taken by the market in terms of sophistication of instruments and participants. In addition, it analyses the impact of monetary policy announcements on volatility of money market rates and spreads. The study shows the significant improvement in market microstructure and its role in determining the behaviour of money market rates and spread, particularly as the money market has emerged from a highly restrictive policy regime only in the 1990s.

The study finds evidence of a structural break from April 2002, signalling the various money market reforms ushered in since that period which have brought about subtle changes in market microstructure. Since 2004 the share of the traditionally dominant over the counter (OTC) market declined in terms of market activity while new collateralized instruments have gained importance, partly induced by policy preference for financial stability. As rate volatility had a positive impact on money market spread, monetary policy aimed at ensuring orderly market conditions in preserving financial stability.

After establishing the relationship between market expectations and actual volatility movements and improvement in money market microstructure in the recent period, the paper concentrated on exploring the impact of various policy instruments on money market volatility. While other policy instruments had mixed impact on the volatility of call rate and/or spread, the paper demonstrates the effectiveness of the announcement impact of CRR changes in reducing volatility of both market rates and spread. Furthermore, while expansionary policy reduced volatility in money market rate and spread, contractionary policy had a negative impact only on spread (which is essentially poll based) volatility but a positive impact on the volatility of the call rate (market determined). As discussed above, the results are a pointer to the evolving market microstructure and its interaction with monetary policy in the Indian money market. Contingent upon the availability of more intensive tick-level and real time data, these findings can trigger off more focussed research on market microstructure which would serve as a useful guide, both in refining operating procedures and furthering money market reforms in India.

Acknowledgements

The authors are grateful to the journal editor and an anonymous referee for valuable suggestions and appreciate the comments received from Professor Vikas Chitre at the 10th Annual Conference on Money and Finance held at IGIDR in February 2008, where an initial version of the paper was presented. Feedback from Shri Chandan Sinha and Shri H.S. Mohanty of the Reserve Bank of India are also gratefully acknowledged. The views expressed in this paper, however, are those of the authors solely and not of the institution to which they belong. Other usual disclaimers apply.

Notes

1. Out of 17 central banks/monetary authorities surveyed by the Bank for International Settlements (BIS) in 2007, as many as 12 targets the overnight/short-term money market rate and/or modulate liquidity in the overnight/short-term money market as the central plank of their monetary policy operations.

2. In the context of the operating procedure of the European Central Bank, standing facility refers to the marginal lending facility – a rate at which funds are injected into the system – and a standing deposit facility – at which funds are absorbed from the system. Together, they form a corridor to the movement in overnight rates with the marginal lending facility as the ceiling and the standing deposit facility as the floor of the corridor. It is symmetric if the marginal lending facility and the standing deposit facility is above and below the main policy rate, respectively, by identical margins (e.g. $\pm 1\%$).

3. Repos are financial instruments for the temporary exchange of cash against securities with a transfer of ownership.

4. In the Treasury Bills market, the bid-ask spread is found to be the best measure of liquidity (Fleming 2003).

5. A more accurate measure of market depth would take into account both actual transactions and potential transactions volume arising out of portfolio adjustments.

6. In recognition of the need for the development of a benchmark rate for the call money market, the National Stock Exchange (NSE) had developed the MIBID and MIBOR for the overnight money market and launched them in June 1998. It was later rechristened as 'FIMMDA-NSE MIBID/MIBOR'.

7. It may be noted that despite the gradual emergence of the collateralized segment as having the largest share in the money market, turnover volumes have increased perceptibly in the overnight uncollateralized segment during 2005–2006 and 2006–2007.

8. In financial time series data, volatility clustering refers to the observation that large changes tend to be followed by large changes, of either sign, and small changes tend to be followed by small changes.

9. In the Indian context, the reserve maintenance period is a fortnight which begins on a Saturday after a Reporting Friday and ends on the 14th day on another Reporting Friday. In order to cover shortfalls in reserve requirements, typically some banks borrowed heavily in the inter-bank market on Reporting Fridays which created temporary tightness in liquidity reflected in widening of bid-ask spreads. Similarly, pressures from advance tax outflows and other year-end considerations cause some tightness in liquidity conditions in March.

10. Typically, all monetary policy measures are announced after the closure of financial markets at the end of the day.

References

Angelini, P. 2000. Are banks risk-averse? A note on the intraday timing of operations in the interbrain market. *Journal of Money, Credit, and Banking* 32, no. 1: 54–73.

Ayuso, J., A.G. Haldane, and F. Restoy. 1997. Volatility transmission along the money market yield curve. *Review of World Economics* 133, no. 1: 56–75.

Bagehot, W. 1971. The only game in town. *Financial Analysts Journal* 27, no. 2: 12–4. 22.

Bartolini, L., G. Bertola, and A. Prati. 1998. Day-to-day monetary policy and the volatility of the federal funds interest rate. EUI Working Paper ECO, no. 98/35, European University Institute, November.

Bartolini, L., G. Bertola, and A. Prati. 2002. Day-to-day monetary policy and the volatility of the federal funds interest rate. *Journal of Money Credit and Banking* 34, no. 1: 137–59.

Bartolini, L., and A. Prati. 2003a. The execution of monetary policy: a tale of two central banks. *Economic Policy* 18, no. 37: 435–67.

Bartolini, L., and A. Prati. 2003b. Cross-Country Differences in Monetary Policy Execution and Money Market Rates Volatility. Federal Reserve Bank of New York Staff Report No. 175, October

Bernhardsen, T., and A. Kloster. 2002. Transparency and predictability in monetary policy. *Economic Bulletin* Q2. Norges Bank.

Bernoth, K., and J. von Hagen. 2004. The Euribor futures market: efficiency and the impact of ECB policy announcements. *International Finance* 7, no. 1: 1–24.

Bhattacharyya, I., and R. Sensarma. 2008. How effective are monetary policy signals in India. *Journal of Policy Modelling* 30, no. 1: 169–83.

Bindseil, U., and F. Seitz. 2001. The supply and demand for Eurosystem deposits – the first 18 months. ECB Working Paper, No. 44, February.

Bollerslev, T. 1986. Generalized autoregressive conditional heteroskedasticity. *Journal of Econometrics* 31, no. 3: 307–27.

Campbell, J.Y. 1987. Money announcements, the demand for bank reserves, and the behaviour of the federal funds rate within the statement week. *Journal of Money, Credit, and Banking* 19, no. 1: 56–67.

Cassola, N., and C. Morana. 2006a. Volatility of interest rates in the euro area: evidence from high frequency data. *The European Journal of Finance* 12, no. 6–7: 529–52.

Cassola, N., and C. Morana. 2006b. Comovements in Volatility in the Euro Money Market. ECB Working Paper No. 703.

Chow, G.C. 1960. Tests of equality between sets of coefficients in two linear regressions. *Econometrica* 28, no. 3: 591–605.

Coppel, J., and E. Connolly. 2003. What Do Financial Market Data Tell us About Monetary Policy Transparency? Research Discussion Paper No.5, Reserve Bank of Australia.

Demiralp, S., and O. Jordà. 2004. The response of term rates to FED announcements. *Journal of Money, Credit, and Banking* 36, no. 3: 387–405.

Fleming, Michael, J. 2003. Measuring Treasury Market Liquidity. *Economic Policy Review*, Federal Reserve Bank of New York, September, 83–108.

Furfine, C.H. 1999. The microstructure of the federal funds market. *Financial Markets, Institutions and Instruments* 8, no. 5: 24–44.

Garman, M. 1976. Market microstructure. *Journal of Financial Economics* 3, no. 3: 257–75.

Gaspar, V., G. Perez-Quiros, and J. Sicilia. 2001. The ECB monetary policy strategy and the money market. *International Journal of Finance and Economics* 6, no. 4: 325–42.

Goldfeld, S.M., and R.E. Quandt. 1973. The estimation of structural shifts by switching regressions. *Annals of Economic and Social Measurement* 2, no. 4, October: 475–85.

Griffiths, M.D., and D.B. Winters. 1995. Day-of-the-week effects in federal funds rates: further empirical findings. *Journal of Banking & Finance* 19, no. 7: 1265–84.

Hamilton, J.D. 1996. The daily market for federal funds. *Journal of Political Economy* 104, no. 1: 26–56.

Hartmann, P., M. Manna, and A. Manzanares. 2001. The microstructure of the Euro money market. *Journal of International Money and Finance* 20, no. 6: 895–948.

Ho, T.S.Y., and A. Saunders. 1985. A micro model of the federal funds market. *Journal of Finance* 40, no. 3: 977–0.

Krueger, J., and K. Kuttner. 1996. The fed funds futures rates as a predictor of Federal Reserve policy. *Journal of Futures Markets* 16, no. 8: 865–79.

Kuttner, K. 2001. Monetary policy surprises and interest rates: evidence from the fed funds future market. *Journal of Monetary Economics* 47, no. 3: 523–44.

Perez-Quiros, G., and H. Rodriguez. 2000. The daily market for funds in Europe: has something changed after the EMU? Paper presented at the ECB conference The Operational Framework of the Eurosystem and Financial Markets, May 5–6, in Frankfurt.

Perez-Quiros, G., and J. Sicilia. 2002. Is the European Central Bank (and the United States Federal Reserve) Predictable? Working Paper No. 192, European Central Bank.

Poole, W., and R.H. Rasche. 2000. Perfecting the market's knowledge of monetary policy. *Journal of Financial Services Research* 18, no. 2/3: 255–98.

Prati, A., L. Bartolini, and G. Bertola. 2003. The overnight interbank market: evidence from the G-7 and the Euro zone. *Journal of Banking and Finance* 27, no. 10: 2045–83.

Reserve Bank of India. 2007. Financial Market Integration. In *Report on Currency and Finance 2006–07*.

Ross, K. 2002. Market Predictability of ECB Monetary Policy: A Comparative Examinations. IMF Working Paper No. 233.

Sánchez-Fung, José R. 2008. Modelling the term structure of interest rates in a small emerging market economy. *Macroeconomics and Finance in Emerging Market Economies* 1, no. 1: 93–103.

Söderlind, P., and L.E.O. Svennson. 1997. New techniques to extract market expectations from financial instruments. *Journal of Monetary Economics* 40, no. 2: 383–429.

Sun, L. 2005. Regime shifts in interest rate volatility. *Journal of Empirical Finance* 12, no. 3: 418–34.

Spindt, P.A., and J.R. Hoffmeister. 1988. The micromechanics of the federal funds market: implications for day-of-the-week effects in funds rate variability. *Journal of Financial and Quantitative Analysis* 23, no. 4: 401–16.

White, H. 2000. A reality check for data snooping. *Econometrica* 68, no. 5: 1097–126.

Appendix

Table A1. Day of the week effect on spread.

Variable	Coefficient	Std. Error	t-Statistic	Prob.
C	0.176361	0.016978	10.38779	0.0000
MON	0.000413	0.023957	0.017249	0.9862
WED	0.014532	0.024046	0.604343	0.5457
THUR	0.008683	0.023957	0.362439	0.7171
FRI	0.097292	0.024082	4.040038	0.0001
SAT	0.066238	0.024211	2.735861	0.1063
R-squared	0.013984	Mean dependent var		0.207169

Note: Among the days of the week, Tuesday is not considered in the above regression to avoid multicolliniarity and dummy variable trap problems.

Table A2. Month of the year effect on spread.

Variable	Coefficient	Std. Error	t-Statistic	Prob.
C	0.164261	0.023615	6.955711	0.0000
FEB	0.088114	0.034222	2.574777	0.1101
MAR	0.079571	0.033844	2.351104	0.0188
APR	0.045809	0.035340	1.296248	0.1950
MAY	0.041445	0.033691	1.230154	0.2188
JUNE	0.075274	0.033591	2.240902	0.9251
JULY	0.011540	0.033166	0.347942	0.7279
AUG	0.079034	0.033397	2.366495	0.1081
SEP	0.031906	0.033844	0.942744	0.3459
OCT	0.046810	0.033792	1.385226	0.1661
NOV	0.023050	0.034056	0.703522	0.4818
DEC	−0.002490	0.033445	0.074449	0.9407
R-squared	0.009597			

Note: The month of January is not considered in the above regression to avoid multicolliniarity and dummy variable trap problems.

Precautionary and mercantilist approaches to demand for international reserves: an empirical investigation in the Indian context

K.P. Prabheesh[a], D. Malathy[a] and R. Madhumathi[b]

[a]Department of Humanities and Social Sciences, Indian Institute of Technology Madras, Chennai, Tamil Nadu, India; [b]Department of Management Studies, Indian Institute of Technology Madras, Chennai, Tamil Nadu, India

This paper empirically investigates the importance of precautionary and mercantilist approaches to international reserves in the Indian context using monthly data from 1993:06 to 2007:03. The ARDL approach to cointegration is used to estimate as in the long-run relationship between reserves and its determinants. The empirical results show that the impact of the volatility of Foreign Institutional Investment which captures the precautionary motive, and that of undervalued real exchange rate which is associated with the mercantilist view on reserves are statistically significant in the long run. We conclude that both the precautionary and mercantilist motives explain reserve accumulation in India over the study period.

1. Introduction

Over the last 15 years, there has been a steep increase in the global international reserves from US$1200 billion in 1990 to US$5960 billion in 2007. This has taken place despite most of the economies shifting from a fixed to a flexible exchange rate regime, which requires countries to maintain lower levels of international reserves to prevent any currency crisis. Interestingly, the developing countries' share in the global reserves has also risen dramatically from 30 to 72% in the same period (IMF 2007). A notable fact is that the Asian economies are the major reserve holders among developing countries. This unprecedented rise in international reserves is a cause of concern among central banks for reserve management policies.

Two alternative approaches are used to explain this unprecedented reserve accumulation, especially in Asian economies. First, the precautionary approach, according to which the financial integration of the developing countries has increased their exposure to volatile capital flows or hot money, which are subject to sudden stop and reversal (Calvo 1998; Edwards 2004). The East-Asian crisis resulted in reducing the accessibility of these countries to the international capital market and exposed their hidden vulnerabilities. This forced the market to update the probability of sudden stop affecting all countries (Aizenman and Lee 2005). The reductions in growth rates due to the crisis induced the policy-makers to follow tight internal and external adjustment policies to stabilize the output. Under such circumstances, holding international reserves can be viewed as an output stabilizer or as a precautionary saving against volatile capital flows, its sudden stop and its reversal. An alternative explanation to the recent reserve accumulation is the mercantilist view. Dooley, Folkerts-Landau, and Garber (2003) argued that the reserve accumulation is the by-product of the undervalued exchange rate polices adopted by the Asian economies to promote their exports and channel domestic and foreign direct investment to the export industries. They viewed Asian countries as periphery regions which follow undervalued exchange rate policies to promote exports to the central region, namely, the USA. This phenomenon can be understood as a new Bretton Woods system. These mercantilist policies resulted in persistent current account surpluses and reserve accumulation with the central banks of these economies. The best example is China, which has been following an undervalued exchange rate to maintain its export competitiveness with its trading partners, and has emerged as the top reserve holding country in the world. In short, the mercantilist approach views reserve accumulation as the outcome of exchange rate and export policies of the country, whereas the precautionary approach to reserves expresses the concern over sudden stop, capital flight, and its volatility.

Empirical investigation of the importance of precautionary and mercantilist approaches is very limited. Aizenman and Lee (2005) tested the relative importance of these approaches in the context of developing countries and found that the variable which captures the mercantilist concern was statistically significant though; its magnitude of impact on reserves accumulation was almost zero. At the same time, the variable related to precautionary motive was found to be highly significant in explaining reserve accumulation. It was also found that undervalued exchange rate polices tended to increase reserves in the context of Korea (Aizenman, Lee, and Rhee 2007).

The present study empirically tests the relevance of precautionary and mercantilist approaches in explaining reserve accumulation in the Indian context. Though India moved to a flexible exchange rate regime after 1992, it holds more than US$200 billion as international reserves as of end of March 2007. This level of reserves accounts for more than 20% of India's Gross Domestic Product (see Figure 1). Of this, foreign investment is found to be the major source accounting for more than 50% of reserve accumulation over the period 1991–2007 (RBI 2007). One of the major policies undertaken during the economic reforms in the early 1990s was to permit foreign institutional investors to invest in Indian stock markets. The cumulative Foreign Institutional Investment touched US$50 billion by the end of March 2007 (RBI 2007). This increased flow of short-term capital to India in the form of Foreign Institutional Investment to stock markets and its volatile nature can be a reason for large reserve accumulation. Though, greater exchange rate flexibility mitigates the impact of short-term capital flight, the cost of a capital market crash as well as the impact of depreciation of domestic exchange rate due to capital flight are expected to be significantly large. Therefore, high reserves with the Reserve Bank of India (RBI) can be considered as precautionary savings to mitigate the risk of short-term capital flight.

It is observed that the RBI has been following a stable exchange rate regime with respect to the US dollar compared to other foreign currencies (Patnaik 2003).

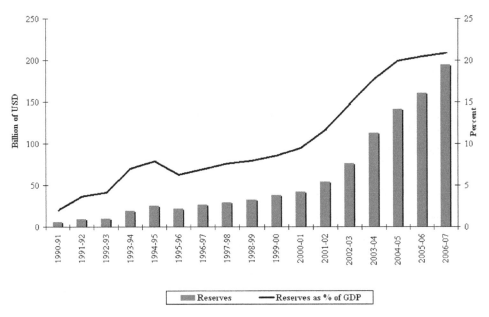

Figure 1. Trends in international reserve holdings in India.

Evidence also suggests that the RBI has been intervening in the foreign exchange market whenever the rupee appreciates but not when the rupee depreciates (Ramachandran and Srinivasan 2007). These observations provide a case for investigating whether it is the mercantilist view that can better explain reserve accumulation in India in recent years.

While a limited number of studies have empirically investigated the behaviour of India's demand for international reserves, not much work has been done on testing the relative importance of mercantilist and precautionary motives. Prabheesh, Malathy, and Madhumathi (2007) argued that India's reserve demand is highly sensitive to capital account vulnerability during the period 1983–2005. Ramachandran and Srinivasan (2007) argued that the reserve accumulation in India seems to be the result of asymmetric intervention of RBI in the foreign exchange market and that the precautionary hypothesis does not explain the upsurge of reserves. There is a dearth of studies examining the reserve accumulation process from the view of precautionary savings against the volatility of short-term capital flows and the implication of keeping an undervalued real exchange rate on the reserve accumulation. This study makes an attempt to test the importance of the two alternative views that seek to explain reserve accumulation, by including specific variables to capture these motives, namely, the volatility of Foreign Institutional Investment for the precautionary motive and a measure of the undervalued real exchange rate of the Indian rupee against the US dollar for the mercantilist motive.

The rest of the paper is organized as follows: Section 2 deals with the empirical model of reserve demand and is followed by a discussion on data and its source in Section 3. The econometric methodology and empirical results are given in Sections 4 and 5. Section 6 presents the conclusion.

2. Empirical model

A reserve demand function is estimated incorporating volatility of Foreign Institutional Investment to capture the precautionary motive of reserve holdings as a response to volatile capital flows and the deviation of real exchange rate from its trend series to capture the mercantilist argument of undervalued exchange rate policies, along with other standard explanatory variables of reserves. The empirical specification of the reserve demand function is as follows:

$$res_t = \gamma_0 + \gamma_1 im_t + \gamma_2 r_t + \gamma_3 fii_t + \gamma_4 td\_reer_t + \varepsilon_t. \tag{1}$$

In Equation (1), res_t denotes the stock of reserves at time 't', im is the value of imports, r is the opportunity cost of holding reserves measured by Treasury bill rate, fii is included to capture the precautionary motive and is measured as the volatility of Foreign Intuitional Investment, and td_reer is included to account for mercantilist motive and is defined as the deviation of real effective exchange rate from its trend. Here γ_1, γ_2, γ_3, and γ_4 are the parameters to be estimated, γ_0 is the intercept, and ε_t stands for the error term. All variables are expressed in logarithmic form except td_reer.[1]

A positive relationship is expected between res and im since higher imports imply higher transactions, which leads to higher demand for reserves. The variable r is expected to have a negative relation with res because a higher opportunity cost is expected to lead to a reduction in reserve holdings as alternative investments become more attractive. The measure of precautionary motive, fii, is expected to have a positive sign because high volatility in short-term capital flows induces high reserve holdings as a precaution. The variable td_reer is also expected to be positively related with res because a positive td_reer indicates an undervalued real exchange rate of domestic to foreign currency and accordingly it would increase res.

The USA is known to be India's major trading partner and a large volume of foreign exchange transactions of the rupee takes place in US dollars. In keeping with this, Equation (1) has also been estimated by replacing td_reer by td_US, where td_US stands for undervalued exchange rate policy and is measured by taking the deviation of a real exchange rate of the rupee against the US dollar. The alternative reserve demand function can be written as

$$res_t = \gamma_0 + \gamma_1 im_t + \gamma_2 tb_t + \gamma_3 fii_t + \gamma_4 td\_US_t + \varepsilon_t. \tag{2}$$

The data sources, measurement of variables, estimation methods, and empirical results are discussed below.

3. Data

The reserve demand functions (Equations (1) and (2)) are estimated using monthly data from 1993:06, the beginning of Foreign Institution Investment in India, to 2007:03. Most of the data are collected from the RBI publications such as *Handbook of Statistics on Indian Economy* and monthly bulletin. The variables, namely, *res, im,* and *fii* are expressed in crores of rupees. The yield rate of the 91-day Treasury bill in

India has been used for measuring opportunity cost of holding reserves. In order to construct the real exchange rate of the rupee against the US dollar, the US Consumer Price Index (CPI) and Indian Wholesale Price Index (WPI) are used. The US CPI is drawn from the website of the US Bureau of Labor Statistics (www.bls.gov). The Indian WPI with base 1993–94 is converted into the base 1981–82 in order to make it comparable with the US CPI which has the base 1980. The variable *td_reer* is based on the monthly average index of Real Effective Exchange Rate (REER) of the Indian rupee (36-currency trade-based weights). The exchange rate is expressed as the number of domestic currency per unit of foreign currency and accordingly a rise in the exchange rate indicates depreciation and decline indicates an appreciation of the Indian rupee.

4. Econometric methodology

4.1. ARCH model

To generate the volatility measure of Foreign Institutional Investment, *fii*, we have applied the Autoregressive Heteroscedastic (ARCH) model developed by Engle (1982). The main advantages of the ARCH model compared to traditional volatility estimation method such as rolling standard deviation etc. are it helps to model the volatility clustering features of the data and incorporates hetero-scedasticity into the estimation procedure.[2] The ARCH(p) model specification can be written as

$$fii_t = \mu + \varepsilon_t$$
$$\varepsilon_t / \Omega_{t-1} \sim N(0, h_t)$$
(3)

$$h_t = \omega + \sum_{i=1}^{p} \alpha_i \varepsilon_{t-i}^2$$
(4)
$$\omega > 0; \alpha_1, \ldots, \alpha_p \geq 0.$$

Equation (3) is the conditional mean equation, where μ is the mean of *fii*$_t$. ε_t is the error term conditional on the information set Ω_{t-1} and is normally distributed with zero mean and variance h_t. Equation (4) is the variance equation which shows that the conditional variance h_t depends on mean ω and the information about the volatility from previous periods ε_{t-i}^2. The size and significance of α_i indicates the presence of the ARCH process or volatility clustering in the series.

4.2. HP filter method

The variables *td_reer* and *td_US*, which capture mercantilist motive, are derived using Hodrick and Prescott (1997) or the HP filter method. The HP filter is a smoothing method which obtains smooth estimates of the long-term trend component of a series. It has an advantage over the simple de-trending procedure based on the linear trend in that it is a time varying method and allows the trend to follow a stochastic process, whereas, the traditional method assumes that the trend series grows at a constant rate. The HP filter method computes the smoothed series of real effective exchange rate $reer^T$ by minimizing the variance of $reer$ around $reer^T$, subject to a penalty that constrains the second difference of $reer^T$. The HP filter chooses $reer^T$ to minimize

$$\sum_{i=t}^{n} (reer_t - reer_t^T)^2 + \lambda \sum_{t=2}^{n-1} (\Delta reer_{t+1}^T - \Delta reer_t^T)^2 \tag{5}$$

where λ is the smoothing parameter and n is the sample size. Here λ takes a value of 1,26,400 for the monthly series (Harvey and Jaeger 1993). The difference between the actual series $(reer_t)$ and the smoothed series $(reer_t^T)$ is the deviation of the real exchange rate from its trend td_reer.

4.3. ARDL approach to cointegration

Equations (1) and (2) are estimated using the Auto Regressive Distributed Lag (ARDL) cointegration procedure developed by Pesaran and Shin (1999) and Pesaran, Shin, and Smith (2001). This model has several advantages as compared to the standard multivariate cointegration test such as Johansen and Juselius (1990). One advantage is that this is a bound test procedure and it is simple to follow. This test can be applied irrespective of whether variables in the model are purely $I(0)$, purely $I(1)$, and mutually cointegrated. Therefore, this method eliminates the pre-testing problems associated with the standard cointegration test such as the classification of variables into $I(0)$ and $I(1)$.

The ARDL cointegration procedure involves two steps. The first step is to examine the existence of the long-run relationship between the variables in the model. If cointegration exists, the second step is to estimate the long-run and short-run coefficients using associated ARDL and error correction models (ECMs). The error correction model of the ARDL model pertaining to the variable in Equation (1) is as follows:

$$\Delta res_t = \alpha_0 + \lambda_1 res_{t-1} + \lambda_2 im_{t-1} + \lambda_3 tb_{t-1} + \lambda_4 fii_{t-1} + \lambda_5 td\_reer_{t-1} + \sum_{i=1}^{p} \beta_i \Delta res_{t-i}$$

$$+ \sum_{i=1}^{p} \delta_i \Delta im_{t-i} + \sum_{i=1}^{p} \gamma_i \Delta tb_{t-i} + \sum_{i=1}^{p} \phi_i \Delta fii_{t-i} + \sum_{i=1}^{p} \theta_i \Delta td\_reer_{t-i} + u_t. \tag{6}$$

In Equation (6), the first part of the RHS with parameter λ s represents the long-run relationship and the second part with β, δ, γ, ϕ, and θ represents the short-run dynamics of the model. To examine the existence of the long-run relationship between the dependent variable res and its determinants, an F-test procedure is followed for the joint significance of the coefficients of the lagged levels of the variables, for instance, $H_0 : \lambda_1 = \lambda_2 = \lambda_3 = \lambda_4 = \lambda_5 = 0$ against $H_1 :$ $\lambda_1 \neq \lambda_2 \neq \lambda_3 \neq \lambda_4 \neq \lambda_5 \neq 0$. If the null hypothesis is rejected then it indicates the existence of a long-run relationship or cointegration. Pesaran, Shin, and Smith (2001) propose lower and upper critical values for the F-statistic assuming all variables are $I(0)$ for the lower bound and all variables are $I(1)$ for the upper bound. If the computed F-statistic exceeds the upper critical value, then the null of no cointegration can be rejected irrespective of the order of integration of the variables. Conversely, if the test statistic falls below the lower critical bound, then the null of no cointegration cannot be rejected. However, if the test statistic falls between the lower and upper critical values, then the result is inconclusive.

If cointegration is established, then the long-run coefficients can be estimated by the ARDL model using the OLS method. Since the ARDL model assumes no serial correlation in errors, an appropriate lag level (m) should be chosen. We estimate a total of $(m + 1)^{k+1}$ different ARDL models, where k is the number of variables, and choose a model based on information criteria such as Akaike's information criterion (AIC) and or Schwarz's Bayesian information criterion (SBC). Then the short-run dynamics are estimated through the error correction model.

5. Empirical results

5.1. ARCH variance of Foreign Institutional Investment

The volatility of Foreign Institutional Investment or variable fii is estimated through the ARCH(2) model.[3] The results reported in Table 1 show that the ARCH effect is significant in the conditional variance. The model diagnostics do not indicate serial correlation in the standardized squared residuals or ARCH effect on residuals. The log of conditional variance series of net Foreign Institutional Investment is shown in Figure 2 and it shows that volatility has a tendency to increase over the period of time.

5.2. HP filter estimates for undervalued exchange rates

The measure of the undervalued exchange rate to capture mercantilist motive is constructed based on two real exchange rates, for instance, REER and the real exchange rate of the rupee against the US dollar. The real exchange rate of the rupee against the US dollar is constructed using the following formula:

$$\begin{aligned} &\textit{Real exchange rate of rupee in terms of US dollar} \\ &= \textit{Nominal exchange rate} * (\textit{US price level}/\textit{Indian price level}). \end{aligned} \qquad (6)$$

where US CPI is taken as the US price level and Indian WPI is taken as a proxy for the Indian price level. The deviation of the real exchange rates from its trend series

Table 1. ARCH(2) results of Foreign Institutional Investment.

$fii_t =$	122.48	$+0.734\,fii_{t-1}$	$+\,\varepsilon t$
	$[1.90]$***	$[33.4]$*	
$h_t =$	166,923.3	$+0.589\,\varepsilon_{t-1}^2$	$+1.12\,\varepsilon_{t-2}^2$
	$[7.93]$*	$[3.91]$*	$[6.557]$*

Log-likelihood $= -1398$, SR LB $\chi^2 = 8.49$ (0.58), SSR LB $\chi^2 = 7.70$ (0.65), ARCH $= 0.82$ (0.60)

Note: SR $=$ standardized residuals, SSR $=$ standardized squared residual, LB $=$ Ljung–Box statistics for serial correlation at 10 lags. ARCH $=$ LM test for ARCH effects in the residuals. * and *** denote significance at 1 and 10% levels, respectively. Figures in square brackets and parentheses show t-statistics and level of significance, respectively.

from the HP filter method is shown in Figures 3 and 4. Figure 3 shows that the series contains more positive values indicating an undervalued real exchange rate of the rupee against the US dollar.[4] However, Figure 4 exhibits somewhat mixed results.

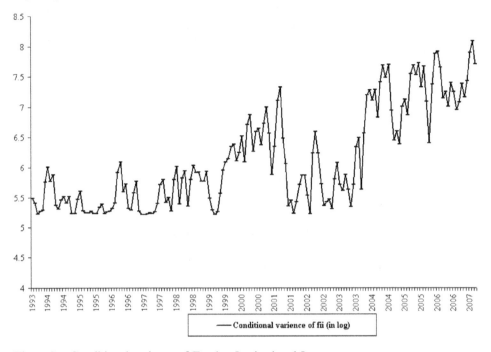

Figure 2.   Conditional variance of Foreign Institutional Investment.

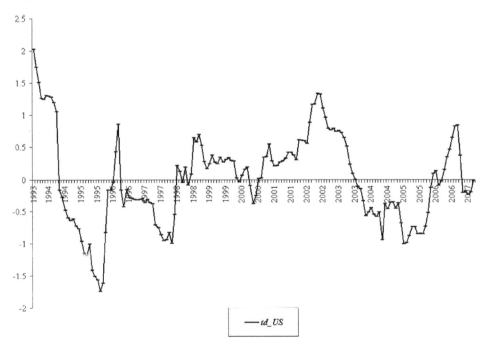

Figure 3.   Deviation of the rupee vs. US dollar real exchange rate from its trend.

5.3. ARDL approach to cointegration

To estimate the reserve demand equations (1) and (2), the ARDL approach to cointegration is used.[5] Table 2 displays the calculated *F*-statistics for the two equations up to level lag 4.

In the case of Equation (1), the estimated *F*-statistic values are below the lower critical value 3.28 at the 5% level. This implies that the null of no cointegration cannot be rejected. However, in the case of Equation (2), the null of no cointegration can be rejected at the 5% level up to lag 4, implying that there exists a long-run relationship or cointegration between reserves and its determinates. The absence of cointegration in the case of Equation (1) may be because the variable *td_reer* may not be cointegrated with *res*. This may be due to the fact that RBI may not be targeting REER (Patnaik 2003).

Having established the cointegration relationship in the case of Equation (2), the next step is to estimate the long-run coefficients of the equation by using the ARDL specification. The ARDL specification assumes that the errors are serially uncorrelated and therefore we choose maximum lag as 4 where no autocorrelation

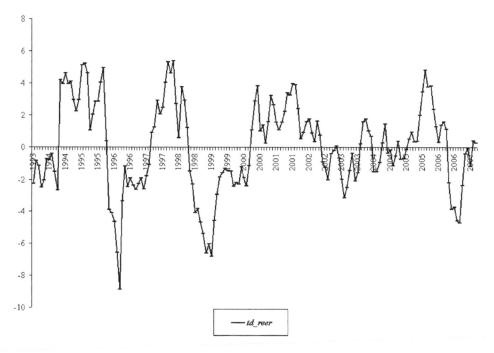

Figure 4. Deviation of REER from its trend.

Table 2. Results from bound test.

Lag	1	2	3	4
Equation (1)	3.03	2.25	2.73	3.34
Equation (2)	5.249*	5.663*	6.580*	6.673*

Note: The critical bound for the 5% level in the case of five variables including constant is 3.28–4.39.

is found in Equation (2). The optimum ARDL order suggested by SBC and AIC is found to be the order of ARDL(1, 0, 0, 0, 0) and ARDL(1, 1, 0, 0, 4). The estimated long-run coefficients of ARDL models suggested by the SBC and AIC criteria are shown in Table 3.

The long-run coefficients show that all regressors in the reserve demand equation exhibit the theoretically expected sign and are statistically significant at the 10% level or better. The import elasticity is found to be 0.51 and significant at 10% in the model selected by SBC criteria, which indicates a 1% increase in imports increases the reserve by 0.51%. The measure of opportunity cost of reserve holdings tb is found to be highly significant in this context. The opportunity cost plays an important role in the theoretical model of demand for reserves. Most of the empirical studies are unable to find its significant effect on reserve demand.[6] However, Ben-Bassat and Gottlieb (1992) argued that when the opportunity cost is measured appropriately, it can be a significant determinant of reserve demand.

The estimated coefficient of fii is 0.1 and is significant at the 10% level. This implies that a rise in volatility in Foreign Institutional Investment by 1% increases

Table 3. Estimated long-run coefficients using ARDL approach.

Regressors	SBC-ARDL [1, 0, 0, 0, 0]	AIC-ARDL [1, 1, 0, 0, 4]
Constant	8.748 [1.94]***	7.90 [2.86]*
im	0.515 [1.94]***	0.554 [1.90]***
tb	−1.426 [−4.05]*	−1.267 [−3.59]*
fii	0.106 [1.76]***	0.116 [1.71]***
td_US	0.267 [2.12]**	0.394 [2.26]**

Note: *, **, and *** denote significance at 1, 5, and 10% levels, respectively

Table 4. Error correction representation for the ARDL model.

Variables	Model selection criteria	
	SBC	AIC
Constant	0.434 [5.60]***	0.370 [−2.77]*
$\Delta\, im_t$	0.0255 [1.255]	0.070 [2.59]*
$\Delta\, tb_t$	−0.070 [−4.67]*	−0.059 [−3.90]*
$\Delta\, fii_t$	0.005 [2.21]*	0.005 [2.33]*
$\Delta\, td\_US_t$	0.0132 [3.23]*	0.002 [0.21]
$\Delta\, td\_US_{t-1}$		0.019 [1.70]***
$\Delta\, td\_US_{t-2}$		0.179 [1.61]
Δtd_US_{t-3}		0.019 [1.70]***
ecm_{t-1}	−0.049 [−3.12]*	−0.046 [−2.77]*
Adjusted R^2	0.211	0.281
χ^2_{AC}	1.60 (0.80)	1.78 (0.65)
χ^2_{ARCH}	3.42 (0.49)	0.74 (0.94)
χ^1_{FF}	0.001 (0.96)	0.033 (0.85)

Note: χ^2_{AC}, χ^2_{ARCH} are LM statistics for serial correlation and for ARCH effect in residual at lag 4, and χ^2_{FF} = LM statistics for functional form misspecification. *, **, and *** are statistically significantly different from zero at 1, 5, and 10% levels, respectively. Figures in square brackets and parentheses show t-statistics and level of significance, respectively.

reserve holdings by 0.1% which is evidence of the precautionary motive of reserve accumulation against volatile capital flows. A more or less similar result is reported by Choi and Baek (2006) in their cross-country study of the effect of portfolio flow volatility on reserve demand.

The variable associated with mercantilist concern, td_US, also exhibits a positive sign and is statistically significant at the 5% level. This finding indicates that a real depreciation of the rupee against the US dollar leads to an increase in reserves. This validates the argument that the undervalued exchange rate policies by the RBI against the US dollar leads to reserve accumulation in India. The short-run dynamics of the reserve demand function is estimated by error correction representation of the ARDL(1, 0, 0, 0, 0) shown in Table 4.

The signs of the short-run coefficients are consistent with theoretical predictions and are statistically significant at the 5% level except imports in the SBC model. The error correction term (ecm_{t-1}) is significant at the 1% level and has the expected sign. The estimated coefficient of error correction term (-0.049) indicates that around 5% of the deviation from equilibrium is eliminated within one month. The diagnostics statistics reported in Table 4 do not show any autocorrelation and

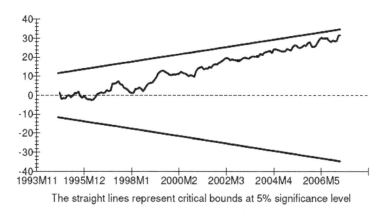

The straight lines represent critical bounds at 5% significance level

Figure 5.   Plot of cumulative sum of recursive residuals.

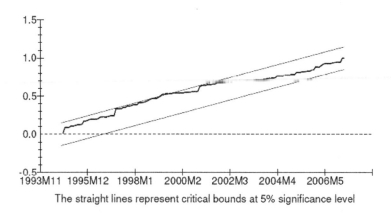

The straight lines represent critical bounds at 5% significance level

Figure 6.   Plot of cumulative sum of squares of recursive residuals.

ARCH effect in the residuals of the error correction model. The functional form test also does not indicate any misspecification in the model. Moreover, the cumulative sum (CUSUM) and cumulative sum of squares (CUSUMQ) plots based on the recursive residual shown in Figures 5 and 6 do not show evidence of any instability of the coefficients across sample periods.

6. Conclusion

This study has empirically investigated the importance of precautionary and mercantilist motives to holding international reserves in the Indian context using monthly data from 1993 to 2007. The empirical long-run reserve demand function includes explanatory variables such as imports, opportunity cost measure, Foreign Institutional Investment volatility to account for precautionary motive, and the deviation of real exchange rate from its trend to capture the mercantilist motive. The volatility series of Foreign Institutional Investment is derived from the ARCH model and the deviation of real exchange rate from its trend is derived from the HP filter method. Two measures of real exchange rate are used in the study, namely, REER and real exchange rate of the rupee against the US dollar to measure mercantilist motive.

The ARDL approach to cointegration developed by Pesaran, Shin, and Smith (2001) is used to estimate the reserve demand function. The cointegration results indicate a long-run equilibrium relationship between reserves and its determinants when the mercantilist motive is measured with the real exchange rate of the rupee against the US dollar, but not with REER. Our estimates of the preferred Equation (2) indicate that the variables associated with precautionary motive as well as mercantilist motive are statistically significant in determining reserves. Further, the mercantilist motive is found to be more significant than the precautionary motive during the period of study.

In sum, our study reveals that accumulation of reserves in India is not only due to greater exposure to volatility of short-term capital flows but also due to the undervalued exchange rate policies of RBI against the US dollar implying that both precautionary as well as mercantilist motive are important in explaining international reserve accumulation in India over the period of study.

Acknowledgements

This is a revised version of the paper presented at the '10th Annual Conference on Money and Finance in the Indian Economy' held at Indira Gandhi Institute of Development Research, Bombay, January 2008. The authors are thankful to Mr Anjaneyulu and Dr Charan Singh, Reserve Bank of India, for their valuable comments and suggestions. The authors are solely responsible for any errors in the paper.

Notes

1. The series of real exchange rate from its trend contains negative values.
2. See Bollerslev (1986).
3. We also estimated the volatility series using the GARCH model. However, the results are not stable.
4. It may be noted that the nominal exchange rate of the rupee against the US dollar appreciated during the period 2003–2007 and steeply after April 2007. However, the present analysis is confined up to March 2007.
5. It is found from the unit root test that all variables are $I(1)$ except td_reer, td_US_t.
6. See the review paper on demand for international reserves by Bahmani-Oskooee (1985).

References

Aizenman, J., and J. Lee. 2005. International reserves: Precautionary versus mercantilist views, theory and evidence. NBER Working Paper 11366, National Bureau of Economic Research.

Aizenman, J., J. Lee, and Y. Rhee. 2007. International reserve management and capital mobility in a volatile world: Policy considerations and a case study of Korea. *Journal of the Japanese and International Economics* 21: 1–15.

Bahmani-Oskooee, M. 1985. Demand for international reserves: Survey of recent empirical studies. *Applied Economics* 17: 359–75.

Ben-Bassat, A., and D. Gottlieb. 1992. On the effect of opportunity cost on international reserve holdings. *The Review of Economics and Statistics* 74: 329–32.

Bollerslev, T. 1986. Generalized autoregressive conditional heteroskedasticity. *Journal of Econometrics* 31: 307–27.

Calvo, G.A. 1998. Capital flows and capital-market crises: The simple economics of sudden stops. *Journal of Applied Economics* 1: 35–54.

Choi, C., and S.G. Baek. 2006. Portfolio-flow volatility and demand for international reserves. *Seoul Journal of Economics* 19: 199–214.

Dooley, M., D. Folkerts-Landau, and P. Garber. 2003. An essay on the revived Bretton Woods system. NBER Working Paper 9971, National Bureau of Economic Research.

Edwards, S. 2004. Thirty years of current account imbalances, current account reversals, and sudden stops. IMF Staff Paper 51 (Special Issue), International Monetary Fund, Washington, DC.

Engle, R.F. 1982. Autoregressive conditional hetroscedasticity. *Journal of Econometrics* 31: 307–27.

Harvey, A.C., and A. Jaeger. 1993. Detrending, stylized facts and the business cycle. *Journal of Applied Econometrics* 8: 231–47.

Hodrick, R.J., and E.C. Prescott. 1997. Post war US business cycle: An empirical investigation. *Journal of Money, Credit and Banking* 29: 1–16.

IMF. 2007. *IMF annual report*. Washington, DC: International Monetary Fund.

Johansen, S., and K. Juselius. 1990. Maximum likelihood estimation and inference on cointegration with applications to the demand for money. *Oxford Bulletin of Economics and Statistics* 52: 169–210.

Patnaik, I. 2003. India's policy stance on reserves and the currency. Technical Report, ICRIER Working Paper 108, Indian Council for Research on International Economic Relations, New Delhi.

Pesaran, M.H., and Y. Shin. 1999. Testing for the existence of a long-run relationship. DAE Working Paper 9622, Department of Applied Economics, University of Cambridge.

Pesaran, M.H., Y. Shin, and R.J. Smith. 2001. Bounds testing approaches to the analysis of long-run relationships. *Journal of Applied Econometrics* 16: 289–326.

Prabheesh, K.P., D. Malathy, and R. Madhumathi. 2007. Demand for foreign exchange reserves in India: A cointegration approach. *South Asian Journal of Management* 14: 36–46.

Ramachandran, M., and N. Srinivasan. 2007. Asymmetric exchange rate intervention and international reserve accumulation in India. *Economic Letters* 94: 259–65.

RBI. 2007. Report on foreign exchange reserves, Reserve Bank of India, Mumbai.

India's fiscal and monetary framework: growth in an opening economy

Ashima Goyal*

Since a crisis is a shock impinging on a system, the response can be used to deduce aspects of the system's structure. Analysis of the crisis and recovery suggests aggregate supply in India is elastic but subject to upward shocks. This has implications for cyclical policy and for fiscal consolidation. Both monetary and fiscal policy should identify measures that would reduce costs, while avoiding too large a demand contraction. Specific policies are identified and Indian policies evaluated.

Introduction

India's opening out coincided with a period of major global crises. The institutional changes that opened out a closed economy were the background in which fiscal and monetary policy had to respond to external shocks and domestic cycles while maintaining high growth with low inflation and ensuring fiscal sustainability. There were clear benefits such as a higher trend growth rate, and emergence of new growth foci. Growth was no longer government driven. But were these outcomes due to good luck or good policy? Was policy able to smooth cycles and external shocks or did it magnify them? India itself did not have a financial crisis although growth became volatile. How did it deal with policy trilemmas created by a more open capital account? What improvements does the experience of crisis and exit suggest for short- and long-term policy strategies? The chapter analyzes the fiscal and monetary policy combination, the extent of stabilization, and extracts lessons for strategies that would benefit India while contributing to global adjustment.

Policies were procyclical in the early reform years, but the response to the Global Financial Crisis (GFC) demonstrated the effectiveness of countercyclical macroeconomic policies, while making clear the importance of supply-side factors for Indian inflation and of demand for output. During exit, early resurgence of inflation before recovery was well established created problems for policy. The chapter argues action consistent with structure and shocks can increase growth yet reduce inflation. Exchange rate regimes can contribute to these objectives, while reducing risk taking and dealing with surges of capital. It also analyzes other ways in which the shocks of opening out can be handled before concluding with an analysis of fiscal sustainability.

---

* This is a revised version of a paper written for the October 2010 ICRIER-InWEnt-DIE Conference in Mumbai. I thank InWEnt for the invitation, Francis Xavier Rathinam, Ina Dettmann-Busch and conference participants for useful comments, Sanchit Arora and Shruti Tripathi for research and Reshma Aguiar for secretarial assistance.

Policy recommendations include further fine-tuning stabilization policies. Short-run strategies include early, forward-looking, and therefore mild, policy responses. Instead of relying solely on reducing demand to bring down inflation, an announced conditional adjustment path to anchor inflationary expectations and prevent the second-round wage-price effects is a supply-side policy that reduces costs. Exchange rate appreciation is another monetary measure. Short-term fiscal measures include tax-tariff rates, freer imports, and better management of food stocks. If policy created shocks work in the opposite direction to temporary supply shocks they may abort inflation, even while demand is stabilized. More flexibility of the exchange rate allows a smoother and more counter-cyclical interest rate. Since the exchange rate contributes to lowering inflation, the Central Bank's ability to adapt interest rates to the domestic cycle increases.

Longer-term strategies to reduce the distortions that create chronic inflation include raising agricultural productivity, improving infrastructure and delivery of public services. Gradual but transparent movement towards capital account convertibility has to deepen domestic markets and risk-taking ability before allowing riskier types of foreign capital inflows. Growth will improve the fiscal position provided reforms ensure the necessary quantity and quality of expenditure for alleviating supply side bottlenecks. Incentives to improve compliance, such as selective expenditure caps and targets for individual ministries as part of better accounting and management systems are required. Caps imply countercyclical deficits as revenue falls in bad times.

Temporary widening of the current account deficit would support India's investment cycle. Short-term exchange rate appreciation would reduce inflationary pressures and the cost of imports required in the high investment phase, while contributing to demand in other countries facing a slowdown. Countries that help finance Indian infrastructure would be benefiting from Indian growth that creates demand for their own products. Reforms in the global financial architecture would reduce the necessity of self- insurance and the cost of engaging with the world, and enable faster liberalization. High transitional growth looks feasible for India but an appropriate fiscal and monetary framework can ensure it is stable and sustainable.

Crisis and Exit

This GFC faulted two myths that the media and mainstream analysts propagate about the Indian macroeconomy. Namely: inflation always indicates capacity constraints, and rising deficits are always a major risk. It is important to point this out because the same myths are reviving as time passes.

There are two types of errors made. The first assumes the final goal applies now so mature economy macroeconomic concepts can be uncritically applied to India. The second that nothing has changed so new policy instruments do not work. Macroeconomic policy had largely aggravated the effects of shocks rather than moderated them. But following the global demand push showed us that countercyclical macroeconomic policy was feasible and it worked. The RBI was able to manage higher government borrowings to limit crowding out of private borrowing, for example through preponing government borrowing in the period of slack private demand.

Table 1 shows the sharp monetary tightening raising short rates above 9 percent in the summer of 2008 precipitated a collapse in industrial output even before the September fall of Lehman. The tightening came after a period of high growth. The economy was feared to be overheating and inflation, following the international spike in fuel and food, was high. A demand shock, with a near vertical supply curve should affect inflation more than

Table 1.   Crisis and Exit: Vs and Us in India.

Indicators	2008-09: Q1-Q4				2009-10: Q1-Q4				2010-11: Q1-Q4			
Growth (Y-o-Y) (%)	Q1	Q2	Q3	Q4	Q1	Q2	Q3	Q4	Q1	Q2	Q3	Q4
Real GDP	7.8	7.5	6.1	5.8	6.3	8.6	7.3	8.6	8.8	8.9	8.2	7.8
Agriculture	3.2	2.4	-1.4	1.3	1.8	1.2	-1.6	1.1	2.4	5.4	9.9	7.5
Industry	5.3	4.6	0.3	2.5	2.9	6.3	10.0	10.8	11.7	8.9	5.7	6.1
Services	9.8	9.6	11.4	8.3	8.5	10.8	9.2	9.2	9.4	9.6	8.7	8.7
Private Final Consumption Expenditure	8.4	7.6	6.4	5.1	7.4	7.7	6.5	7.2	8.9	8.9	8.6	8.0
Government Final Consumption Expenditure	3.7	7.5	59.0	2.5	14.9	30.2	3.8	0.6	6.7	6.4	1.9	4.9
GFCF	6.5	7.3	-0.1	2.7	-2.2	-1.2	6.3	19.5	17.4	11.9	7.8	0.4
Inflation (Y-o-Y) (%)												
WPI	9.6	12.5	8.6	3.2	0.5	-0.1	5.0	10.2	11.0	9.3	8.9	9.3
CPI- Industrial Workers	7.8	9.0	10.2	9.5	8.9	11.6	13.2	15.1	13.6	10.5	9.3	9.0
Money and Credit Growth (Y-o-Y) (%)												
Broad Money	22.3	20.3	19.9	19.9	21.0	20.4	18.7	16.9	15.1	15.5	17.5	16.5
Banks Credit	24.9	25.5	26.8	19.2	16.5	14.4	10.4	15.9	18.3	15.8	16.4	16.9
Interest Rates (%)												
Overnight (call) money	6.8	9.5	7.8	4.2	3.2	3.2	3.2	3.3	4.2	5.4	6.6	6.8
10-year g-sec	8.3	8.9	6.6	8.5	6.7	7.3	7.6	7.8	7.6	7.9	8.0	8.1
Foreign Trade (Y-o-Y) (%)												
Export Growth (%)	57.0	39.6	-8.4	-20.2	-16.0	-17.9	-9.1	3.6	10.0	10.7	24.8	25.0
Import Growth (%)	49.0	61.2	7.4	-25.8	-8.8	-16.2	0.6	18.1	15.5	11.6	0.4	10.3
Balance of Payments (US $ billion)												
Current Account Deficit (-)	-3.4	-12.3	-11.9	-0.4	-4.2	-9.1	-12.2	-12.8	-12.5	-16.8	-9.7	
Net Capital Flows	5.0	4.3	-5.1	1.6	13.1	17.2	8.7	12.2	7.5	21.8	8.4	
Reserve Outstanding	312.1	286.3	256.0	252.0	265.1	281.3	283.5	279.1	275.7	292.8	297.3	304.8

Source: RBI, CSO, and GOI websites
http://mospi.nic.in/Mospi_New/upload/mospi_press_releases.htm

output. But the reverse happened. The wholesale price index (WPI) did not fall until November when Indian fuel prices fell, but the consumer price index remained high. The V shaped recovery also indicates a reduction in demand rather than more intractable destruction of capacity.

A rise in government consumption compensated, in a well-calibrated countercyclical fiscal impulse, for the fall in private consumption and investment, and contributed to the quick recovery. An expanding fiscal deficit made this possible. Countercyclical deficits are compatible with overall fiscal consolidation.

The episode also countered the belief that demand is interest inelastic in India, and output is supply determined. The impact of recently freed interest rates on elasticities, in particular on consumer durable spending, housing, etc. was yet to be fully understood. The table shows only a short lag from policy rates to industry; 2-3 quarters for a fall and one quarter for a sharp rise. Policy rates have impacted output growth since 1996.

The table also shows that a rise in policy rates almost immediately impacts gross fixed capital formation (GFCF) while a cut takes effect after a 3-4 quarter lag. The revival of foreign inflows had an almost immediate impact on both industry and capital formation. The rise in exports followed the industrial recovery. Growth in GFCF was negative for a year starting from the quarter that Lehman collapsed even though real interest rates remained very low since inflation continued high.

The crisis response was fast but the resurgence of inflation before recovery was firmly established led to policy dilemmas regarding exit. The sharp resurgence of WPI inflation by Q3 of 2009 was regarded as surprising since industry had barely recovered. But it should have been expected given the impact of sustained high CPI inflation on wages. Because of the latter, the manufacturing price index fell only for a few months, and had risen to its November 2008 value of 203 by April 2009. A booming economy does add pricing power, but supply side shocks explain even manufacturing inflation. Arguments that the economy was overheating were probably incorrect because of the sharp rebound in investment after the four-quarter slump, while growth in private consumption and bank credit remained low. Growth in government consumption also slowed sharply as investment recovered. But not enough was done to anchor inflationary expectations and to reduce constraints in agricultural markets. A poor monsoon in 2009 and protracted rains in 2010 aggravated food price inflation. CPI inflation finally began to fall with a bumper harvest in 2011.

The response to early signs of industrial inflation was delayed, given the very large cut in interest rates that had to be reversed. The delay led to too fast a pace of increase in interest rates[1] and to quantitative tightening. The latter contributed to volatility in interest rates and in industrial output. Government expenditure pumped into the informal sector increased demand for food. Demand for currency actually increased and financial disintermediation occurred. Financing for firms was coming from abroad as domestic credit growth remained slow. Firming oil prices added to wage pressures from food inflation and costs rose. Liquidity remained tight and demand contracted. Growth in industrial production softened and that in investment also fell sharply in Q1 of 2011.

If policy is better based on structure and shocks, it could more successfully smooth cycles and maintain growth. As elasticities increase and systems become more complex, blunt instruments should be phased out, and policies designed to reduce sharp changes. The next section extracts the structural aspects that are consistent with the crisis shocks and outcomes before examining implications for policy.

Structure and Shocks

Mainstream macroeconomic analysis is adapted to a modern economy. Issues relating to the large informal sector, which still accounts for the major share of employment, are relegated to development economics. But once a populous emerging market crosses a critical threshold and high catch-up growth is established, higher labor mobility blurs the distinction between formal and informal sectors. A macroeconomics of the aggregate

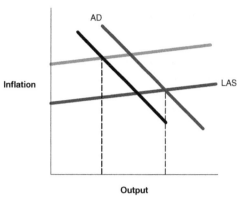

Figure 1. Aggregate demand and supply.

economy is both necessary and feasible. Aggregate labor supply is elastic as a large labor force shifts to more productive occupations.

In India, even as higher productivity releases labor from traditional occupations, the demographic profile ensures a steady stream of youthful entrants to the work force. Improvements in education supply, and more important, the returns to acquiring an education, ensure that new entrants have adequate skills. Finance is no longer a constraint. A larger share of earners and higher per capita income growth with sticky consumption habits raise aggregate savings; financial deepening improves intermediation of savings, and freer capital inflows complement domestic savings.

For all these reasons, the modern NKE apparatus (Woodford, 2003), which takes labor as the input into aggregate production, and allows specific distortions to be included, can be applied. In this framework capital is not a binding constraint since it is a produced means of production. The major distortion to be modeled, for an emerging market (EM) like India, is the dualistic labor market.

The longer-run aggregate supply (LAS) is elastic (Figure 1), since increasing output levels do not increase marginal cost, as capacity can be expanded and labor is available without a rise in wages. But inefficiencies, distortions and cost shocks tend to push costs upwards over the entire range, rather than only at full employment. For example, a rise in administered prices will raise costs independently of the level at which output is produced. The LAS becomes vertical only as the economy matures and full productive employment is reached. This framework differs from the early idea that output cannot be demand determined in a developing economy because of supply bottlenecks (Rao, 1952). Here output is demand determined but the supply-side raises costs. It also differs from the structural school that while industrial output is demand determined agricultural output is fixed at a time period. The difference arises because in an open economy supply bottlenecks are easier to alleviate. Even agricultural commodities can be imported, and the share of agriculture shrinks.

Even so, the food price wage cycle is an important mechanism propagating price shocks and creating inflationary expectations in India, given low per capita incomes, and the large share of food in the consumption basket. If markets are perfectly clearing and prices and wages are flexible, then a fall in one price balances a rise in another with no effect on the aggregate price level. But prices and wages rise more easily than they fall. So, a rise in a critical price raises wages and therefore other prices, generating inflation. Some relative prices, among them food prices and the exchange rate, have more of such an impact.

Food prices are critical for inflation in India and, since international food inflation now influences domestic, the exchange rate becomes relevant.

Political pressures from farmers push up farm support prices, with consumption subsidies also going up. But these are inadequate due to corruption and failures of targeting, so nominal wages rise with a lag pushing up costs and generating second round inflation from a temporary supply shock. This political economy indexes wages informally to food price inflation. Political support also raises wages through minimum wages and employment schemes such as MGNREGA. If the rise in subsistence wages exceeds that in agricultural productivity, prices rise propagating inflation. This happened after 2008 with MGNREGA as States competed with each other in raising minimum wages since the Centre was footing the bill. Given an exit option, workers' could extract large jumps in wages.

Monsoon failures or international oil price shocks have been dominant inflation triggers. But sustained inflation requires monetary accommodation. Prior to the nineties monetary policy routinely accommodated the populist rise in deficits. After the reforms, discontinuation of ad-hoc treasury bills, and other measures of monetary autonomy, prevented automatic financing of deficits. But the reforms did not resolve supply side issues. Government spending continued to be populist. Sharp monetary tightening to reduce demand was the response to a cost shock, given political sensitivity to inflation. But a leftward shift of the demand curve along an elastic supply curve, pushed up due to supply shocks or cost creep, results in a high output loss with little effect on inflation. Administered prices would be increased after monetary tightening. So while sometimes they served as inflation triggers, at others they formed a floor ratcheting prices upwards and imparting an upward bias to inflation.

Structural VAR based tests, time series causality tests, GMM regressions of AD and AS, and calibrations in a DSGE model for such an economy (Goyal, 2011b) all support the elastic longer-run supply and the dominance of supply shocks[2].

Calibration of exit based on this structure would include a mild early tightening, signaling reversal of accommodation, together with supply-side polices. This should be sufficient to anchor inflationary expectations and shift down the supply curve. Lower interest rates would further encourage the supply response. This is an example of successful anticipation and prevention given knowledge of structure and behavior. Instead of relying solely on reducing demand to bring down inflation, both short-term monetary and fiscal policies should shift down the supply curve. For example, exchange rate appreciation, or fiscal measures such as tax-tariff rates, and freer imports. Policy created shocks working in the opposite direction to temporary supply shocks could abort inflation. Longer-term strategies to reduce distortions that create an upward creep in the supply curve, include raising agricultural productivity, changing the composition and effectiveness of public spending, improving infrastructure and delivery of public services.

Since the exchange rate regime can contribute to the above, to managing capital flows, and to coordination of the global exit, we examine it in more detail in the next section.

The Exchange Rate Regime

There has been considerable evolution in India's exchange rate regime over the reform years. The shift has been from a nominal fix to one-way movement over the nineties to two-way with low volatility implying a tightly managed exchange rate, to greater volatility and nominal movement after the global crisis (Figure 2).

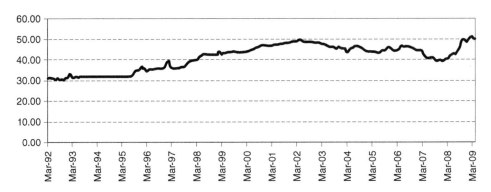

Figure 2.   End of Month Exchange Rate.

Concerns to prevent appreciation in the context of a trade deficit, large but volatile inflows, and higher Indian inflation, led to reserve accumulation, a tendency for nominal depreciation, and relative constancy of the real exchange rate around the real effective exchange rate (REER) established after the double devaluation in the early nineties.

But theory (Cordon, 2002, Svensson, 2000) suggests the exchange rate regime can aid other policy objectives in addition to encouraging exports and contributing to macroeconomic stabilization. It can neutralize inflationary commodity shocks, and reduce the risk taking that leads to a currency crisis. With more two-way short-term variation, more objectives can be accommodated, through more sophisticated strategies

The average daily turnover in Indian foreign exchange (FX) markets had the fastest world growth rate from about US $3.0 billion in 2001, to US $34 billion in 2007, but has slowed down since (BIS, 2010). Since deepening occurred from very low levels, FX markets still have a long way to go. So periods of high volatility tend to be associated with external shocks such as the East Asian crisis (1995-98), the dot com bust and dollar decline in the new century, and the sub-prime and global economic crisis since 2007. In between there were large stretches of time with low volatility. Movements in the Euro Dollar rate strongly affected Rupee movements.

Even so, development helped the economy absorb much larger movements in capital and reserve changes in the global crisis compared to the East Asian crisis with a smaller growth contraction (Table 2). This time the interest rate defense was not used—more exchange rate flexibility was accepted. The rise in policy rates in 2008 was more in response to food and oil price shocks. It preceded the outflow-induced depreciation, and was reversed when outflows started.

After the immediate crisis, the RBI intervened less[3], letting portfolio capital flows affect the exchange rate although continuing restrictions on debit flows did moderate flow volatility. The guiding hand deserted the markets. Swings in nominal and real exchange rates exceeded ten percent. Intervention may have been lower in order to conserve reserves at a time of great uncertainty, as the fear of floating gave way to a fear of reserve depletion, and also because reviving inflows more or less matched a widening current account deficit. But the resulting changes in the exchange rate were often opposite to what was required for macro stabilization.

Table 2.   Comparing volatilities during two external crises.

Year	Foreign portfolio inflows (FPI)(USDb)	Call money rate (CMR)	Change in reserves (- increase) (USDb)	Rate of Growth (GDP)
1994-95	3.8	15.32	-4.6	6.4
1995-96	2.8	34.83	2.9	7.3
1997-98	1.8	28.7	-3.9	4.3
1998-99	-0.1	10.04	-3.8	6.7
2007-08	29.4	8.33	-92.2	9.0
2008-09	-13.9	10.62	20.1	6.7

Note: The CMR is the highest average rate in any month of a year.

Figure 3 shows monthly changes in WPI, CPI, IIP and average inflation. In 2007 an appreciating exchange rate helped keep inflation low although oil and food prices were firming up internationally. But outflows began just as cost shocks pushed up prices. In March 2008 WPI inflation was at 7 percent. In May depreciation began and in June the WPI reached 12 percent. The supply shocks turned out to be temporary, as oil prices crashed in September, so avoiding depreciation could have moderated inflation. Instead inflation contributed to the decision to raise policy rates sharply although industrial growth was softening, and the growth collapsed.

Outflows and depreciation contributed to high CPI inflation despite a WPI which was negative due to the slump in world oil prices. The exchange rate fluctuated, reached its lowest level, falling below 51 in March 2009, and began sustained appreciation in April as inflows revived with Indian growth. Appreciation before export growth had recovered worked against the macroeconomic stimulus. It could not reduce the CPI inflation because of the effect of failed monsoons in raising food prices, which have a large weight in the CPI. As CPI finally fell in February 2010, outflows due to the Greek crisis depreciated the exchange rate and both WPI and CPI rose again.

Thus the depreciations in May 2008 and May 2010 due to external events and a resulting flight to safety aggravated inflation. In thin markets large foreign capital movements can cause excessive exchange rate fluctuations, which also hurt the real sector. If a central bank does not buy/sell a currency that is not freely traded internationally, sharp spikes occur.

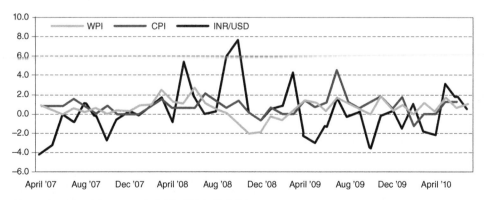

Figure 3.   Monthly change in WPI, CPI, INR/USD.

India cannot as yet let capital flows determine the exchange rate as a full float under capital account convertibility would imply. But the middle ground is large, and more flexibility is feasible. In the exit, since Indian inflation is higher than in the rest of the world, short-term appreciation can import low inflation at the same time increasing export demand from other countries and increasing their output. By reducing the need for a sharp rise in interest rates it will help maintain higher Indian growth, and contribute to world demand. Otherwise the inflation differential will anyway cause a real appreciation. Depreciation can follow, depending on the current account balance, after inflation subsides. Recovering world demand would help India reduce its trade deficit. In addition, active non-price polices, including diversification of destinations, could encourage exports. This was demonstrated as exports grew sharply from end 2010 without substantial depreciation of the exchange rate.

The exchange rate has the shortest lag among monetary policy transmission channels. Oil dominates India's imports. Since these are quoted in dollars pass through of the exchange rate is high. As border prices begin to affect domestic food prices, the exchange rate also becomes important for the domestic political economy. Some agricultural liberalization and falling world food prices in the nineties did reduce political pressures on procurement prices. Inflation fell. Since appreciation following an adverse supply shock lowers intermediate goods and food prices, it pre-empts the effect of temporary supply shocks on the domestic price-wage process. Lower food price inflation would reduce the necessity for subsidies and administered prices that distort incentives and lower efficiency. Building in a rule whereby there is an automatic exchange rate response to a supply shock avoids the tendency to do nothing until it becomes necessary to over-react. Actions linked to exogenous shocks also avoid moral hazard.

Such nominal changes can counter temporary shocks. But permanent shocks require productivity improvements. Without a rise in productivity, inflation would add real to the nominal appreciation, requiring nominal depreciation to correct overvaluation.

Some exchange rate volatility also forces hedging to reduce currency risk. As risks reduce so does the probability of currency crises. But too predictable or unidirectional movements encourage speculative positions. Despite steady reforms in Indian foreign exchange (FX) markets and some two-way rupee movement, firms lost large amounts from bets on a trend appreciation when the global financial crisis led to large depreciation. Movement in a 10 band is sufficient to make such positions unattractive since potential losses from an incorrect position become large. Volatile movements above that level invite excessive entry of uninformed traders and below that level reduce the risk to speculative one-way bets on the exchange rate. So a plus minus five percent band is the volatility level a managed float should aim at.

Limited volatility is consistent with maintaining a trend competitive real effective exchange rate. There is evidence such volatility does not have a large effect on trade while currency crises adversely affect trade. If crises are avoided, interest rates lowered, and the exchange rate kept near competitive rates, trade is benefited.

Free capital flows and a fixed exchange rate make monetary policy ineffective since it is tied to maintaining the fixed exchange rate. The domestic interest rate must equal the international rate since any policy induced departure would lead to a flood of inflows and in order to maintain the fixed exchange rate policy must absorb the inflows, changing money supply in the process until the domestic interest rate is back in alignment with the international rate. For example, buying dollars to prevent appreciation when dollars flood in, if the domestic short interest rate exceeds the US interest rate, raises money supply and reduces the domestic interest rate. The incompatibility of independent monetary policy with free capital flows and a fixed exchange rate is known as the impossible trinity. Since the interest rate also has to cover expected depreciation it becomes volatile. Relative variation in nominal interest exceeded that in exchange rates initially following reforms. In the nineties, the volatility of capital flows was less than that of the current account deficit implying policy instead of smoothing shocks from openness magnified them.

More flexibility of the exchange rate allows a smoother and more counter-cyclical interest rate. Its contribution to lowering inflation increases the Central Bank's ability to adapt interest rates to the domestic cycle. Sequenced capital account restrictions and flexible exchange rates help to navigate the trinity and retain some degrees of freedom for monetary policy. That capital flows were never able to close the large differential between domestic and foreign interest rates in India suggests these degrees of freedom existed.

Capital Account Restrictions

Private Foreign Investments[4] have many benefits. But especially in EMs they are subject to sudden stops or reversals. These could be due to external shocks or to infectious panics unrelated to fundamentals. India's policy strategy of "middling through" helped to reduce these risks and manage the surges. Liberalization of the capital account distinguished between types and direction of flows and was much greater for equity compared to debt flows including bank loans, and for foreign compared to domestic residents. Among debt flows long-term debt was to be liberalized before short-term. The rationale was equity, in contrast to debt, shares in and therefore reduces liabilities in a crisis. Inflows have to be allowed to go out if they are to come in, but continuing restrictions on domestic capital outflows can reduce the reserve cover required. Reversible volatile inflows were largely accumulated as reserves—a costly form of self-insurance.

Research and empirical estimation has found that only countries with strong domestic institutions, markets and government finances benefit from foreign inflows. These features determine absorptive capacity that reduces volatility and also gives countries the ability to withstand volatility. Thus the Indian strategy followed a well thought out sequence whereby full capital account liberalization was to come after deepening domestic markets, and improving government finances. Liberalizing, deepening markets and improving institutions and policy form a package. One alone is dangerous without the others. Strict sequencing is also necessary. The crisis showed that improvement in the international financial architecture and regulation are also preconditions for full capital account liberalization.

There is a perspective that regards any departure from full liberalization as a failure of reforms. But it is beginning to be recognized that it is actually a better strategy of liberalization. Lobbyists who want free foreign entry without the other harder preconditions would put the country to unnecessary risk.

Partial capital convertibility gives flexibility along the line of control, making selective tightening feasible if necessary. Additional instruments become available to tackle the policy trilemma. For example, stricter end use criteria were imposed for firms bringing funds in during periods of excessive inflows.

The strategy paid off as India avoided East European-type crisis due to excessive entry and loan pushing by banks. Despite higher volatility in narrow markets, the FPI inflows benefited firms. Loans became easier to get and more venture capital entered. Higher equity inflows were associated with higher level of domestic investment. But households did not benefit. Retail participation shrank in volatile markets. Thus foreign entry cannot resolve all problems. Other conditions also have to be in place. Eventual internationalization of Indian financial services is required as Indian companies go global. But the sequencing has to be correct. Better intermediation of the high domestic savings ratios would make markets more stable.

The Indian debt market is underdeveloped. There is zero retail participation, and caps on foreign rupee debt funds. Banks are forced to hold the large government debt through high statutory liquidity requirements (SLR). This must be brought down and more government debt held by households in a domestic retail market as a first step. The Greece sovereign debt crisis, and the post crisis explosion in government debts, suggests that risks associated with excessive external holding of sovereign debt will be large. India is not yet ready to face high interest volatility. Fiscal consolidation is a precondition and will be analyzed in the next section.

Sustainable Debt and Fiscal Reform

In the beginning stages of the global crisis India was regarded as high-risk because high government debt and deficit ratios limited the scope for fiscal stimulus. In the event the stimulus worked and it was one of the first countries to resume fiscal consolidation. A concept of counter cyclical deficits or cyclically adjusted fiscal balance is required.

The perception of risky deficits extrapolates unconditionally from Latin American crises, where savings rates and population densities were low, and sovereign debt was held abroad. But Indian private savings are high enough to cover for some government dissaving, thus preventing a large current account deficit and potential currency crises. Like in Japan, where the debt ratios are more than double Indian, the debt is held internally. Moreover, once high catch-up growth is established in a populous country, with a demographic profile that ensures sustained entry of youthful workers, the denominator increases so deficit and debt ratios reduce. Government expenditure that increases the supply response is sustainable. Higher growth also contributes more revenues[5]. Average Indian nominal interest rates exceed international and have been falling, while Indian inflation tends to be higher. A lower real interest rate means lower interest payment on past debt so lower additions to expenditures and therefore deficits. The section below demonstrates these aspects formally.

Deficits and the evolution of Government debt

The maturity value of nominal government debt B_tP_t, changes over time as follows:

$$B_tP_t = (1+i_t)B_{t-1}P_{t-1} + (P_tG_t - T_t)$$ (1)

B_t is the maturity value of real public debt; real government purchases are G_t and nominal net tax collections are T_t so that real tax collections are $\tau \equiv T_t/P_t$. The real debt to output ratio is b_t. Dividing by Y_t, and making other manipulations, (1) can be written as:

$$\frac{B_t}{Y_t} = (1+i_t)\frac{B_{t-1}}{Y_{t-1}}\frac{Y_{t-1}}{Y_t}\frac{P_{t-1}}{P_t} + \frac{G_t}{Y_t} - \frac{T_t}{P_tY_t}$$ (2)

Next using $1+g_t - Y_t/Y_{t-1}$, $1+\pi_t = P_t/P_{t-1}$ and the approximation:

$$(1+i_t)/(1+g_t)(1+\pi_t) = 1+i_t - g_t - \pi_t$$ (3)

Gives:

$$b_t - b_{t-1} = (i_t - \pi_t - g_t)b_{t-1} + \frac{G_t}{Y_t} - \frac{\tau_t}{Y_t}$$ (4)

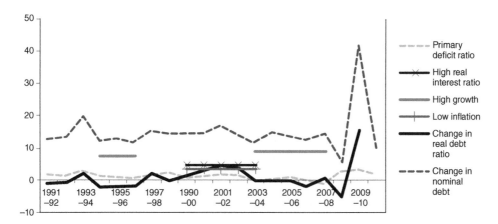

Figure 4.   Macroeconomic Variables and Government debt.

That is, the evolution of the real debt ratio. The latter rises with the debt level, nominal interest rate, and primary deficit ratio (*pd*) or the excess of real government expenditure over taxation as a ratio to output. Therefore high debt levels can imply unsustainable exploding debt.

Falling real interest rates and rising growth rates effectively reduce government debt. Inflation and growth rates do not affect the nominal value of public debt, B_tP_t, which increases in any year by nominal interest payments on debt plus the PD, P_tG_t - T_t. The latter is the non-interest budget deficit, while the fiscal deficit (FD) includes interest payments and is the total government-borrowing requirement to finance current and capital expenditure net of tax and non-tax revenue. The revenue deficit (RD), or deficit on current account, is the amount the government needs to borrow to finance its own consumption. If the real interest rate equals the rate of growth, the PD ratio alone would add to the debt ratio.

Figure 4 shows how the Indian debt and *pd* has tended to fall in periods of high growth, and rise when inflation has been low and real interests high. But the fall was more convincing in the mid-nineties than it was in the mid 2000s when B actually kept rising, ending in a sharp spike in government borrowing.

After 2003-04 nominal interest rates fell, and inflation began to rise again, driving real interest rates very low. Growth peaked at average rates of above 8 percent. The Fiscal Responsibility and Budget Management (FRBM) Act was also passed in 2003. The *pd* fell along with the mandated fall in FD and RD. It turned into a surplus for the first time in 2004-05. Tax revenue was buoyant. But the fall in debt was not as much as these favourable conditions warranted. The goal of inclusive growth encouraged large government expenditures, as tax revenues rose with growth. Despite the FRBM, actual deficits were probably higher than reported deficits as budgetary tricks like oil bonds shifted liabilities to the future. The growth dividend was blown up in large expenditures. Therefore the *pd* shot up in the year of the global financial crisis, and reached 3.2 percent in 2009-10. Uncovered expenditure items helped create the steep rise despite modest tax cuts, and explained the speed of the fiscal stimulus.

Goyal (2011b) allows high transitional growth in a populous low per capita income EM to reduce debt ratios as in equation (4) in a DSGE model of optimal monetary-fiscal policy adapted to EMs. A relation similar to (4) holds since there are multiple steady-states in a transitional economy. Results include: in response to a consumption shock change in government debt rises with growth, tax response, and the level of debt. Although lags and other structural features make for greater stability, a permanent rise in expenditure in excess of taxing capacity can lead to instability. Both the model and India's recent experience, where high growth was unable to reduce government debt, suggest improved incentives for expenditure management are required, to build robust space for countercyclical fiscal measures, and allow a cyclically adjusted fiscal balance.

In the steady state, when b and other variables are constant, equation (3) reduces to $b = pd/$ g-r. The budget estimate of pd for 2010-11 is 1.9. Inflation reduces the real interest rate. Since it was coordinating with international policy, the Government put more weight on reviving growth than on reducing inflation. Inflation around seven percent reduces r to 1. Taking $g = 8$, $pd = 1.9$, the steady-state b reduces to 27 percent, compared to a current debt ratio[6] of around 0.8. But inflating away debt imposes a large cost on the populace and destroys goodwill for the Government. Fiscal prudence is the better way to reduce debt. Without high growth, debt can explode, so the path to a steady state would lie through a crisis.

Although reforms aimed to improve fiscal health, the norm of political populism sought inclusion through short-term transfers. The FRBM Act was not designed to protect investment, so productive expenditure was cut to continue populist spending. The former would have improved human, social, and physical capital, and therefore the supply response. The FRBM legislation brought down only reported deficits. But the global shock exposed the inadequate attention paid to incentives and escape clauses in formulating the Act. Loopholes were used to maintain the letter of the law even while violating its spirit. Targets were mechanically achieved, compressing essential expenditure on infrastructure, health and education, while maintaining populist subsidies. A new path of fiscal consolidation proposed by the 13th Finance Commission draws heavily on and seeks to maintain India's growth dividend. There is only a gentle attempt to prevent the Centre's favorite ploy of reducing capital expenditure. Stricter constraints on the revenue deficit and more bite for the medium term fiscal plan are suggested. But more incentives are required for compliance, such as selective expenditure caps, and detailed targets for individual ministries, and levels of government, as part of improved accounting, including shifts from cash to accrual based accounts. This would contribute to better governance, reducing pressures that raise costs.

There is ongoing improvement on the tax side. Apart from buoyancy due to higher growth, there were reforms in tax administration such as TIN, a proposed shift to GST and a new Direct Tax Code. If the composition of fiscal expenditure changes to improve the supply response, monetary policies can also support cyclical adjustment and growth on a more sustained basis, allowing better fiscal-monetary coordination.

Conclusion

Good luck in the shape of diversified sources sustaining Indian growth, gives some leeway for policy errors. Positive factors include domestic demand, agriculture, openness, technology, the demographic profile, the infrastructure cycle, high savings and having crossed a critical threshold. While foreign capital does not contribute much to aggregate resources it is useful in financial intermediation and in improvements in organization. Periods of outflow have been brief. India was one of the few economies continuing to grow even as most economies contracted in the aftermath of the financial crisis. The country may have crossed a critical threshold in its transitional catch-up phase of growth.

Good management was evident in some flexibility of exchange rates, reserve accumulation in response to volatile inflows, the strategy of graded restrictions on the capital account, steady market, institutional and regulatory development, countercyclical prudential regulations, improvements in tax administration and the enactment of the FRBM. All these helped India side-step crises, and achieve respectable growth despite financial turbulence.

So India's good performance was due to good luck and to good management. The inherent strengths of the economy helped absorb both policy mistakes and external shocks. The policy strategy did contribute, but it was arrived at by fluke and did less than it could have, precisely because it was not properly understood or owned. It is beginning to be recognized that sequenced reforms may be a better reform strategy rather than a failure of reform.

Improvements include more forward-looking response of policy, with exchange rates contributing to smoothing of interest rates, better composition and quality of government expenditure and of governance, and faster more focused development of domestic financial intermediation. All this would better adapt macroeconomic policy to the structure of the economy. Analysis of the crisis and recovery suggests aggregate supply in India is elastic but subject to upward shocks. This implies both monetary and fiscal policy should identify measures that would reduce costs, while avoiding too large a demand contraction.

Although improvements are possible, and one can debate timing, mix, degree and direction, policy came pretty close to finding the correct combination of reforms and of caution. On the whole regulators exhibited a healthy contrarian attitude, and democratic pulls and pressures resulted in a middling through process. This has a better chance of success in EMs needing development over several fronts to achieve robust diversified growth.

This paper is due to be published in *Macroeconomics and Finance in Emerging Market Economies,* volume 5, issue 1 (March 2012).

Notes

1. The operative rate went from the reverse repo at 3.25 in March 2010 to the repo at 6 by September 2010.
2. The analysis in this paper draws on and extends earlier work (see Goyal 2011a). More references not given to save space are available at www.igidr.ac.in/~ashima.
3. Intervention was exactly zero from mid 2009 to mid 2011, and FX market growth slowed in this period.
4. These include Foreign Direct Investment (FDI), Foreign Portfolio Investment (FPI) and other long- and short-term investment flows. This section draws on Goyal 2011c.
5. The ratio of Indian tax revenue to GDP, which had long stagnated in single digits, peaked at 12.6 in 2007-08 with high growth, before falling in the next crisis year to 11.8.
6. According to the RBI website Indian Central and State Government debt was 73 percent of GDP in 2009-10. Of this 53.9 percent constituted domestic liabilities of the Centre, 2.21 its external liabilities, and 26.26 was aggregate liabilities of State Governments.

References

BIS (Bank of International Settlements). 2010. Foreign Exchange and Derivatives Market Activity in 2010. *Triennial Central Bank Survey.*

Corden, W.M. 2002. *Too Sensational: On the Choice of Exchange Rate Regimes*, Cambridge MA: MIT Press.

Goyal, A. 2011a. 'Exchange Rate Regimes and Macroeconomic Performance in South Asia'. *Routledge Handbook on South Asian Economies*, (ed.) Raghbendra Jha, (2011a).

Goyal A. 2011b. 'Sustainable Debt and Deficits in Emerging Markets', *International Journal of Trade and Global Markets.* 4 (2): 1-23.

Goyal A. 2011c. 'Inflows and Policy: Middling Through', *India Development Report 2011*, D.M. Nachane (ed.), New Delhi: IGIDR and Oxford University Press.

Rao, V.K.R.V. 1952. 'Investment, Income and the Multiplier in an Underdeveloped Economy', *The Indian Economic Review*, February, reprinted in A.N. Agarwala and S.P. Singh (eds.) *The Economics of Underdevelopment*, pp. 205-218, London, Oxford, New York: Oxford University Press, 1958.

Svensson L.E.O. 2000. 'Open-economy inflation targeting'. *Journal of International Economics*. 50:155-183.

Woodford, M. 2003. *Interest and prices: Foundations of a Theory of Monetary Policy*, NJ: Princeton University Press.

Index

Page numbers in *Italics* represent tables.
Page numbers in **Bold** represent figures.

For Product Safety Concerns and Information please contact our EU representative GPSR@taylorandfrancis.com Taylor & Francis Verlag GmbH, Kaufingerstraße 24, 80331 München, Germany

Batch number: 08165852

Printed by Printforce, the Netherlands